Growing Architecture

Ferdinand Ludwig
Daniel Schönle

Growing Architecture

How to Design and Build with Trees

With a Preface by
Sonja Dümpelmann

Birkhäuser
Basel

Graphic design, layout and typesetting: niessnerdesign

Translation into English: Julian Reisenberger

Copy-editing translation: Ferdinand Ludwig, Ria Stein

Project management: Ria Stein

Production: Anja Haering

Paper: Soporset Premium, 120 g/m²

Printing: Beltz Grafische Betriebe GmbH

Lithography: Repromayer GmbH, Reutlingen

Library of Congress Control Number: 2022944008

Bibliographic information published by the German National Library
The German National Library lists this publication in the Deutsche Nationalbibliografie; detailed bibliographic data are available on the Internet at http://dnb.dnb.de.

ISBN 978-3-0356-0332-3
e-ISBN (PDF) 978-3-0356-0339-2

This book is also available in a German-language edition with the title *Wachsende Architektur*, print-ISBN 978-3-0356-0331-6

First reprint 2024

P.O. Box 44, 4009 Basel, Switzerland
Part of Walter de Gruyter GmbH, Berlin/Boston

Printed on acid-free paper produced from chlorine-free pulp. TCF ∞

Printed in Germany

9 8 7 6 5 4 3 www.birkhauser.com

This publication was financially supported by the Werner Konrad Marschall and Dr-Ing Horst Karl Marschall Foundation at the Technical University of Munich and by special funds from the University of Stuttgart.

MIX
Papier | Fördert gute Waldnutzung
FSC® C089473

Contents

Preface: Buildings and Trees

Sonja Dümpelmann

The origin of all architecture is vegetal. This recurring hypothesis has captivated the imagination of architectural theorists since Vitruvius in the 1st century BC, and especially his counterparts in the 18th century, who saw the model of the primitive hut as a prototype for basic rational architectural principles. According to the French Jesuit Abbé Marc-Antoine Laugier, the primitive hut represented the fundamental form of human shelter and comprised no more than four living tree columns supporting beams and a gable made of dead branches. For the Frenchman, it was the precursor of classical temples. In returning to the vegetal origins of architecture and the structural significance of the classical order of columns, Laugier was responding to what he saw as the excessive superficial ornamentation of the Baroque style at that time. His primitive hut gave a rational form to organic nature.

Some 270 years after Laugier, the architects Ferdinand Ludwig and Daniel Schönle are now ushering in a new paradigm shift with "Baubotanik" and *Growing Architecture*. Here, Baubotanik is a building technique and trees are no longer just an intellectual construct but the actual material of architectural constructions that also extend into the vertical dimension. But Baubotanik goes much further than just questions of form. It concerns the future of living in cities, the future design of our environment and how interactions between humans and non-human nature can be actively shaped for the benefit of both. In short, it is about overcoming the traditional opposition between the permanence of architecture and the dynamic flux of nature. How can living trees be combined with inanimate materials to create pleasant spaces that promote biodiversity and protect the climate? Ludwig and Schönle explore this question, combining fundamental scientific research with visionary architectural design. In this book, they not only study the growth behaviour and physiology of different tree species and present the advantages and disadvantages of different techniques for stimulating the growing together of branches, trunks and roots, as well as the incorporation of objects. They also revisit inspirational historical examples and show new designs, some of which are taken from their own practice.

The new research field of Baubotanik that Ludwig and Schönle describe builds on diverse practices and insights from botany, environmental engineering, forestry, arboriculture and horticulture. Gardeners have been grafting and pruning trees into shape for thousands of years in order to optimise their growth characteristics for fruit and wood production as well as to create spatial environments in ornate gardens and designs for outdoor spaces. As plants, trees are continually growing, which is both an opportunity and a challenge for Baubotanik. On the one hand, the physiological processes of plant growth are what make the fusion of trees and buildings possible in the first place. On the other, these processes are difficult to plan with because numerous external factors can influence tree growth and development. At the same time, the varying seasonal and cyclical nature of baubotanical structures lend them a characteristic quality, especially in the temperate climate zones.

While there are some obvious parallels to the integration of trees into the urban realm, Baubotanik differs from the planting of trees in parks and on streets. It interweaves trees directly into building structures, often in confined spaces, to create diverse forms of growing architecture. If one considers the urban fabric as a holistic form of architecture, trees here also play an integral part as living green (infra)structures fitted into pockets between houses, lining streets and forming green islands. Indeed, most of today's cities are hard to imagine without trees, even though in the past they did not always shade pavements, parks, balconies or roof terraces, nor did they enliven the urban townscape through their changing shape, appearance and colour to the same extent as they do today. The presence of trees in townscapes is also not without its own conflicts: some trees can cause allergies, all trees require maintenance, their foliage can be a safety hazard on pavements, their roots may damage underground pipes, and they can obstruct light, occupy space and restrict airflows in streets. However, the denser and larger cities become, and the more trees they displace in the process, the more important it becomes to plant and maintain trees in private and public urban spaces. While cities have become "naturalised" by this process, trees have also become "urbanised". Tree nurseries, for example, have for some time now been breeding new "industry-resistant" cultivars that bear little or no fruit and can withstand air and soil pollution as well as heat stress.

Over the past 300 years, various utopian urban visions and design paradigms have proposed integrating trees and green spaces into the urban realm. For Abbé Laugier in the 18th century, for example, trees were not only the basis of the original human-made dwelling, but also of urban planning. He wanted the city to be conceived of like a forest. Although he criticised the rigid linearity of the gardens of Versailles, he saw the interplay of human organisation and non-human nature in parks and forests as a model for urban planning. This idea took on a more concrete form in the garden and forest cities that were developed from the late 19th century onwards in response to the effects of increasing industrialisation on society and the environment. Nature was now supposed to help create not only a better living environment but also a better society. Social utopias and at times a critique of civilisation also lay at the heart of many subsequent "nature-oriented" architectural designs that emerged as part of environmental movements. One example is Frei Otto's eco-houses built as part of the Berlin IBA 1984/87, for which he designed not only the structure but also the supply infrastructure. The houses use solar energy, recycle grey water, incorporate vegetation into the façades and roof design, and were conceived around the provision of outdoor space. Around the same time, Frei Otto also founded the special research unit "230 — Natural Constructions: Lightweight Construction in Architecture and Nature" at the University of Stuttgart to learn from nature for the design of lightweight constructions. Scientists examined aspects of plant biomechanics and morphology, cell mechanics, the density and strength of wood from different tree species and how tree branches and trunks break — all aspects on which Ludwig's and Schönle's current work is based. The University of Stuttgart later also became home to the new field of Baubotanik. Founded by Ferdinand Ludwig in Stuttgart, it is now part of his professorship for Green Technologies in Landscape Architecture at the Technical University of Munich and is also applied in projects undertaken by the Office for Living Architecture (OLA) founded by Ferdinand Ludwig and Daniel Schönle together with Jakob Rauscher.

While the form and anatomy of trees have repeatedly provided models for architecture and urban planning, it is primarily their material and growth processes that have contributed to the building and evolution of our living environment over the millennia. This is also the focus of Baubotanik: trees, both living and dead, are a functional building material that shapes the built environment through its specific material and aesthetic qualities. It is no coincidence that the word "baum", which has been documented as existing in German since the 8th century, can be traced back to the West Germanic "bauma" and the Old English word "bēam", which referred both to "beam" and to "tree". Even more than in Abbé Laugier's primitive hut, this linguistic dualism becomes apparent in the work of Ludwig and Schönle's *Growing Architecture*. Here, the synthesis of buildings and trees is closer than ever before. Baubotanik therefore represents a vital component of plant-friendly urbanism — an urbanism that employs plants and takes their needs into account, and an urbanism that promotes plant culture without abandoning and restricting urban culture and density.

Philadelphia, October 2022

1

1 Introduction

Archetypes of growing architecture

Living bridges

Probably the most impressive examples of living architecture are to be found in the remote tropical mountain forests of the eastern Indian province of Meghalaya. Here, the indigenous Khasi people have been utilising the growth processes of trees to create living bridges for centuries. The constructions, some of which span more than 20 m, enable the Khasi to safely cross deep gorges and raging rivers. Aerial roots, which have merged to create truss-like structures, form the main supporting structure and also serve as railings (→ Fig. 1) while flat stone slabs that have been incorporated into this living, growing construction provide an even walking surface (→ Fig. 2). Rooted in the earth and overgrown with mosses and lichens, the living structures fit seamlessly into their natural ecosystem and appear almost to have sprung from a fairy-tale world in which humans and nature live together in perfect harmony. Their creation, however, is the product of farsighted planning, special techniques and, above all, patience: to begin with, rubber trees (*Ficus elastica*) are planted on the banks of a river, stabilising the soil with their roots to form the future "foundations". Once the trees have grown sufficiently, a temporary supporting structure is usually erected over the river along which the aerial roots emerging from the trees' branches and trunks are trained. As they grow, they are repeatedly knotted together to form a network-like structure (→ Figs. 3, 4). It can take decades for the structure to acquire sufficient thickness and strength to bear loads and serve as

1 The "Double Decker Bridge" is one of several bridges that can be used to reach the village of Nongriat in Meghalaya, India (photo: 2011).
2 The merged roots of the bridge between the new and the old part of Nongbareh village have, over a period of several hundred years, developed into bizarre gnarled structures. Stones have become incorporated by the living structure and form the walking surface (photo: 2017).
3, 4 The aerial roots of the *Ficus elastica* that emerge from the trees are knotted in such a way that they merge (photos: 2014).

2

3

4

a functioning living bridge (→ Figs. 5—7). The "construction" of such a living bridge is therefore a project that spans multiple generations in which the work begun by the parents is continued by the children, and mostly for the benefit of the grandchildren.[1]

Today, such long-term thinking and foresighted behaviour is virtually unknown. However, it is vital if we are to live and build sustainably: increasingly we are realising that our own economic activity oriented around short-term profits is destroying our own livelihood as well as that of future generations. What makes the achievements of the Khasi all the more remarkable is that the "production" of a living bridge consumes neither fossil nor renewable resources; rather than emitting greenhouse gases, the bridge itself binds carbon dioxide and sequesters it through photosynthesis in the fabric of the "living wood". At the same time, the bridge stabilises the forest ecosystem, prevents erosion of the fertile soil and releases oxygen. And at the end of its useful life, fungi and microorganisms will convert the structure into humus, and thus into the basis for new life.

5 As part of the regular upkeep, new aerial roots are repeatedly woven into the structure (photo: 2015).
6 The knotting of the roots together with the increasing thickness of the roots results in strong living truss structures (photo: 2017).

7 Nearly 53 m long, the bridge at Mawkyrnot is probably the longest living bridge, making it the largest historical botanical building structure in the world (photo: 2019).

7

Dance linden trees

While it is perhaps no great surprise that the ways of living and building of indigenous peoples are prime examples of sustainability, it is certainly more extraordinary to find centuries-old examples of living, growing architecture in Central Europe. The so-called "dance linden trees" (dance lime trees or "Tanzlinde" in German) are a type of structure that arose out of the tradition of planting linden trees in village or town squares. As focal points in communities, lime trees had social significance as places where locals met, held court or celebrated festivities. The branches of these trees, which were typically summer lime trees (*Tilia platyphyllos*), were trained to extend horizontally, sometimes in several tapered tiers and sometimes as one wide spreading tier. In such cases, the intention was to form broad canopies of foliage that could provide extensive areas of shade for a large number of villagers or townsfolk.

Where the manipulation of these trees reached extreme proportions, it sometimes became necessary to erect supporting structures to prevent them from collapsing under their own weight

8 The horizontally trained branches of the dance linden tree in Effeltrich rest heavily on the wooden supporting structure (photo: 2008).

9 The walkable treetop of the dance linden tree in Peesten is an example of the interplay of living and constructed architectural elements in a botanical building structure (photo: 2020).

8

10 The “façade” of the dance linden tree in Peesten with its “leaf walls” and the window openings framed by the wooden construction (photo: 2020).

(→ Fig. 8). In the simplest cases, wooden posts were placed beneath the branches, but constructions were often more elaborate and some even featured stone pillars. The result was a hybrid structure in which the tree branches spreading from a central trunk rested on a custom-made supporting framework like "living wooden beams". In some places, the musicians performing for the May Day celebrations played not beneath the branches but sat in the artificial tree canopy. Over time platforms were built on top of the branches, initially for the musicians, and later as semi-permanent dance floors. Ultimately, entire festive congregations sat in the treetops resulting in an elaborate structure that was at once tree and building. A particularly impressive example of this tradition is the "Tanzlinde" in Peesten in Upper Franconia in Germany which, after its restoration in 2001, is once again actively used (→ Fig. 9). A stone spiral staircase was even constructed to help reach the 90 m^2 dance floor of oak planks. From within the structure, eleven window openings offer magnificent views of the Main valley. The lattice-like wall construction serves as a framework along which the shoots of the lower branches were trained (→ Fig. 10).[2]

Aspects of living architecture

The Khasi bridges and the dance linden trees are each impressive, but also quite different examples of how architecture can be created as a living structure. As structures, the living bridges serve in the first instance as vital parts of an infrastructure for accessing remote villages. They need to be functional and reliable. Under the social, technological and ecological circumstances that prevailed at the time and place of their creation, one must assume that they were the best solution to the problem they address. One of their greatest attributes is their long lifetime: although it is hard to date them exactly, it is thought that the older examples are several hundred years old.[3] Given the simple technical means required for their construction and the fact that a construction made of timber would have rapidly succumbed to rot in the warm and humid tropical climate, the constructions are a remarkable technological achievement. The living structure is protected against harmful influences and damage by its bark, and minor damage is repaired by the bark's own self-healing mechanism. In addition, as the roots grow thicker over time—assuming they remain vital and are well cared for—the bridges gain stability. As such, the Khasi's predominantly pragmatic, functional approach makes use of trees and their growth processes for primarily constructive purposes.

The name dance linden already tells us that these structures were created for a very specific reason. They fulfilled no functional or practical purpose, but rather arose out of the desire to make a unique place for special occasions in the crowns of lime trees, which bore particular significance as a centre point of local communities. The resulting platform is a space where one can experience the aesthetic qualities of the tree from close-up—its bark, scent, fruits and the play of shadows on its leaves—while also being set apart from the dusty routine of daily life. Using horticultural means, the trees were shaped to create the desired conditions. At the same time, this manipulation of the tree's own natural form also aimed to eliminate the randomness of tree growth, in the process "enhancing its beauty", which at that time meant shaping it to have a perfect geometric form. It was accepted that this often resulted in the tree's no longer being able to support itself without some kind of artificial structure. From today's point of view, this seems quite unnatural, as if forcing the tree into a corset that leaves it little room to breathe. As it turns out, lime trees have tolerated such treatment remarkably well. The dance linden tree at Schenklengsfeld, which is said to have been planted in 760, still sprouts anew every spring, even though only fragments of its trunk are preserved, and the branches weigh heavily on the wooden frame. At an estimated age of some 1200 years, it is very likely the oldest tree in Germany and thus older than all "naturally" growing summer lime trees untouched by human hands.[4] Perhaps this suggests a symbiotic relationship between human and tree, and between nature and technology, prompting us to reconsider the possibilities of living architecture. A new form of contemporary architecture using trees could contribute to solving the pressing ecological problems of our time and enrich the design of buildings, cities and landscapes with a range of aesthetic qualities.

Baubotanik — a new field of research

This is where Baubotanik comes into play as an interdisciplinary field of work and research where scientific and botanical, architectural and conceptual, and horticultural and practical approaches come together to explore the possibilities of designing and building with living plants. The term “Baubotanik” was first coined at the Institute of Architectural Theory and Design (IGMA) at the University of Stuttgart as part of a research initiative founded in 2007 as a cross-disciplinary and cross-institutional network. After ten years of intensive research, the field now has its own professorship for Green Technologies in Landscape Architecture situated at the Technical University of Munich. As the name suggests, Baubotanik encompasses all conceivable approaches in which living botanical organisms can be used in construction, and in turn all forms of architecture that employ diverse kinds of vascular plants, as well as mosses, fungi or algae. Given the breadth and variety of topics covered, the number of architects, artists and scientists working in the field around the world is increasing, and with it the range of different objectives and methodologies. The work in the field of Baubotanik focuses on architecture using trees, which is therefore the subject of this book. Trees — and especially their trunks, branches and roots — can function directly as “living building materials” while their leaves convey a sensory impression of their vitality. It is possible, using comparatively simple technical means, to influence their growth form quite significantly and to transform them into structures and works of architecture. Trees serve here as a building element and can be considered as a “living semi-finished product”. At the same time, they are biological entities that are constantly interacting with their environment and must be considered and treated accordingly.

Baubotanik in this context is a form of architecture in which structures are created through the interaction of natural plant growth and technical joining methods, whereby trees, or parts thereof, are influenced in their growth in such a way that, through their interconnection and connection with non-living components, they fuse to form an entity that is both organic and technical. Research into Baubotanik draws on aspects discussed in the 1970s and 1980s at the University of Stuttgart, when Frei Otto and his interdisciplinary team at the legendary Institute for Lightweight Construction (IL) explored natural constructions and their potential for architecture. At that time, it seemed obvious not just to draw inspiration from trees as a source of ideas for constructions, such as the well-known branched tree supports, but also to explore the possibilities of living plant architecture. In this context, the architect Rudolph Doernach, for example, developed “biotecture” as his vision of living architecture,[5] which inspired, among others, the willow structures of the group “Sanfte Strukturen” (Gentle structures).[6] Research on the dance linden trees by the building historian Rainer Graefe also established the first historical foundations of Baubotanik.[7] Similarly, the engineer Lothar Wessolly developed the first beginnings of a new discipline, tree statics,[8] which is still used today to establish the load-bearing capacity of trees and proving their stability. The research field of Baubotanik aims to compile and systematically incorporate these approaches, and to develop theoretical and practical foundations that have been lacking up to now through its own testing and experimental structures. Ultimately, the goal is to generate design knowledge to facilitate the conception, planning and realisation of architectures with living trees so that they can be made applicable on a wider scale.

The chances and challenges of growing architecture

In Baubotanik, the architect is in effect a co-designer creating a structure together with the tree. As such, it will never be "finished", even though at some point a desired stage of development will be reached. How it will eventually look in future depends on many factors and events that cannot be entirely planned in advance. Forecasts are possible, but they are at best only general statements. The further ahead one looks, the less distinct the forecast can be. This contrasts markedly with architecture which has traditionally been built in opposition to nature as something that is as permanent as possible. An architect can neither determine the exact size or proportions of a baubotanical structure. Not only that, its appearance changes with the seasons, at least in temperate climes: in autumn it first changes colour and then loses its leaves; in winter it is bare and gnarled; in spring it sprouts again, perhaps even blossoming; and in summer it may be so leafy that it is barely recognisable as a building. One can see this transformation very clearly in a project entitled the Baubotanik Footbridge, which was built as an experimental demonstration structure by members of the Baubotanik research team on moorland near Lake Constance (→ Fig. 11; → Chapter 6, pp. 144—149). It also makes clear how carefully baubotanical projects can fit into the image of an evolved (cultural) landscape and how responsive they are to sensitive ecosystems. This results in possible applications in nature reserves and landscape conservation areas and, in general, wherever buildings are to merge visually with the landscape.

Unlike conventional technical approaches to ecological building, which attempt to minimise their impact on an ecosystem, baubotanical projects actively interact with their environment on an ongoing basis through their life-sustaining processes. They both influence their environment and are shaped by it: their shape adjusts to wind and light conditions, and their growth responds to drought, heat or frost. Storms may break off branches or hail impacts on bark such that the scars remain visible even after it heals. As with every tree, every baubotanical structure also has its own specific life story, a distinctive individual character that develops over the years. This unique character explains the sense of attachment and deep personal affection many people develop towards trees that they have lived with for extended periods. And there is every reason to believe the same emotional bond can arise with architecture in which living trees play an integral part.

The trees that we love and value are, however, only rarely purely natural specimens. Very often they are the product of cultural intervention and have arisen through cultivation, planting and pruning. One example is the case of orchards, which can exert a certain attraction through the interplay of their natural growth forms and artificial arrangement. Another example is the free-standing trees commonly found in pastureland, as immortalised in the paintings of Caspar David Friedrich. Their form derives from the action of grazing animals gnawing on the trunk and lower-lying branches, giving them a strong limb-like appearance. Baubotanical projects are similarly shaped by this interplay between the artificial and natural, except that here the artificial component is that much greater, often becoming clearly visible or even overtly expressive where botanical and technical elements are joined together. One sees the successful symbiosis of nature and technology most clearly in connection details where technical components have over time become incorporated by organic parts.

Natural growth processes are directed in such a way that forms are enclosed and connected in a way that would not have been possible by other technical means. At the same time, one can also see this interplay as an act of violation where, for example, a cold steel bar penetrates the trunk of a tree (→ Fig. 32, p. 147).

Baubotanical structures require a certain amount of care and attention over their lifetime because they can quickly become unusable if they grow (too) unregulated. As such, the designer's responsibility does not end with the construction work: maintenance concepts need to be developed and continually adapted to the actual state of development. While this is nothing new to gardening and landscaping, it is comparatively new for works of architecture. Baubotanik should therefore be seen as a form of horticultural architecture and considered in terms of ongoing processes. Patience and waiting are as much a part of this as foresight and forward-looking action. Landscape architects and also urban designers are familiar with such aspects, even if they are rarely explicitly outlined in a design concept.[9] After all, decades can pass before trees reach their full size and properly meet the expectations placed on them. In that same period, a city can change greatly: a tree planted around 1800 may still be in its prime today and will have experienced the urban expansions of industrialisation, the destruction of the Second World War, and the reconstruction and zoning of the city with housing estates and business parks in the 20th century (→ Fig. 12). We can, of course, only predict these dynamics to a limited extent because the future is always speculative. That said, we should try and relate plant development processes, which are similarly hard to predict, to urban, social and ecological transformations so that baubotanical construction can present an open invitation for the future.

Rapid global population growth together with equally rapid urbanisation has focused attention on the urgent need to improve urban spaces. Now that climate change is no longer impending but well and truly upon us, we are finding ourselves facing overheated street spaces. Trees with adequate canopies provide shade and cool such environments, however it takes decades for them to reach a sufficient size to have a noticeable climatic effect. Baubotanik is thus well placed to enrich urban spaces through the introduction of living architecture at the scale of mature trees, but it must develop solutions that are ready to deploy now. Initial tests and experimental structures such as the Baubotanik Tower (→ Chapter 6, pp. 158—161) and the Plane Tree Cube (→ Chapter 6, pp. 162—169) suggest that it is possible to create living structures at the scale of mature trees using techniques such as the newly developed plant addition. Baubotanik could therefore rise to the challenge of providing adequate green infrastructure in densely built-up inner cities and rapidly developing urban conurbations within a comparatively short space of time, and in turn introduce many of the ecological qualities found in mature trees without waiting decades for them to grow. These include microclimatic effects such as cooling through evapotranspiration, and air purification through binding dust. The design for the House of the Future in Berlin (→ Chapter 8, pp. 206—209) by the Office for Living Architecture (OLA) makes use of such effects to create a building that is — at least partially — air-conditioned by trees and at the same time positively influences the local microclimate.

Numerous studies have shown that such conditions can make a marked contribution to improving people's health and well-being. People who live in neighbourhoods with many tree-lined streets suffer significantly less from cardiovascular and metabolic diseases than residents of the same age group and income in neighbourhoods with fewer trees. Residents in neighbourhoods with more trees also subjectively rate their quality of life significantly better. The quality of life among residents in streets without trees was only rated similarly high by residents who were either seven years younger or earned at least

11 The Baubotanik Footbridge, built in 2005 near Lake Constance, shows how humans can inhabit the treetops of growing architecture (photo: 2011).

US $10,000 more per year than the comparison group in green streets.[10] This not only illustrates the added value for individual residents, but also documents an economic benefit of urban trees. If it is possible to use Baubotanik to build structures that have such beneficial health, psychological and socio-economic effects, the not inconsiderable expense of their construction and maintenance is more than justified.

Up until now, such studies have not yet found their way into planning practice. Although architects are increasingly building functional, aesthetically pleasing and ecologically sophisticated buildings, these still often have a negative impact on the quality of life in their immediate urban surroundings. Landscape architects are then frequently charged with compensating for these effects in the best possible way by designing the residual areas. Some approaches, such as "landscape urbanism", "ecological urbanism" or "biotope city" attempt to address this contradiction by taking a processual approach to developing the city as a landscape or ecosystem.[11] Baubotanik ties in with such approaches because it understands buildings as being part of their environment and aims to strategically develop interactions between the two. Through the provision of a variety of spaces and environmental conditions, it aims to foster a graduated system of complex interactions and diverse opportunities for both inhabitants and ecological processes.[12]

12 Juxtaposition of the development of a tree alongside the schematic development of a Central European city showing the considerable changes that a tree, and thus also a botanical structure, experiences over the course of its life.

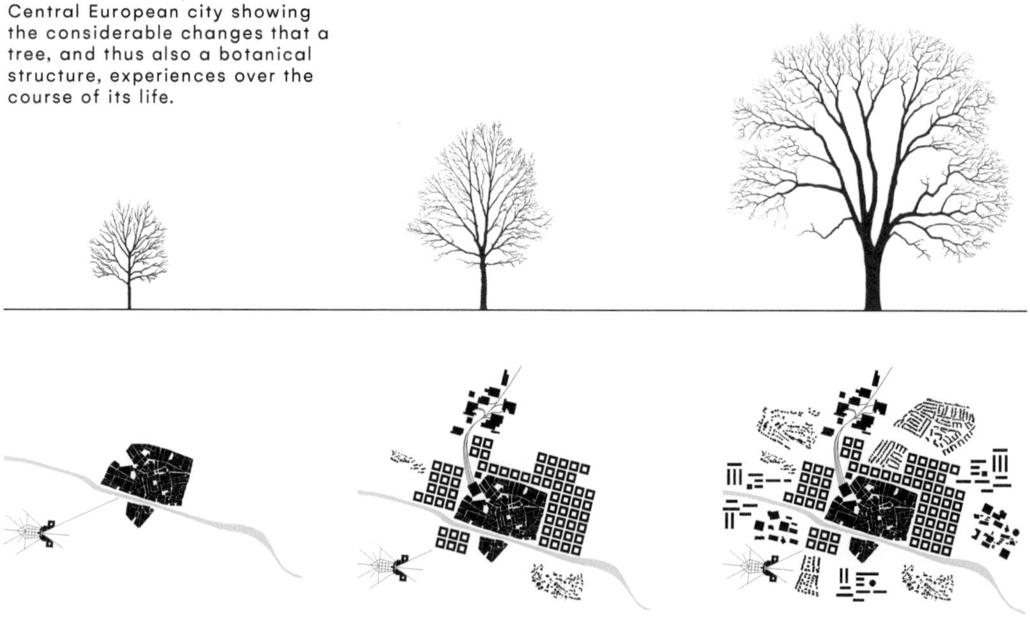

About this book

With this book, we hope first and foremost to comprehensively outline the challenges and opportunities that designing and building with living trees presents and the work currently being undertaken in this experimental and innovative field. Our intention is to introduce Baubotanik to a broader circle of readers. On the one hand, we wish to stimulate the reader's own imagination and visions and on the other to show concrete possibilities for its use and potential applications for different design tasks and areas of application. The fusion of the built and natural environment in living architecture presents new, largely unexplored aesthetic possibilities and also provides potential answers to current pressing ecological questions. At the same time, designing and building with organic growth processes necessitates a design attitude and corresponding design methods that do justice to the tree as a "living building material". Using living trees in designs and constructions requires that we understand the underlying patterns and conditions of plant growth and recognise these as essential design parameters. Only then do living structures stand a chance of flourishing according to the designer's vision, rather than dying off prematurely. Not only that: if we are to make full productive use of the aesthetic, ecological and constructive potential of trees, we must also understand the diverse ways in which plants adapt and self-optimise in their interactions with their environment, so that we may use this potential in the design and construction of these structures. In the chapter "Botanical Foundations", we summarise the primary basic patterns and important phenomena of tree growth as a basis for the interdisciplinary challenge of designing and constructing with trees. In the chapter on "Techniques and Tree Species", we present the current state of the art of the techniques of Baubotanik using test series from ongoing research and discuss the suitability of different tree species.

At a conceptual level, Baubotanik picks up on two trends that we can currently observe in architecture: On the one hand, trees are increasingly being used for greening buildings, and on the other, more and more projects are emerging that concentrate on the aesthetic qualities of trees and make it possible to experience tree crowns. In the chapter "Fusion of Trees and Building", we trace this development and attempt a classification of Baubotanik and its designs in the context of current architectural discourse.

Baubotanical structures can maintain and repair themselves, improve the microclimate of their immediate environment and serve as a habitat for animals and people. To do this, however, they must also be situated in an environment that provides the necessary resources for healthy growth and/or employs vegetation techniques that can ensure adequate growing conditions. As such, the organic and technical elements are interdependent. Baubotanical structures can be very robust, adapting to the specifics of their location, but they can also be quite fragile—especially in the early phases of development. The chapter "How Living Structures Interact with Their Environment" discusses the productivity of baubotanical structures in relation to the conditions necessary to support them.

A characteristic of baubotanical structures is that they are never finished. As such the design process is not about designing finished buildings but rather their ongoing development processes. Designing entails envisioning desired conditions that will occur at a certain point in time and also last for a certain period of time. As a designer, one must take into account the limited influence one has on growth conditions and on extreme weather events such as droughts or storms, as well as the fact that, as living buildings, baubotanical structures can grow but also die. The chapter "Designing with Trees and Time" provides a systematic overview of current and historical projects that show how such questions of temporality can be dealt with conceptually.

In the chapter "Utopias and Visions: Living Architecture between Science and Fiction", we present projects that for the most part have not been realised or perhaps seem unrealisable, that postulate unattainable goals or take the principle of manipulating living trees to an excessive degree. Despite their questionable realism, they present ideas and visions, and sometimes also interim results, that make an essential contribution to the development of Baubotanik. This leads naturally to the final chapter, "Vers une Arbotecture: Towards a Future Tree Architecture", which examines what a future architecture with living trees could look like in concrete terms. Illustrated using current research projects in the field of Baubotanik and selected designs by the Office for Living Architecture (OLA), the chapter builds on the botanical principles and design strategies discussed in the preceding chapters and explores new possibilities for designing with living trees (→ Fig. 13).

Finally, this book cannot and does not intend to be a comprehensive textbook on all aspects of the planning and construction of baubotanical structures. At present the discipline is too young for that. Instead it conveys a cross-section of knowledge from an interdisciplinary standpoint using generally understandable language so that it may encourage cooperation between protagonists from different backgrounds in the realisation of growing structures. It is therefore of equal interest to architects, planners, scientists, practitioners and potential builders. Unlike many other design handbooks, it does claim to convey a set of categorical rules for construction, in part due to a lack of adequate practical examples and scientific research. Instead, it takes a predominantly speculative standpoint. Many of the projects shown do not conform to normed building construction methods and thus require special permission and the participation of receptive experts, authorities and companies who are willing to think outside the box. Last but not least, these projects are frequently the product of an open-minded building community with a pioneering spirit and sometimes also alliances that dispense with typical classifications of roles. It is precisely for this reason that this book aims to inspire and encourage people to undertake new projects, to continue searching for solutions to open questions and to nurture and elaborate new visions.

13 Installation of pre-cultivated baubotanical elements. Plane Tree Cube, Nagold → Chapter 6, pp. 162—169 (photo: 2011).

2 Botanical Foundations

Since trees are comprised primarily of wood, Baubotanik can be described as a building method using "living wood". But while material properties such as strength and durability are certainly relevant for built constructions, defining Baubotanik according to the dominant material of its structures is only part of the equation. Far more important is that every living element of a baubotanical structure is considered as part of a larger whole. The focus lies on the organism of a tree, which is a self-maintaining and continuously developing system that interacts constantly with its environment. A fundamental aspect of all baubotanical design and construction projects is therefore maintaining the integrity of the organism and preserving its systemic equilibrium. As such, Baubotanik is guided as much by biological and processual factors as it is by the laws of physics and statics. In the first instance it is botanical principles that determine what is possible and what is not, what is easy to achieve and what is particularly problematic.

Understanding the structure, composition and functions of the different organs of a tree is fundamental to learning how trees develop as complex organisms along with the basic patterns of their growth. In this respect, the practice of Baubotanik shares the same foundation as fruit growing, horticulture, forestry or tree maintenance. In these disciplines, the problem areas and corresponding tasks that address them are usually well defined. For example, the primary goal of tree maintenance is to ensure the tree's ongoing health and long-term structural stability.[1] Baubotanik differs from these in that it is not about solving known problems but instead focuses on creatively exploring the new design and functional possibilities of tree growth. This chapter aims therefore to provide an overview of fundamental botanical principles and specific adaptation and optimisation phenomena with a view to determining their usefulness for the creative process of baubotanical design and construction. To begin with, however, we shall outline the most important dimensions and parameters of tree growth so that we can better quantitatively classify biological processes in the context of human construction activities.

The capacity and contribution of trees

Trees can grow to a vast size and incredible age and make an enormous contribution over their lifetimes. The largest tree in the world today is probably a coastal redwood (*Sequoia sempervirens*) in Redwood National Park in California, USA, which has a height of 115.55 m and an estimated wood volume of 530 m^3.[2] The probably oldest individual tree, with an age of 4852 years, is a Western Green Pine (*Pinus longaeva*) in the White Mountains (also in California, USA).[3] So-called "clonal colonies" of trees can grow to become even older. The record is held by a colony of quaking aspen (*Populus tremula*) known as Pando (Fishlake National Forest, Utah, USA), whose more than 40,000 trunks extend over an area of 43.6 hectares and spring from one common root system.[4] Computational modelling has estimated the age of this root system to be about 14,000 years.[5]

This means that some individual trees are older than the pyramids of Giza, which are known for their enormous durability. And at the time when the first saplings of the Pando germinated, around the beginning of the Neolithic period ca. 9500 BC, humankind had not even invented agriculture. Trees also have the capacity to reach the height of 30-storey buildings or expand over an area equivalent to that of about 20 Manhattan street blocks. As with all plants, these impressive "structural" feats are the product of a single biochemical process—photosynthesis. Using only the energy of the sun, they convert water and CO_2 into sugar and oxygen to produce the basic constituents of their entire biomass. Aside from this, they need only a few nutrients and trace elements, which they absorb with water sucked up from the soil (→ Fig. 1). This and all other processes that contribute to a tree's growth take place at ambient temperature and under normal pressure — unlike the energy-intensive processes needed to produce modern building materials such as steel or concrete. In stark contrast to conventional construction, which results in vast quantities of greenhouse gas emissions, building with living trees not only binds CO_2 but also produces oxygen.

Limits of tree growth

Given how impressive these facts are, one would be forgiven for believing that trees — and therefore also Baubotanik — provide an almost inexhaustible potential for construction. For a true and fair assessment, however, one should be aware of the limits of tree growth. The first question is how much "construction mass" can trees provide, in what timescale, and how effective are they at providing it? The field of forestry uses the parameters "annual wood growth" and "wood stock"[6] to denote the potential yield of an area of woodland. For example, woods and forests in Germany have an average wood stock of somewhere between 200 and 400 m³ (cubic metres of solid material) per hectare of woodland.[7] In visual terms, this translates into a 2 to 4 cm thick slab of wood covering the base of the forest. This same volume, however, also indicates the order of magnitude of wood volume that can be created and survives in baubotanical structures. It corresponds roughly to the volume of wood contained within a highly optimised lightweight construction. For example, the wood lattice shells of the Multihalle in Mannheim, built in 1974 and designed by Frei Otto and Carlfried Mutscher, contain about as much wood as there would be in the same area of woodland.[8] This was a highly efficient structure built by designers who became world-famous for their economic use of material. The quantities of material utilised in conventional architecture is typically many times higher. By comparison, a single-family house built as a mass timber structure contains up to 90 m³ of wood,[9] which corresponds to approx. 2500 to 3000 m² of forest, i.e. more than 20 times the floor area of the house. And while such a wooden house is erected in a few days or weeks, it takes about 80 years for that quantity of wood to grow in the forest.

By way of illustration, the amount of wood that grows each year in an area of woodland corresponds roughly to a 1 mm thick layer of wood across the entire forest floor.[10] This volume of wood can embody about 3 kWh of energy[11] — which corresponds to about 0.3 % of the solar energy that the surface is exposed to each year. This is obviously a very low value, especially when one considers that a modern photovoltaic system would generate about 100 kWh, i.e. about 30 times as much (electrical) energy, on the same surface area.[12] The comparatively low efficiency of trees is explained by the fact that photosynthesis uses only a small part of the light spectrum (blue and red light) and that its most important raw material — CO_2 — is only present in the atmosphere in extremely small concentrations of 0.3 %. In addition, a tree consumes a large part of the energy it absorbs for its life processes and a not inconsiderable part of a forest's biomass dies over the course of a forest's development.

We can draw several conclusions from this for Baubotanik. Firstly, it would be presumptuous to believe that entire houses with massive walls, ceilings and roofs can be made of "living wood" created by growing trees. The above-mentioned figures show that this lies outside the realm of the possible (→ Chapter 7, pp. 174–176). Rather, the potential of Baubotanik — as outlined in the first chapter — lies in utilising the constructional possibilities of trees in symbiosis with their ecological and aesthetic qualities so that they make a beneficial contribution to our built environment. Secondly, it is important to note that although ancient trees can grow to an extraordinary size and mass, the growth of the biomass of the tree is an extremely tedious process and it is therefore in constant short supply. While this may at first seem paradoxical, the comparative inefficiency of photosynthesis means that trees have to manage the resources at their disposal well and use them as efficiently as possible: through ingenious branching and leaf positioning, they try and capture as much valuable sunlight as possible without using more wood than necessary to "build" the capturing surfaces. At the same time, the resulting construction must be strong and stable enough to withstand high forces, such as wind and snow, over a long period of time. Living trees are therefore highly optimised structures that not only produce their own construction but also maintain it over many decades or even centuries using a combination of protective mechanisms, continuous adaptation and self-repair.

Formation and functions of the basic organs of a tree

Despite their enormous size and extraordinary complexity, trees in principle have a very simple structure and develop according to relatively straightforward processes. They consist of the basic organs shoot axis, leaf and root. The flowers and fruit that subsequently form are ultimately just metamorphoses of the basic organs of shoot axis and leaf. Since they are not specifically relevant for baubotanical design and construction, we shall not detail them any further in the following. The roots can be further subdivided into main and fine roots and the shoot axis into branches, twigs and stems. These organs or units can be grouped into two functional groups: The leaves and fine roots serve to exchange nutrients with the environment and are therefore optimised for maximum surface area and occupy as much growth space as possible. The twigs, branches, stems and the main or coarse roots can be described as transport and support organs whose task it is to connect the fine roots and leaves as efficiently as possible, usually by the shortest route, and to facilitate their physical and spatial distribution.

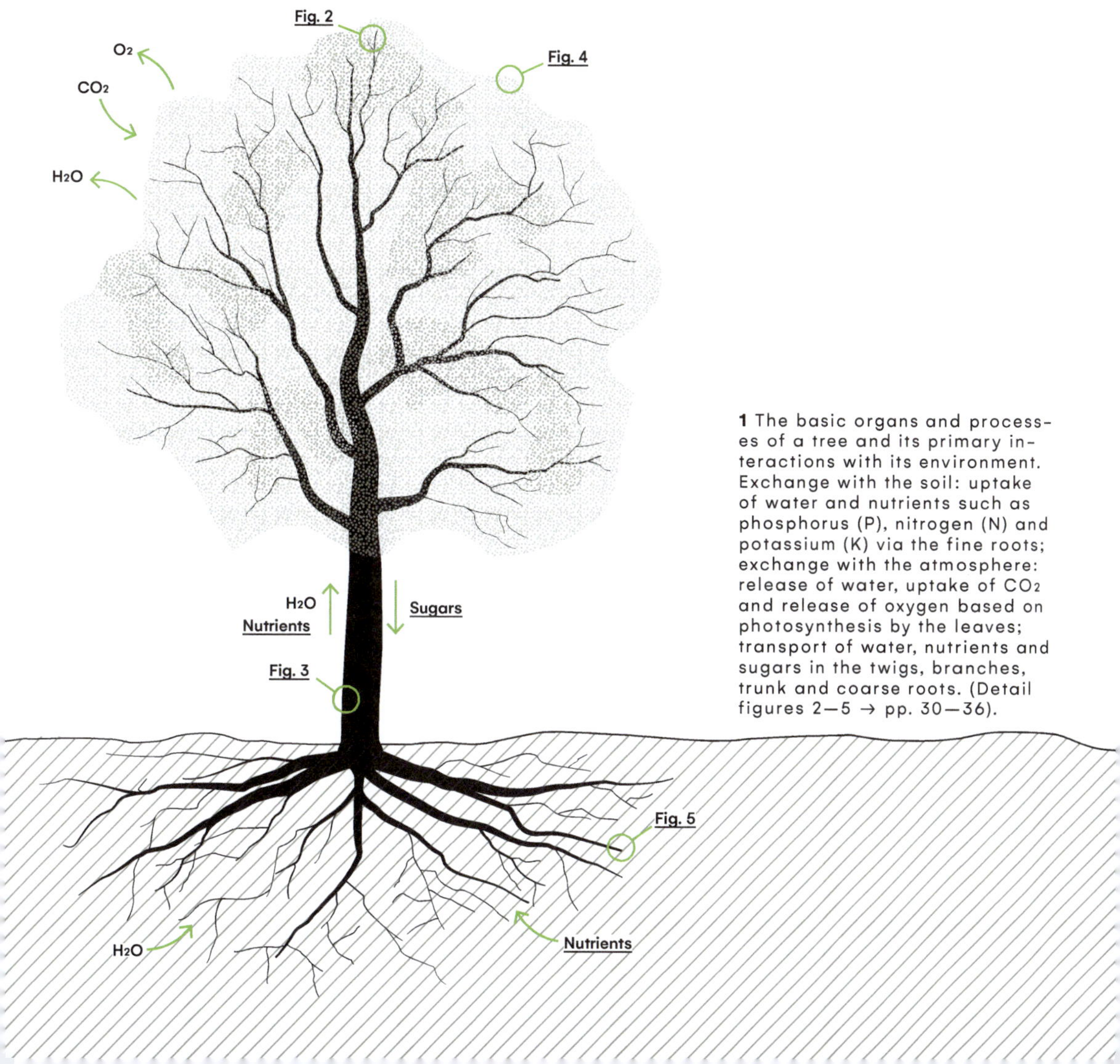

1 The basic organs and processes of a tree and its primary interactions with its environment. Exchange with the soil: uptake of water and nutrients such as phosphorus (P), nitrogen (N) and potassium (K) via the fine roots; exchange with the atmosphere: release of water, uptake of CO_2 and release of oxygen based on photosynthesis by the leaves; transport of water, nutrients and sugars in the twigs, branches, trunk and coarse roots. (Detail figures 2–5 → pp. 30–36).

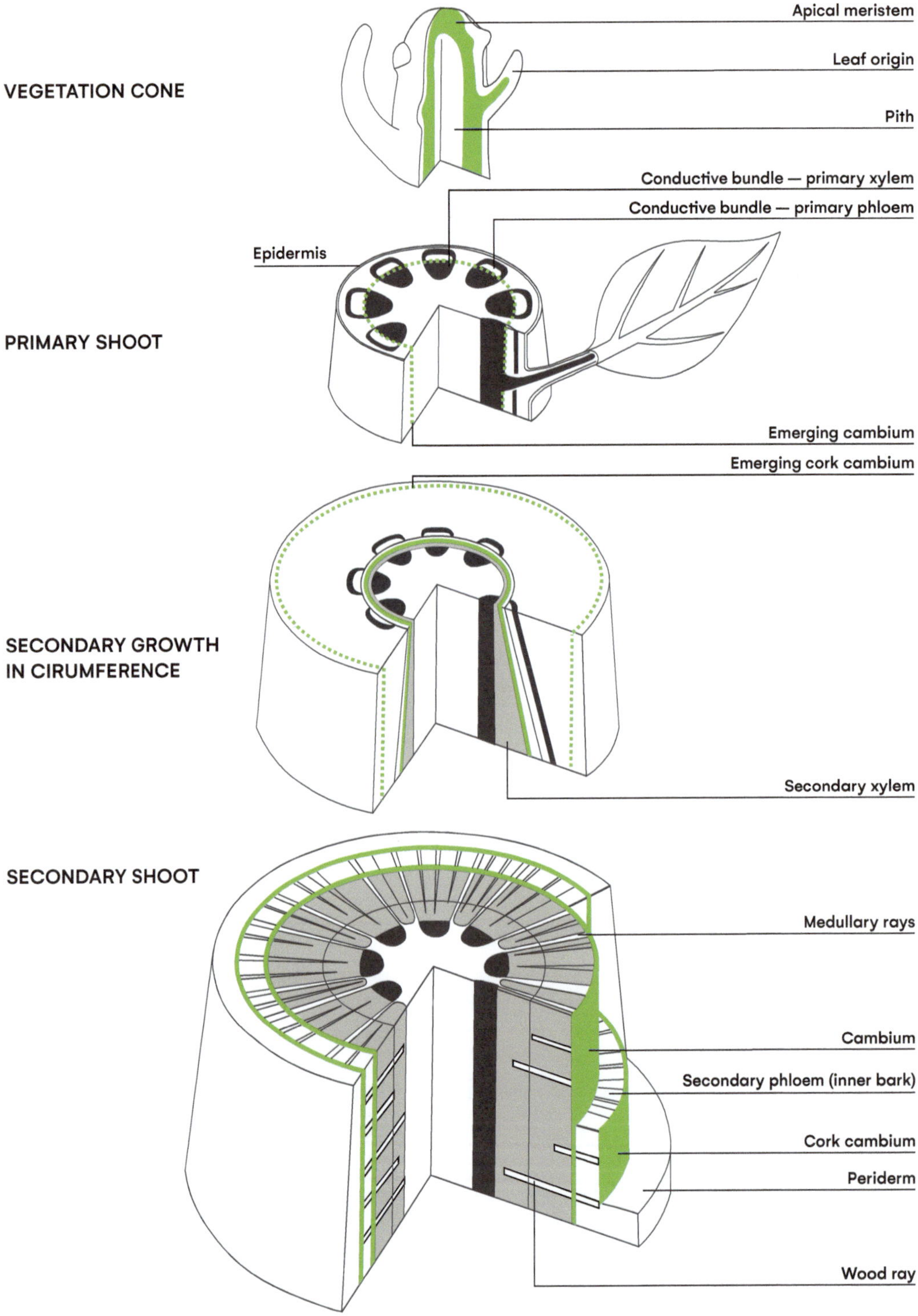

2 Development of the shoot axis of a tree.

Shoot axis

The shoot axis is of particular relevance to Baubotanik as it is this part of a plant's structure that is typically altered by cutting, shaping and joining. The development of the shoot axis is also indirectly influenced by changes in growing conditions.

Formation and structure of a young shoot axis

At the tip of each shoot or shoot axis is the vegetative cone (shoot apex), a region of rapid cell division (meristem) that constantly produces new cells. This is where all the primary tissue of a young shoot axis develops: the ground tissue (parenchyma), the conductive and stabilising tissues and the outer tissue (epidermis). In the growth process, straight sections of shoot axis, the internodes, form in a species-typical pattern that spans between nodal points that either serve as the basis for a leaf or the point from which a lateral shoot branches off. This zone of cell division is followed by an area in which the cells elongate and differentiate. As a result, the primary shoot axis increases somewhat in circumference and the vegetative cone at the growing point is pushed further upwards, while at the same time the leaves unfurl.

The conductive tissues of the young shoot axis consist of bundles of two different types of tissue, the xylem and the phloem. While the xylem transports water and nutrients from the root upwards to the leaves, the phloem conducts assimilates, typically sugars formed in the leaves, to the places where they are consumed. The conducting bundles are arranged in a star shape (in cross-section) around the inner core of ground tissue, the central pith, which in a tree is usually a few millimetres in diameter, with the xylem oriented inwards and the phloem outwards. Narrow radial bars of ground tissue, the medullary rays, extend outwards between the conductive bundles to the primary bark (→ Fig. 2 top). The ground tissue consists of generalised, living cells which, in contrast to the axially elongated cells of the conductive bundles, have no specific orientation. Unlike the more specialised tissues, the cells of ground tissue can subdivide relatively easily, which is why they play a significant role in many of the most important developmental steps in Baubotanik.

Secondary growth in circumference

After cell elongation is complete, the shoot no longer exhibits longitudinal growth in that area, which can be seen when the length of the internodes no longer changes. At the same time primary growth in circumference also ends. Meanwhile, the vegetative cone remains active, constantly forming new tissue, which leads to elongation at the tip of the shoot and also to the development of further leaves and side shoots. The longer this gets, the greater the transport tasks and mechanical demands on the shoot axis. Trees meet these demands through secondary growth in circumference: as cells of the medullary rays subdivide, a ring of meristematic tissue—the cambium—develops starting from a layer of divisible cells between the phloem and xylem in the conductive bundles. Through tangential division, radial cell stacks form, creating a secondary xylem facing inwards—the woody stem of the tree—and a secondary phloem facing outwards—the bast or inner bark (→ Fig. 2, middle and bottom).

Formation, structure and function of the cork layer and bark

This growth in thickness increases the girth of the shoot. It becomes more stable and can transport greater amounts of water and nutrients. At the same time, the increasing circumference causes the primary outer tissue (epidermis) to tear, necessitating a secondary protective outer tissue (periderm) around it. This forms when the cells in the ground tissue of the inner bark become capable of subdivision and another ring of divisible cells develops—the cork cambium. The outer tissue of the inner bark produced by the cambium thus only fulfils its conductive and retentive functions for a short time, as they soon become assimilated into the outer bark due to the activity of the cork cambium. The cork cambium in turn forms cork cells on the outside and a smaller amount of ground tissue on the inside that often contains chlorophyll. This is the reason why young shoots are mostly green and can also contribute—to a small extent—to photosynthesis. Over time, however, the initially transparent cork cells on the outermost layer die, turning brown or grey and obscuring the green colouring (→ Fig. 2 bottom). In some tree species, such as the European beech (*Fagus sylvatica*) or the hazel (*Corylus avellana*), this secondary outer tissue remains intact. This is made possible by the fact that in these species the cells of the cork cambium grow laterally to accommodate the circumferential growth. In many other tree species, however, the cork cambium cannot expand sufficiently to cope with such strong growth in thickness, and also tears open. Each new tear in the outer tissue causes a new cork cambium to develop further inside, in the area of the bast. Parts of the bast are then repeatedly cut off from the supply of nutrients and die. Together with the old periderm, they form a tertiary outer tissue—the outer layer of bark. The task of this layer of dead cells, which can often grow to several centimetres or even decimetres thick,[13] is to protect the inner bark and the wood from negative influences from the environment such as extreme temperatures, mechanical damage or penetration by fungi, bacteria or insects. The structure and appearance of the bark changes greatly as a tree grows and often acquires a characteristic appearance that can be traced back to the specific formation and growth patterns of that species' cork cambium. Typical bark variants include striped bark (e.g. *Thuja plicata*), reticulated bark (e.g. *Fraxinus excelsior*) and scaly bark (e.g. *Pinus sylvestris*). In some species, such as the plane tree (*Platanus × hispanica*), layers of tissue separate at regular intervals, causing the outermost bark layers to peel or blow off in relatively large flakes as they grow thicker (→ Chapter 3, pp. 88—89).

Formation, structure and function of the wood

Although the bark of some trees can grow to a considerable thickness, the largest mass of a tree's shoot axis is almost always its woody core, as the cambium produces much more woody tissue than bark tissue. Due to tangential cell division, cells of the same kind are usually "copied" in the cambium. That means that around the primary conductive bundles, the cambium produces mainly conductive tissues for transporting water and wood fibres for stabilisation, while in the area of the medullary rays, more ground tissue is produced. As a result, the medullary rays continue radially in the newly formed wood. Their task is essentially the storage of reserves and in this context the lateral transport of assimilates between the bark and the wood body. The storage of reserve materials takes place in trees of temperate latitudes[14] in late summer and autumn, when growth is complete. When new leaves are formed in spring and the cambium begins to grow, the tree can draw on these reserves. To enable this exchange, the medullary rays extend as bast rays into the bark (→ Fig. 3).

The conductive and stabilising tissues between the medullary rays make up 60 to 80 % of the tree's wood and consist largely of tracheids. These elongated cells typically have substantially thickened cell walls, stiffened by the incorporation of lignin, and thus form extremely stable and durable structures. Tracheids die shortly after their formation and are usually hollow. In conifers (gymnosperms) they serve both as stabilisation and to transport water. To enable water transport from one cell to the next, the cell walls of the tracheids are perforated, especially at their upper and lower ends. In deciduous trees (angiosperms), tracheids arranged above one another merge by dissolving the horizontal cell walls to form vessels that are particularly efficient at transporting water. The strengthening function is then taken over by specialised tracheids (wood fibre or sclerenchyma cells), which have much thicker, non-perforated cell walls. As the shape and composition of these tissues change over the course of a year, a distinct pattern of annual rings forms (→ Fig. 3 bottom). Conifers, for example, increasingly form very thick-walled tracheids for stabilisation towards the end of a growing season. Many deciduous trees form both vessels and wood fibre tracheids throughout the entire growing season, but towards the end of a growing season the vessels grow smaller (diffuse-porous woods such as maple, willow or birch species). Other species, however, only form vessels at the beginning of the vegetation period and then (practically) only stabilisation tissue (ring-porous tree species such as oak or ash species).

To accommodate the increase in circumference, the cells of the cambium divide repeatedly in a radial direction (lateral growth). In the process, further regions of parenchymatous tissue are created at regular intervals, which extend radially outwards as the tree thickness grows, complementing the original medullary rays (wood rays). As a result, each species develops a specific pattern of radially arranged ground tissue and axially aligned conductive and stabilising tissue as it continues to grow.

The tree wood serves a physiological function for only a few years. This is because only the outermost annual rings, the sapwood, conduct water and store nutrients. In the case of ring-porous tree species, water is only transported in the newly formed annual ring. The inner layers of the sapwood lose their conductive function and the cells of the wood rays die. Therefore, as a tree grows older the core of the shoot axis consists increasingly of dead wood cells. Although this core is no longer physiologically active, it plays an important part of the tree's structural supporting system. In some tree species, secondary plant substances such as tannins become incorporated into the cell walls and the connections between the cells close in the no longer active conductive tissues. This process of heartwood formation, often recognisable as a darker coloration in the cross-section, prevents capillary water transport and makes the wood more stable and durable.

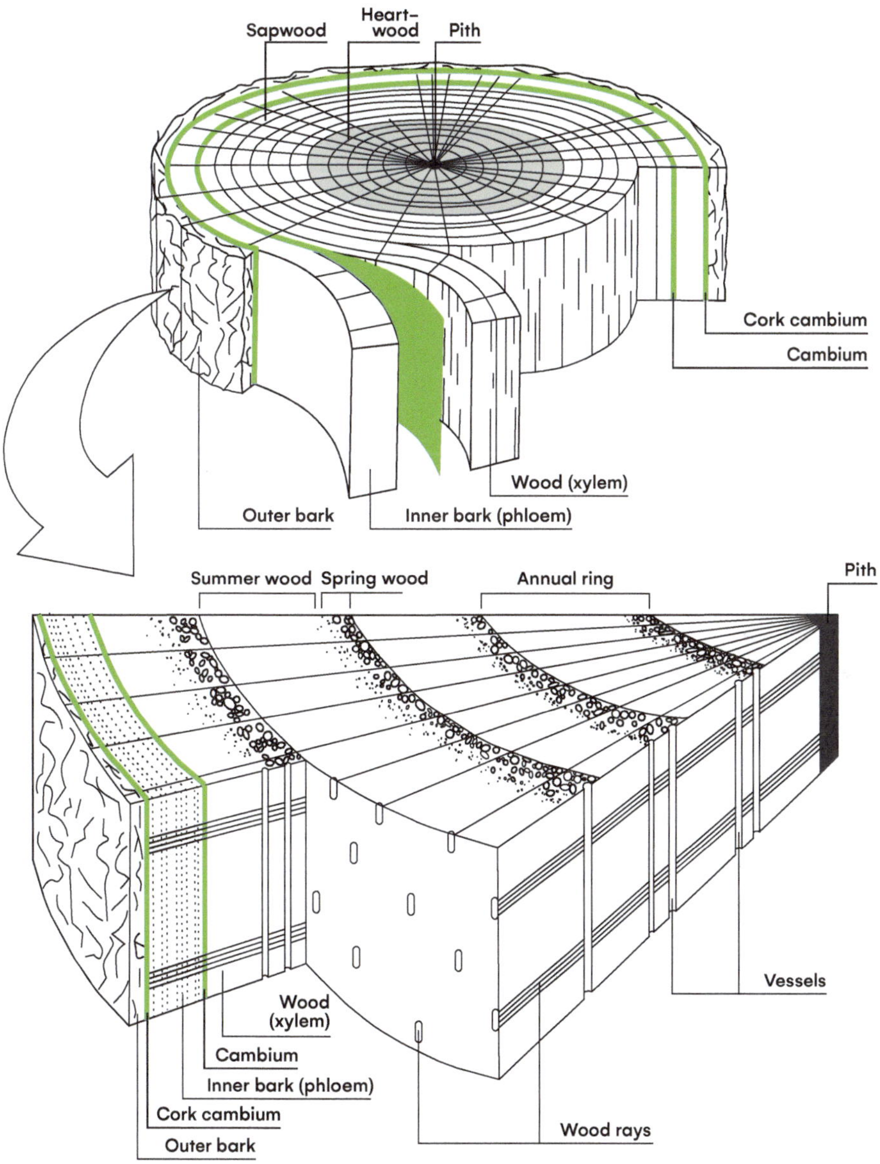

3 Structure of the wood and bark of a perennial shoot axis (trunk).

Leaf

Aside from the essential function that leaves serve for the plant itself, they play an important architectonic role in Baubotanik as a structure's green "clothing". Accordingly, they serve both a spatial-volumetric as well as a climatic purpose. They are not, however, themselves the focus of baubotanical design because their form and structure are not directly altered. Instead, their appearance is only influenced indirectly, for example through changes to growing conditions or manipulation of a plant's growing form at the level of the shoot axis. It is nevertheless still useful to understand their formation and anatomical structure in the context of the development and function of the tree as a whole.

Formation and shape of a leaf

As described above, leaves emerge from the leaf nodes on a young shoot axis that are created as the vegetative cone grows. The arrangement and especially the shape of the leaves are a characteristic feature of each tree species. Leaf shapes can vary enormously, from the simple heart-shaped leaves, for example, of the "foxglove tree" (*Paulownia tomentosa*) to the pinnate leaves of the "tree of heaven" (*Ailanthus altissima*) or the palmately compound leaves of the horse chestnut (*Aesculus hippocastanum*) to the extremely long and thin needle leaves of the common spruce (*Picea abies*). These diverse forms arose through evolutionary adaptation to different environmental factors. But even within a single tree, the shape, size and colour of the leaves can vary greatly depending on the respective growth conditions. On the outer part of a tree crown exposed to the sun, the leaves are smaller and thicker, whereas leaves in the inner, shady part of the crown are thinner and larger to make the most of the lower levels of light. Over the course of time, many other forms of leaf organs have evolved with special functions, such as bud scales, leaf spines, or leaf tendrils.

Anatomical structure of a leaf

Seen in cross-section, the core of a leaf consists of two layers of ground tissue (parenchyma). In the upper area is palisade tissue, which is formed by one to three layers of elongated cells arranged perpendicular to the leaf surface. The primary task of this layer is photosynthesis, which is why approx. 80 % of the chloroplasts are located here. Below this is the sponge tissue, which consists of irregularly shaped cells with numerous cavities between them to ensure aeration of the leaf. At the top and bottom, these tissues are enclosed by a thin, translucent layer of cells, the leaf epidermis, which forms a waxy water-impermeable layer (cuticle) on the outer surface that is also translucent. This permits as much light as possible into the leaf, while preventing gaseous exchange with the environment. The latter takes place almost exclusively via the stomata on the underside of the leaf (→ Fig. 4). The epidermis also contributes to a small extent to the mechanical stabilisation of the leaf. However, the greatest support for the predominantly thin leaf surface is provided by the leaf stalk and leaf veins. These consist of conductive bundles which, just as in the shoot, serve both as veins transporting nutrients and water and as mechanical stabilisation.

Main functions of the leaves and their control

The primary function of the leaves is photosynthesis: the production of energy-rich, organic compounds from energy-poor carbon dioxide and water with the help of sunlight. This process of assimilation — the precise chemical details of which are not relevant here — takes place in the chloroplasts with the help of chlorophyll. The re-

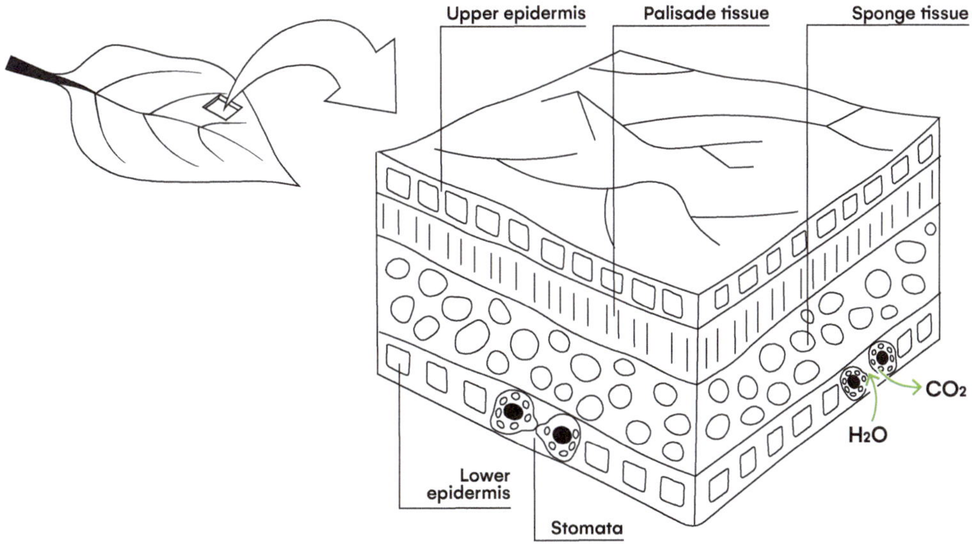

4 Schematic structure of a leaf.

sulting assimilates are essentially sugars which are transported through the phloem part of the leaf veins to the shoot axis and then to where they are needed or for storage. Water flows in the opposite direction through the xylem part of the leaf veins into the palisade and sponge tissue. Only a small part of this water is used for photosynthesis; the vast majority evaporates and is released into the atmosphere. Water serves therefore not just as "building material" for the plant but also a solvent and transport medium for absorbing and distributing nutrients from the soil. Water evaporating via the leaf is therefore not "wasted" but drives the process of water transport by creating suction (→ pp. 47–48). This process of transpiration means that leaves indirectly serve an essential transport function. The leaves can also regulate water transport through the stomata, allowing them to manage the plant's water balance. When the water content in the surrounding cells decreases, the stomata close to prevent excessive water loss. When the water content replenishes, they open again. The plant therefore actively regulates the exchange of gases with the environment via its leaves. For example, if the soil dries out, the stomata close, reducing water transport and consumption. This, however, also impacts on the diffusion of carbon dioxide into the leaf and reduces the release of oxygen. If there is sustained insufficient water supply, photosynthesis will stop and ultimately plant growth will cease.

Root

The underground roots of plants, like the leaves, are not themselves the subject of baubotanical design. The aerial roots of some plants like rubber trees, however, offer excellent potential for baubotanical construction in certain climates, and are the primary construction element of the living bridges seen in → Chapter 1, pp. 10—13. The roots do, however, serve an important mechanical and physiological function for the plant, and for this reason it is important to understand the interrelationship between their anatomical structure, formation and functional processes, despite the fact that the above-ground parts of plants and trees are of most interest to Baubotanik. Unlike the shoot axis and leaves above ground, the various underground functions are not performed by different organs but by differently specialised parts of the root system, which can change function as the root system develops.

Structure and development of a root

Many aspects of the formation and development of a root are similar to that of a shoot axis. The root tip, like the vegetative cone of the shoot axis, creates the new cell tissue of the young root. Behind this region of cell division at the tip of the root is a region of cell elongation measuring just a few millimetres, followed by a region of cell differentiation. While the vegetative cone of the shoot is enveloped by young leaves that shield it from the surrounding air, the root tip is enveloped by the root cap (calyptra) which protects the sensitive divisible tissue (meristme) against injury resulting, for example, from friction with the soil. In addition, the root cap secretes a gel-like mucilaginous layer that makes it easier for the root to penetrate the soil (→ Fig. 5).

In cross-section, the structure of a young root is quite different to that of a shoot axis. At its centre is only one central bundle with the primary water-conducting xylem in the middle, which has a star-shaped cross-section. The primary phloem fills the spaces between the rays of this star. This vascular bundle may also contain strengthening tissue (sclerenchyma) to give the young root a higher tensile strength. Around this is the pericambium (pericycle), a layer capable of growth, from which the lateral roots and secondary bark later emerge. Together, these tissues form the central cylinder.[15] Surrounding this cylinder is

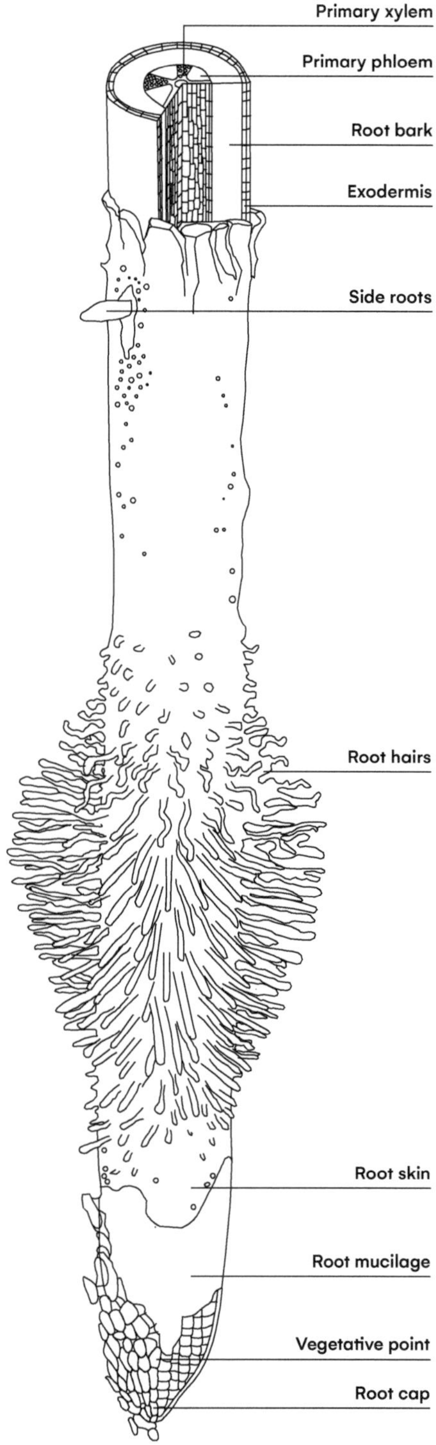

5 Structure of a young root. The structure of older roots is similar to that of perennial shoot axes.

another layer of living cells, the endodermis or innermost bark layer of the root which controls the absorption of water and nutrient salts. This is followed by the actual root cortex, which usually consists of colourless ground tissue that serves a storage function and facilitates the exchange of substances between the central vascular bundle and the root skin. The root skin (rhizodermis), in turn, is an outer tissue consisting of a single layer of cells, which, unlike the epidermis of the shoot, does not form a cuticle. Instead, in many tree species,[16] tubular protrusions grow out of the rhizodermis cells.[17] These root hairs effectively enlarge the surface area of the root so that it can absorb water and minerals more effectively. Like the root cap, the cell walls of the root skin are thin and mucilagous, which also helps improve water and nutrient uptake. The rhizodermis cells have a lifespan of just a few days, after which they die. Consequently, they are found only in the differentiation zone of young, growing roots and only this zone can therefore absorb water and nutrients. Nevertheless, the vast number of root hairs means that the water-absorbing root surface of a plant is usually larger than that of the water-releasing leaf surface.[18] Even before the root skin dies, a secondary, largely water-impermeable outer tissue of cork cells, the exodermis, forms from the ground tissue of the bark. Once this stage is reached, the root functions solely to conduct water and no longer to absorb it.

Differentiation into coarse and fine roots

Roots fulfil different tasks that are strongly predetermined by their diameter. One therefore differentiates between coarse and fine roots. Coarse roots usually result from a particularly strong root tip and are comparable to the stem and the main branches of the shoot. They exhibit secondary growth in circumference and can grow to a high age. Their main function is to transport water and nutrients and to anchor the tree in the soil. The roots nearest to the base of the trunk are most subject to bending stresses (like the trunk and main branches), while coarse roots in more peripheral areas primarily experience tensile stresses.

Fine and very fine roots (also called fibrous roots) are usually lateral roots that emerge from a typically thin root tip and exhibit little to no growth in thickness. They die back after a relatively short space of time and their function is to absorb water and nutrients. As this happens only in the very young roots, which are a few days old and grow longitudinally, they continue to grow and branch, penetrating an ever larger volume of soil.

Secondary thickness growth

Parallel to the growth in thickness of the shoot axis, secondary thickness growth also takes place in the (coarse) roots. A layer of divisible cells forms in the central cylinder along the xylem, creating a closed, initially star-shaped cambium mantle. Through cell division, this cambium now produces xylem elements on the inside and phloem elements on the outside. As xylem growth is initially stronger it leads to a rounding of the cambium, which eventually becomes cylindrical. As growth continues, primary medullary rays and secondary wood rays are formed similar to those in the shoot axis. Soon, the exodermis, the primary bark and the endodermis cannot accommodate the growth in circumference and tear, causing the cells to die. As a tertiary outer tissue, the pericambium forms a periderm and with time a bark can also form as the root continues to grow. Accordingly, the structure of coarse roots that are several years old resembles that of shoot axes. The most significant structural differences are in the arrangement of the primary conducting elements at the centre. The wood of the root is usually wider-lumened (i.e. has a large inner diameter) and therefore more similar to the spring wood of the stem. As a consequence, the annual rings of root wood are also often less pronounced.

Formation of the tree shape

Background knowledge on the three basic structural components of trees—shoot axis, leaf and root—is useful for understanding the development and internal anatomy of the organs of a tree and how they function together. But to understand how trees grow to form such large and complex organisms and how they acquire their respective characteristic form and appearance, one needs to know not just how but also where these organs arise and the pattern of their disposition in space. The spatial aspect of tree growth therefore has parallels with architecture—and it is therefore no coincidence that this is often termed the architecture of trees.[19]

Development of the shoot system

As a tree's biomass increases with growth, it needs ever more photosynthesis products to supply its material and energy requirements. To this end, it must produce new leaves and expose them optimally to the sun, arranging them in space in such a way that they do not shade each other. Evolution's answer to this problem is the branching of the shoot axis. Alongside length and thickness growth, branching growth is therefore the third principle that shapes the development of the shoot system. As the shoot axis grows, the vegetative cone produces cell structures in the angle between a leaf stalk and the shoot that can develop into a side shoot. The spatial configuration of the shoot system is a product of how these side buds and leaf stalks are arranged on the parent shoot. There are three typical patterns—alternate, opposite and whorled arrangement—and it is these that determine the characteristic form of a tree species, especially in young trees. As trees grow older, these basic geometric patterns play a lesser role, and it is the pattern of which leaf systems actually produce side shoots that determine its continuing development. Thus, the ability of the main shoot axis to control the development of lateral shoots determines the development of the tree. This principle is known as apical dominance and is mainly a product of the plant hormone auxin, which is formed in high concentrations in the vegetative cone of the main shoot, and is then transported downwards together with the assimilates from photosynthesis into the inner bark. This hormone is responsible for inhibiting the development of lateral buds, suppressing their development—they are then "dormant"—or inhibiting side shoot growth so that they grow much more slowly than the main shoot. Unlike the main shoot, the side shoots do not grow vertically upwards but at a diagonal angle to the main shoot. When the main shoot is removed or damaged, it loses its apical dominance, allowing formerly dormant buds to sprout and side shoots to orient themselves upwards.

Depending on how the main shoot controls the development of the side buds or side shoots, different growth forms result. If the main shoot remains strongly dominant throughout the tree's life, an upright trunk with flat branching side branches develops, resulting in a conical crown as is typical for many conifers, such as the common spruce (*Picea abies*). Most deciduous trees start off with a similar shape in the first few years but as the tree grows older, the main shoot can lose its dominance, causing a larger number of nearly vertical axes to develop, resulting in a rounded crown at the top.

As the width of the crown increases, the lower branches and the branches inside the crown become increasingly shaded, and their photosynthetic output decreases accordingly. If they produce a smaller amount of assimilates overall than they need to sustain themselves, they become inefficient for the tree. They then either die or are actively cast off by the tree. Through this process of branch or twig cleaning, the tree simplifies its branch structure and frees itself from the ballast of superfluous mass. As a result, the lower part of the trunk becomes increasingly free of branches and the crown gradually moves upwards (→ Fig. 6).

In summary, the shape of a tree is a product of the interplay of patterns of length, thickness and branching growth, of apical dominance and dying off. With the annual repetition of these patterns, the tree grows in size and complexity with the crown form being largely determined by the orientation of the branches to one another and their change in orientation over time. Different tree species have characteristic geometric patterns, but these result predominantly from differences in the way the tree controls growth and not from fundamentally different growing processes.[20]

When trees are used in Baubotanik to form architectural structures, the trees naturally retain their basic patterns and principles. The sequential succession of length, thickness and branching growth also means that the basic geometry of a baubotanical structure does not change as a product of growth in length, since elongation only occurs at the very young shoot tips. However, growth in thickness does occur, making the structure gradually stiffer. Where a baubotanical structure does change is when the tree sheds branches or other parts of its structure that it no longer needs for self-preservation and have therefore become excess ballast.

6 Ideal development of a deciduous tree.

Development of the root system

Unlike the shoot system, the root system is only partially determined by specific geometric patterns. Roots do not develop according to the pattern of nodes and internodes seen in the shoots, and lateral roots do not form from the root tip but develop as a secondary growth from the innermost bark layer, the pericambium. This much more open growth principle is a factor of the frequently very variable growth conditions in the soil and the task of the root system. Unlike branches, roots do not need to be self-supporting and there is no factor that determines the pattern of growth underground like the sun does above ground. Roots have two primary goals: to find suitable soil and then multiply there very quickly to absorb water and nutrients as effectively as possible, and to provide anchorage.

The shape of the root system changes greatly over the course of its development. The young main root of a germinating tree usually grows vertically downwards. As root systems develop, one can identify three basic patterns: deep-rooted trees, for example, typically drive a taproot vertically downwards towards the groundwater, while shallow-rooted trees usually have horizontally oriented roots close to the surface which absorb percolating rainwater.[21] The root growth of heartroots lies somewhere between these two variants. More than anything, however, the shape of all these root systems is influenced by the soil conditions: a root ultimately always seeks the path of least resistance through the soil and then branches out where growth conditions are good and sufficient resources are available.

As we do not experience or see roots growing underground, we often underestimate their dimensions. General statements or schemas are more often than not misleading. In natural environments, well-developed root systems comprise wood roots that extend more or less horizontally at a certain depth beneath the surface. It can frequently extend far beyond the base of the tree crown[22] and the majority of the roots are found in the layers close to the surface, with the root tips often in the uppermost 15 cm.[23] Tree species with a strongly developed taproot system, such as the English oak (*Quercus robur*), can in extreme cases reach depths of up to 10 m, but more usually they extend not much deeper than 1.5 to 2 m into the soil.[24]

The distinction between coarse and fine roots described earlier suggests that the root system has a similar mechanism to apical dominance in the shoot axes. Similarly, the fact that fine roots usually have a short lifetime compared to coarse roots suggests a mechanism similar to branch cleaning. And indeed, older sections of coarse roots rarely have any fine roots branching off them.

While the root system and its development plays a lesser role in Baubotanik, because these structures are almost always formed from the branches and trunks of trees, a healthy root system is always essential for the above-ground parts of a tree to develop properly and be well anchored in the soil. Consequently, knowledge of root systems and their development is essential to ensure adequate root space is available, especially when designing in the proximity of buildings.[25]

Trees and their context

In their natural habitat, few trees are solitary and most grow in groups or as part of larger wooded areas. Baubotanical structures likewise rarely consist of a single plant and are usually formed by many relatively densely planted trees. The conditions and processes that shape the development of groups of trees are therefore also relevant for Baubotanik.

Every tree requires growing space both above and below ground to meet its need for resources (→ Fig. 7). As a tree's biomass increases, so too does its demand for resources and thus for space. If many young trees grow within a small space, they will at some point inevitably end up competing for the available resources. Weaker specimens will increasingly lag behind the others and may eventually die. This process of the loss of plants is known in forestry science as "self-thinning". Tree stands are, therefore, also subject to the same processes seen at the level of plant tissue, plant organs and the plant organism: dying processes are as much part of development as growth processes.

The possible plant density depends on various site-specific factors, and on the tree species. In principle, however, the maximum possible number of plants on a specific area is always a function of the biomass.[26] For trees, the stem diameter is often used as a reference unit, as it provides a good measure for estimating the biomass. Because the relationship between biomass or stem diameter and growth space is linear, trees within a group of trees can be represented abstractly as a sphere, with the crown and the root space each forming a hemisphere. As shown in → Fig. 8, this means that the number of spheres that fit into a given space decreases as the spheres grow larger. While this geometrically derived model is highly simplified, it nevertheless corresponds closely to empirical values from the field of forestry.[27] The corresponding formulas for calculating self-thinning for certain tree species and locations can therefore serve as a schema in Baubotanik for calculating the diameter at which competition-induced loss of individual trees may result at a defined planting density. One must, however, bear in mind that the arrangement of trees in baubotanical structures is usually more complex than in natural environments, and that the boundaries between individual specimens can blur due to inosculation.

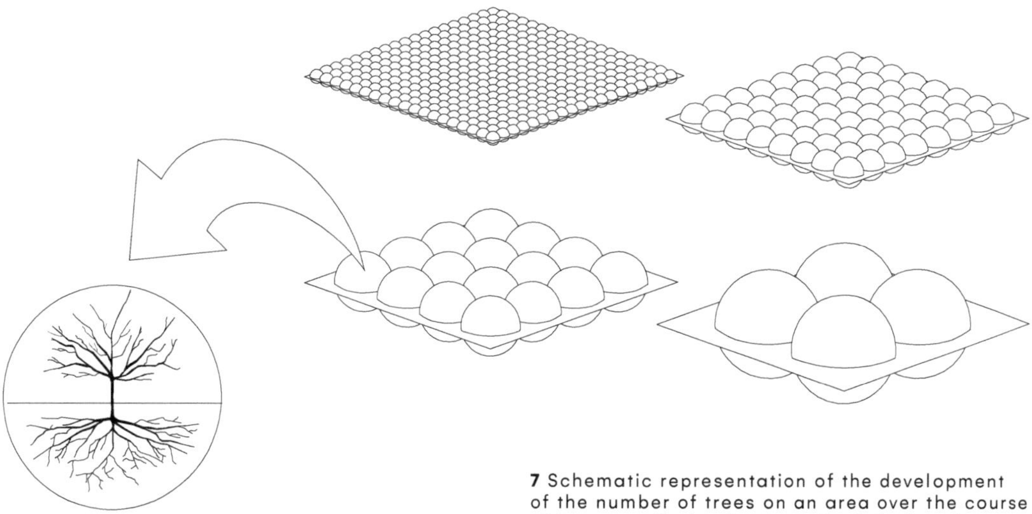

7 Schematic representation of the development of the number of trees on an area over the course of tree growth. As shown on the left, the above-ground and below-ground growth space of trees is represented as a hemisphere.

Regeneration

That tissue, organs or even entire parts of the shoot or root system die is therefore an integral part of the natural development of trees. Over the course of their often long lives, however, they will also have to cope with other losses or damage that are not part of this idealised process: animals of different kinds may eat leaves, roots or branches, and storms or snow loads may cause branches or entire trunks to snap or break off.

That trees can survive such losses is a product of their open, modular structure. Unlike humans or animals, plants are never fully grown but continue to grow throughout their lifetime, constantly producing new limbs and organs. This process of constant self-renewal is also activated by the loss of organs. When part of the shoot system is lost, other shoots compensate by growing stronger. Dormant buds, whose growth may have been suppressed by the apical meristems, may start to sprout, producing replacement shoots (→ Fig. 8[1]). A similar process happens in the root system when, for example, many new lateral roots form after the loss of a root from the pericambium (→ Fig. 8[3]). These replacement organs may develop directly at the site of the loss or also in other places if that is more advantageous for the organism as a whole. The horticultural practice of branch pruning and root pruning in tree nurseries makes use of these principles.

But the regenerative capacity of trees goes much further. As shown earlier, an important process in the formation and development of the basic organs is that tissue that has already differentiated can become capable of further division to produce other forms of tissue. For example, the cambium mantel can form from the ground tissue of the medullary rays. In principle, any living tissue of a plant is capable of dividing to produce any other conceivable tissue providing particular conditions prevail, with plant hormones providing the necessary stimulation. This so-called "totipotency" means that, in principle, a minute piece of living tissue can be the basis for the regeneration of an entire plant. Commercial plant nurseries utilise this fundamental process of regeneration for propagating selected clones from cell cultures in sterile laboratory conditions. While such methods have not yet been used in the field of Baubotanik, they offer potentially very interesting possibilities.

In trees in nature, the regeneration of entire organs from tissue that has regained its capacity to divide also plays an important role. New shoots can form not only from existing shoot nodes, the dormant buds, but also from tissue that has become divisible again, for example when large parts of the shoot system have been lost. These adventitious buds can also form in large numbers from wound tissue, the so-called "callus" (→ pp. 52–54), and often immediately grow into replacement shoots. This form of regeneration is stimulated in horticultural practice through the act of pollarding, or the more drastic coppicing of hedges, in which a hedge or bush is cut back almost to the ground to stimulate its rejuvenation through the formation of basal shoots from the wound tissue that ultimately grow into a new hedge.

The formation of adventitious shoots is not always the result of loss of part of the shoot system. They can also be triggered solely by changes in local growing conditions. For example, if part of

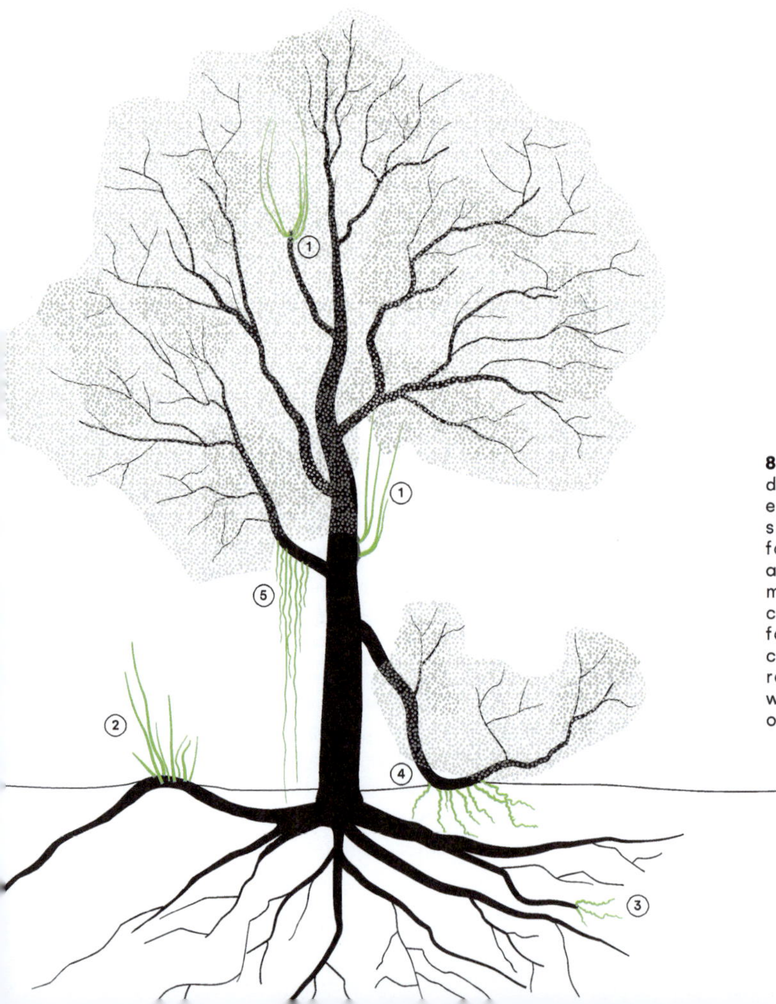

8 Schematic representation of different forms of the regeneration of new organs or new shoot and root systems [1]. New formation of shoots in different areas of the crown [2]. Formation of shoots from a root close to the surface [3]. New formation of roots, e.g. after cop- picing [4]. Formation of roots from branches in contact with the ground [5]. Formation of aerial roots.

a previously shaded trunk becomes exposed to the sun, some tree species may form adventitious roots at that point so that more leaves for photosynthesis can form at a point favourable for the organism. Following the same principle, adventitious shoots can also emerge from roots growing close to the surface (→ Fig. 8[2]). In some species, this regeneration process is part of the plant's development and propagation strategy. Pando at Fishlake National Park in Utah, the clonal colonies of quaking aspen mentioned earlier, are one such example: over the course of development, the original connection to the mother tree may be lost, resulting in many independently growing, but genetically identical plants (vegetative propagation).

Conversely, adventitious roots can also form on the shoot system. Many tree species exhibit this phenomenon when a branch bends downwards far enough to come into direct contact with the soil (→ Fig. 8[4]). The formation of adventitious roots provides a means of supplying the branch with water and nutrients more directly than via the main stem. Tree species that grow on flood plains form adventitious roots on their trunks and branches as a way of absorbing water and nutrients from floodwater. When the water level falls, these extra roots die back. Some species, such as the rubber tree *Ficus elastica*, have a special form of aerial adventitious roots (→ Fig. 8[5]). Like the adventitious shoots of the clonal colonies, they are part of this tree's growth pattern. Apart from providing additional water and nutrients, they also fulfil a supporting function for widely projecting branches. The formation of adventitious roots is used in horticultural practice as a way of propagating cuttings in tree nurseries. Short shoot sections are usually inserted into a special substrate where new roots then form, sometimes with the added help of plant hormones. This propensity to form adventitious roots varies from species to species. For example, many willow species exhibit a particular tendency to form such roots. These different forms of organ regeneration are the foundation of all horticultural pruning techniques, and accordingly also the basis for many baubotanical techniques. In combination with methods of grafting and inosculation, they present many possibilities for baubotanical construction, such as that of plant addition (→ Chapter 3, p. 81).

Biomechanics

Trees are exposed to a variety of mechanical stresses throughout their lives. As they grow, the mechanical demands increase dramatically with increasing size, mass and wind attack surface. External factors can also change significantly over a tree's lifetime. The loss or felling of a neighbouring tree, for example, can suddenly expose a tree to much greater wind forces. Wind forces are an important mechanical variable that shapes a tree's development. In mechanical terms, trunks and branches can be described as cantilevered elements clamped at one end that are subject to flexion stresses and vibrations by the wind.[28] High bending stresses can result that in extreme cases can lead to failure. Trees respond to this with a twofold strategy. The young shoots are comparatively thin and made of soft, flexible tissue so that they can bend flexibly in the wind, reducing the overall load acting on the tree. As they grow, the shoots become thicker and stiffer and at the same time develop a woody core that is increasingly resistant to bending. Over time, a shoot's modulus of elasticity — a technical material parameter that describes the elastic behaviour of plant axes — can increase by a factor of five to six.[29] A tree's mechanical strategy therefore comprises a combination of flexible yielding, especially of the young, thin axes at the tree's periphery, and stiff resisting in the central, older and thicker shoot axes. In Baubotanik, the task is to translate the tree species' mechanical strategy into a coherent structural design strategy (→ Chapter 6, p. 122).

Adaptation of the tree shape

When trees are exposed to wind or comparable mechanical loads, their branches and trunks are constantly bent back and forth. This flexing produces alternating tensile and compressive loads in the outer areas of the shoot axes causing the bark and young sapwood, and thus also the living, dividing cells of the cambium, to be alternately compressed and stretched. This stimulates cell division activity in the cambium and the tree invests more in thickness growth and less in length growth at the shoot tip.[30] Consequently, trees that are regularly exposed to strong winds exhibit more compact growth and have thicker trunks and branches for their size. They simultaneously reduce their wind attack surface and increase their mechanical resistance. However, this also means that the photosynthetically active leaf area remains smaller, and the tree grows more slowly overall. Trees that are constantly exposed to extreme winds often develop special growth forms. Windswept trees have very short branches on the side facing the wind and longer branches on the side facing away from the prevailing wind direction. This is explained by the higher mechanical stresses acting on them, but also by the fact that the shoots most exposed to the wind dry out more through evaporation and thus also partly suffer drought stress.

By sheltering trees from the wind and/or reducing their exposure to vibration, for example by anchoring or tethering them, less alternating bending occurs, and thickening growth is not stimulated. The trees can concentrate on length growth, and thus grow taller and slimmer, as well as more quickly. They are, however, less resistant to bending stresses (→ Fig. 9 a, b).

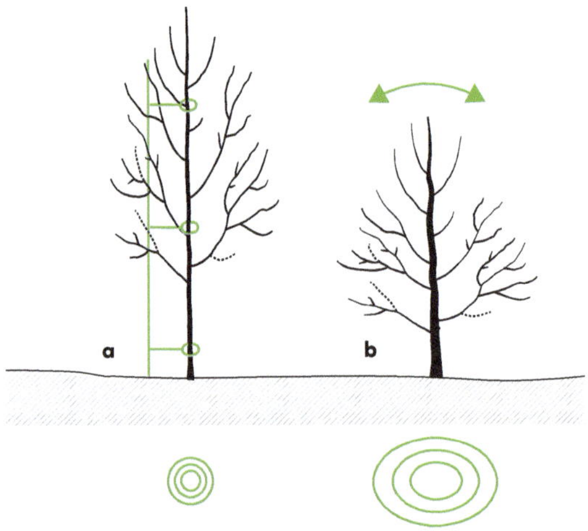

9 a Growth pattern under sheltered wind conditions and when anchored.
b Growth pattern under the influence of alternating bending caused by wind.

Local adaptive thickness growth

Alongside the effects of mechanical stress on the overall tree shape, tree growth of thickness can result in response to localised mechanical stimuli and have a corresponding effect on the tree's development. For example, in a trunk subjected to bending stress by wind acting on the crown, the bending moment is greatest at the base of the trunk, where it is anchored in the ground, and least towards the top. The trunk develops in a conical shape, its diameter decreasing towards the top in response to the load acting on its cross-section. This shape represents an efficient utilisation of the material available to the tree. At the base where the trunk transitions into the roots, the trunk rounds towards the ground. The localised accumulation of material at this point helps reduce stress peaks at the junction—so-called "notch stresses"—so that less material is needed overall. A similar principle applies where branches attach to the trunk (→ Fig. 10). This material-optimised growth can ultimately be attributed to reactions of the cambium to recurring loads and stress peaks: local thickness growth is stimulated, contributing to a more even distribution of forces. Alongside such conical shoot development and roundings at junctions, one also sees this principle in the changing cross-sectional geometry of shoot axes. Where trees are exposed to a predominant prevailing wind direction, they develop an elliptical cross-section so that their modulus of elasticity is greater in the main direction of the applied force. The same applies to branches, which are often subjected to strong vertical bending loads due to their horizontal elongation and self-weight. Branches therefore often have a vertical elliptical cross-section in the area of the branch connection. Such optimisations are even more apparent in roots, which can exhibit a T-shaped or even I-shaped cross-section similar to an engineering beam when subjected to alternating bending stresses.[31]

The connection between mechanical stimuli and tree growth has been known for a long time, especially in the field of forestry. As early as 1893, the thesis was put forward that growth is determined "by the tree's need for mechanical strength" and that the tree trunk is therefore a "carrier of equal [mechanical] resistance".[32] Following on from this, subsequent research and numerous experiments have demonstrated clear correlations between the growth of a plant and its mechanical stress. Although the results differ in detail, one can generally state that the diametrical growth of an axis increases with mechanical stimulation.[33] The "axiom of uniform stress" that derives from this, and is often cited in tree mechanics, says that for a unit of time there is always a uniform distribution of stresses over the entire axis system.[34] However, empirical studies have shown that trees do not have the same stresses everywhere. While this does not invalidate the fundamental relationships described here, it suggests that an axiom, as a universally valid law, is not sufficient to describe the complex processes of tree growth, or at least only in a highly simplified manner, and only from the standpoint of mechanics.[35]

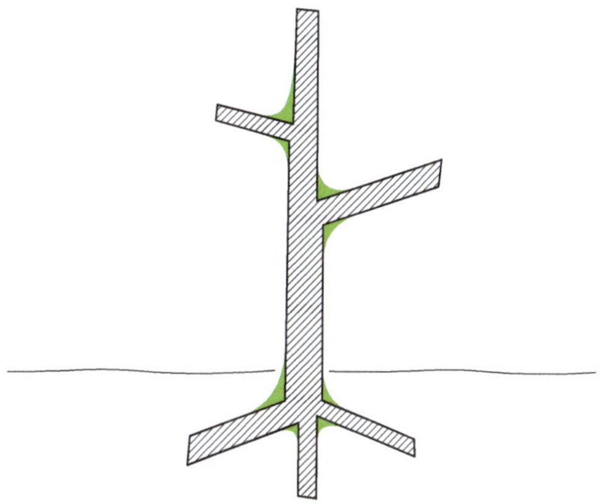

10 Rounding at the transition from root to trunk or trunk to branch caused by local adaptive growth makes optimal use of material where mechanical stresses are greatest (highly simplified).

The significance of mechanics for Baubotanik

These relationships and principles are highly relevant for Baubotanik. Constructions that not only originate out of themselves but can make optimal use of the material available to them and can also adapt continuously to new loads sound like an engineer's dream. And indeed, the aerial roots of the living bridges of the Khasi exhibit developmental patterns that one could describe as self-optimising. The horizontal lying roots of these bridges, which are in effect equivalent to beams subject to bending forces, often exhibit an either strongly elliptical or inverted T-shaped cross-section. Whether these cross-sections have arisen solely in response to bending stimuli has not yet been categorically determined, and it is more likely that the horizontal orientation of the roots already causes this growth response.[36] What is undisputed, however, is that this growth form results in a significant reduction of the tensile forces at the bottom and the compressive forces at the top compared to a circular cross-section. As this makes better utilisation of material, this form of local adaptive growth can be seen as self-optimisation on the part of the plant.

Most baubotanical structures are, however, constructed from the trunks and branches of trees and their assessment starts from a different premise. Such constructions aim to make better use of the material of freely growing trees through the use of constructive measures. While trees are highly optimised structures, their natural growth form, with freely swinging trunks, branches and twigs fixed rigidly at one end, is not very efficient from a mechanical standpoint. As described above, the resulting bending stresses cause high tensile and compressive forces in the outer edge areas of the limbs while the wood within is subject to little or no stress. Constructions subject only to tensile or only to compressive forces are fundamentally more efficient compared to those subject to bending forces, as the forces act only axially and can be absorbed by the entire cross-sectional area. In lightweight construction, material use is minimised by translating bending stresses acting on a structure into a system of tensile and compressive forces distributed across individual members. In baubotanical structures, this is achieved by joining several trunks or trees, often with supporting technical construction elements, to form an overall structural system. By reducing the bending stresses caused by wind, one can make more use of the underutilised load potential of the tree cross-sections for bearing additional live loads, such as the snow load of a roof or traffic loads of a platform or walkway. A logical consequence of this is that thickness growth in the cambium is no longer stimulated, due to the lack of bending stresses. Axial loads are borne primarily by the stiffer core of the wooden body, practically eliminating the stresses and strains in the cambium area that could stimulate corresponding growth of thickness.[37] A consequence of this is that plant axes in connected baubotanical framework structures exhibit less thickness growth than freely growing shoots, and that different axial loads do not lead to differences in growth of thickness, so the load is not a factor determining thickness growth. In this respect, the mechanical optimisation of the structure through adaptive growth in circumference is not typically seen in baubotanical structures, and corresponding observations made on baubotanical prototypes seem to confirm this hypothesis, although no reliable quantitative measurements are yet available.

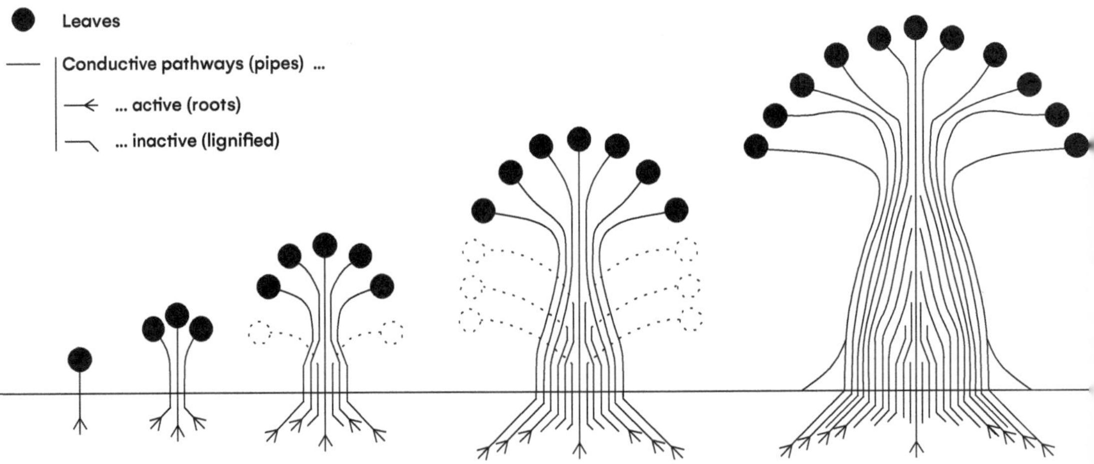

11 Illustration of the development of a tree according to the "pipe model theory".

Water transport

Alongside mechanical stimuli, the influence of transport flows in the plant axis has long been discussed as a possible factor influencing thickness growth, with water transport in the wood (xylem) seen as being particularly relevant. As early as 1913, the plant physiologist Paul Jaccard hypothesised that there is a certain relationship between the water-conducting cross-sectional area of a stem or branch and the leaf mass it supplies and thus the water requirement.[38] This is also the main premise of K. Shinozaki's "pipe model theory", in which plant axes are considered in simplified terms as a bundle of pipes of constant cross-section that connect root areas with crown areas and supply a certain leaf mass with water. Pipes that are no longer in use, for example because the leaves it supplied have fallen from the tree, remain in the stems and branches, which, according to this theory, explains the typical conical shape of the stem or branch (→ Fig. 11).[39]

According to this theory, rather than striving for a state of uniform mechanical stress distribution through adaptive thickness growth, trees strive for a state of uniform water transport resistance in the wood. Even if—as mentioned above with the "axiom of uniform stress"—the actual conditions are far more complex and the values sometimes vary significantly depending on the position in the tree,[40] there is no reason why this model for explaining growth in circumference as a product of transport requirements is any less plausible than the mechanical explanation. To be able to realistically assess or predict the thickness growth of baubotanical structures, one must ultimately determine which of these explanatory models better describes the actual development observed in artificially modified tree structures. To this end, it is useful to take a closer look at how the water conduction system functions and the connection between water transport and thickness growth.

Functioning of the vascular water system

In contrast to the transport of assimilates in the bark, which is driven by metabolic mechanisms, water transport in the xylem is mainly passive. The driving force for water transport is the difference between water potential (i.e. water availability in a system) of the atmosphere and that of the soil. According to the law of diffusion, water flows from a region of high water potential to a region of low potential, i.e. from the soil (liquid) to the air (vapour). In this sense, a plant extends the high water potential of the soil up into the air. This physical phenomenon causes water to flow from the soil into the plant and from there it evaporates into the surrounding atmosphere. The vascular system that conducts the flow of water comprises tracheids, the vessels of the xylem, which create an uninterrupted pathway from the root tips to the branches within the leaves for water to flow through (→ Fig. 12). Within these capillary channels, the water molecules form "water threads" that have a high resistance to "tearing". This tearing, which would interrupt the flow, is mostly prevented by the fact that the water threads adhere relatively strongly to the walls of the capillary channels. This adherence, however, leads to a relatively high flow resistance which in turn requires greater suction forces, i.e. a higher water potential differences, to overcome. The more conductive paths are available—i.e. the larger the conductive cross-section of a plant axis—the lower the resistance. It would therefore seem logical that trees create new conductive pathways where there is disproportionate conductive resistance. According to the principle of efficiency, this allows trees to employ minimal material to maximise the transport capacity of the axis system.

One should, however, note that water transport is not driven solely by external physical forces; it is also distributed among the existing conductive pathways according to the laws of physics. How much water flows in which capillaries or axial sections depends on the resistance these present to the water flow. Water ultimately

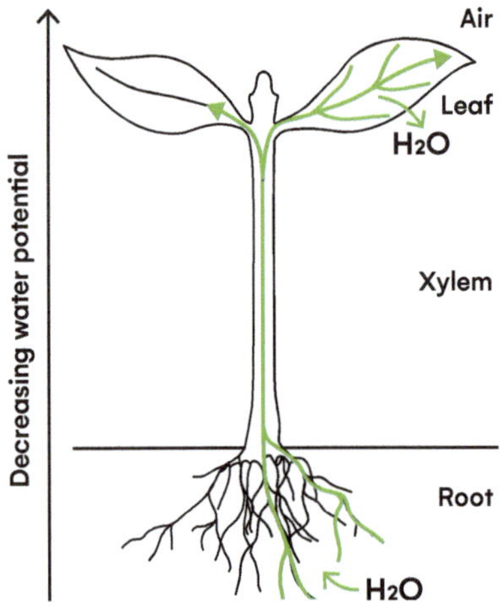

12 Principle of water transport. Left: Water potentials in the soil, air and the corresponding areas of the plant. Middle: Water transport from the soil through the roots, plant axes and leaves into the air.

follows the path of least resistance, and because transport resistance is (approximately) proportional to the conductive cross-section and also the length of axial section, water invariably takes the shortest possible path. Conductive pathways can have very difficult lengths, especially when adventitious roots form on low branches and create more direct connections to the soil (→ Fig. 8), shortcutting the usual conductive pathway. Despite their shorter length, these connections initially have a relatively high transport resistance due to their smaller cross-sectional area as young shoots. However, it is much more efficient for the tree to increase the conductive cross-sectional area of this shortcut than to continue investing in the original, longer connection. This pattern can be observed in the thickness growth of trees where aerial roots regularly create such direct connections between branches and the soil (e.g. *Ficus benghalensis*). Once the aerial roots reach the ground and establish a more direct connection to the water source, they start to grow thicker extremely fast, while the main branch section between the aerial root and the trunk hardly exhibits any thickness growth.

The significance of the vascular water system for Baubotanik

In naturally growing trees with their open branching structures, the successively decreasing diameter of the shoot axes from the base of the trunk to the upper branches can be explained equally well by the mechanical approach (→ Chapter 2, pp. 43–46) and the hydraulic model discussed here. It would seem that a tree's structure addresses the requirements for water transport and the mechanical requirements of a freely cantilevered mechanical system subject to bending loads more or less equally well. When, in a baubotanical structure, plant axes are artificially joined to form truss-like or framework structures, this has implications for both the mechanical and physiological structure. Mechanically, it stiffens their structure, converting bending loads into tensile and compressive forces, which in turn causes less local stimulation of thickness growth. Physiologically, once the physical connections at the nodes grow together, they also form new physiological units. This enables the transport of water and assimilates across the boundaries of individual plants and — as with plants with adventitious or aerial roots — results in different possible pathways for water transport. The flow of water is then a product of the water flow resistance. At the same time, the tree would have to invest most in growth of circumference where there is maximum potential for increasing transport capacity using the least possible material input. Typically, this is the shortest connections, which would accordingly then grow in thickness—regardless of how much axial load they sustain in tension or compression. Working from these assumptions, simulations of thickness growth in complex, network-like intergrown structures have been conducted that correspond well to the actual observed pattern of development (→ Chapter 8, pp. 196—197). The hydraulic model therefore appears to offer a better explanation for describing and predicting growth of circumference in baubotanical structures than the mechanical model. At the same time, these findings have led to a general rule for the baubotanical design of network-like, intergrown constructions: their structure should be devised as far as possible in such a way that the expected water flow coincides with the expected distribution of forces so that mechanically necessary axes, or those subject to particular stresses, exhibit corresponding thickness growth.

Arrangement of the shoots

The distribution of the main and side shoots of a tree in space is a balance between the best possible use of sunlight and the lowest possible mechanical stress. When plant limbs are joined together to form baubotanical structures, the orientation of their trunks, branches and twigs changes significantly, for example, an entire plant may be inserted into the ground at an angle, or a branch may be bent to alter its orientation. Trees respond to such changes in equilibrium by either attempting to restore the original orientation by bending back or adapting their growth patterns to the new spatial orientation. Botanically, these are a reaction caused by the gravity-sensing capability of specialised cells (statocytes) and subsequent changes in plant hormone concentrations in the affected regions.

The bending back to the original orientation (gravitropic response) results from the formation of reaction wood. Deciduous and coniferous woods take different approaches. In deciduous trees, the cambium grows more strongly on the tension side, forming cells that shorten as they differentiate. This shortening gradually pulls the shoot back to its original orientation (→ Fig. 13 a). In conifers, the cambium grows correspondingly stronger on the compression side, forming cells that lengthen as they differentiate, gradually pushing the shoot back to its original orientation (→ Figs. 13 b, 14 a).

Changes in growth or branching patterns caused by altered positioning in space are referred to as gravimorphic responses. These become most apparent when branches are fixed in a new position, i.e. when some form of restraint prevents a plant's gravitropic response (→ Fig. 14 b). If a plant is tilted from the vertical, the growth and branching pattern controlled by the apical dominance of the main shoot initially weakens. If the main shoot is diverted to be horizontal, the apical dominance is virtually inverted. Dormant buds then start to sprout at the base while the shoot tip exhibits barely any longitudinal growth.[41] Inclining the main shoot also changes the orientation of the side shoots, which previously grew diagonally upwards. The

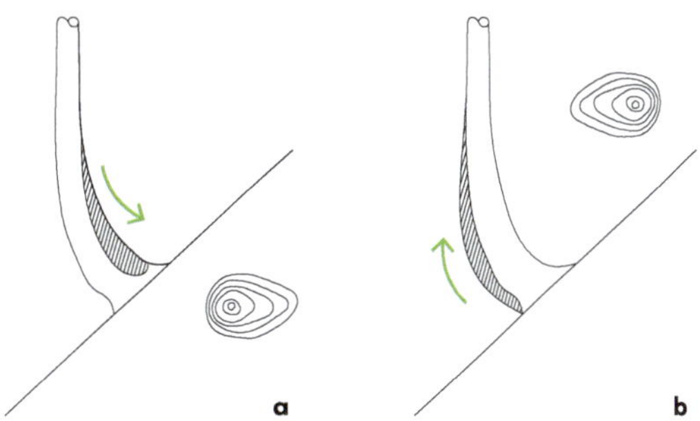

a b

13 a Formation of tension wood in deciduous trees.
b Formation of compression wood in conifers.

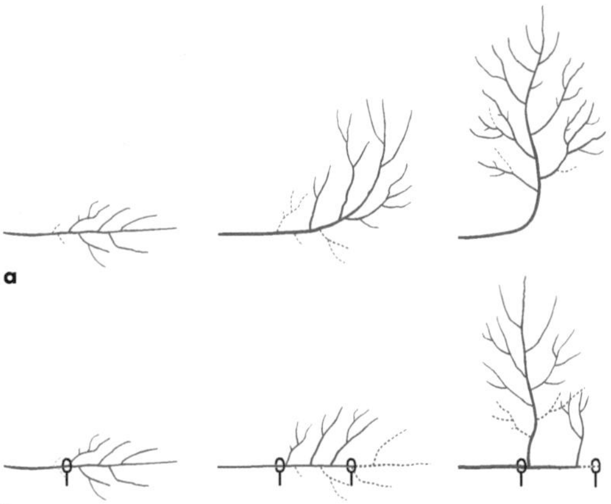

a

b

14 a Gravitropic straightening of a horizontally aligned tree.
b Gravimorphic response of a horizontally aligned tree fixed in this position.

side shoots that now point downwards either die or their growth stagnates, while those that now point upwards tend to grow more vigorously, with the upward-oriented side shoots nearest the base growing most strongly. One or more new main shoots emerge from these or other newly formed side shoots (→ Fig. 14 b), while the original main shoot often dies back from the tip. A comparable development can be seen when the orientation of an axial section is changed by bending. For example, if plants are bent into an arc (semicircle) in such a way that the basal area is oriented obliquely upwards and the shoot tip vertically downwards, the side shoots at the highest point of the arc exhibit greatest length growth and are oriented vertically. As a rule, it can be stated for curved axes that the growth of the side shoots is greatest in the area that is, on the one hand, situated highest and, on the other hand, closest to the base of the main axis.[42] This phenomenon can also be explained by the efficiency principle, because the tree can utilise these responses with the least amount of resources to build up a new axis system that provides the best possible alignment of the leaves to the light with the least possible mechanical stress.

The relevance of shoot orientation for Baubotanik

For the development of botanical structures, gravitropic and especially gravimorphic responses are highly relevant. When a plant is significantly inclined or bent to a new shape, it is very likely that it will develop one or more "leader shoots" in the basal area. This can then lead to the plant's suppressing growth of the tilted axial section above it, or even causing it to die off in the long term—which is highly undesirable when this axis is important to the baubotanical structure. This means that with increasing inclination or deviation from the vertical, or for sections with corresponding bends, an internal developmental mechanism is triggered in the plant that contradicts the intended direction of baubotanical development. The greater the modified development deviates from the plant's natural development, the more likely it is that the desired development goal will be compromised because the axes will grow only weakly or not at all in the intended places. One can counter this development through the removal or cutting back of unwanted shoots—but the more the modified alignment deviates from the natural growth direction, the more diligent one will need to be. This sensitivity to changes in position or alignment varies according to tree species.

Baubotanical structures that are constructed using (aerial) roots rather than shoots are not subject to the same risks. Roots have quite different and typically much lower gravitropic or gravimorphic responses as they do not follow a predetermined branching pattern and their growth and orientation is guided primarily by the growth conditions in the soil. This explains why the complex geometries of the living bridges of the Khasi, with axes that extend both upwards and downwards, are possible, and why such structures could not be realised with shoots.

Light

Since sunlight is the only source of energy for plants, their entire growth pattern is optimised to make the best possible use of the available light energy. Similarly, adaptation strategies to special or changing light conditions also play an important role in their development. As with a plant organism's responses to gravity, one can distinguish between two primary responses to light: phototropic responses that affect growth movements and photomorphic responses that cause changes in growth patterns. With the help of these, plants can adapt their development to changes in brightness (available light energy), light quality (spectral composition of light) and light direction or distribution in space.

When trees grow in groups, they inevitably shade one another and light becomes a scarce, and often limiting commodity (→ pp. 40–41). To survive under such conditions, trees attempt to reach areas of greater light intensity above the crowns of their competitors as quickly as possible. To do this, they promote length growth at the expense of thickness growth: the growth activity of the cambium decreases, while growth at the shoot tip accelerates and the cells of the internodes stretch more. At the same time, the branching pattern changes, with fewer lateral buds sprouting and existing lateral shoots developing more slowly or dying prematurely (→ Fig. 15 a). The result are long, slender, often poorly branched shoots with typically low mechanical strength. This adaptive shift in growth patterns is usually triggered not just by a decrease in the availability of light but also by a change in the spectral composition of light, which is typical where there is competition for the available light. When the leaves of neighbouring plants absorb primarily the blue and red portion of light through photosynthesis, only the yellow and green light, as well as a dark portion of red light barely perceptible to the human eye, passes through or is reflected (the so-called "green shadow"). In particular, the reflection of the dark red (near infra-red) radiation acts as a signal for the adaption of growth patterns before shading occurs. This shade avoidance response helps trees outgrow a potential competitor and thus react quickly to a deterioration of their growth conditions.[43]

In addition to lack of light due to competition, trees are often exposed to growing conditions in which light is only available at sufficient levels in a part of the growing space, or just from one side. Such asymmetrical conditions lead firstly to the fact that better-lit areas of the tree crown flourish while poorly lit branches and twigs lag behind and die, and secondly to phototropic growth where the tree tries to grow towards the light. This is an active reaction that can only take place at the shoot tip as the cells in the internodes that face away from the light stretch more during longitudinal growth. Reaction wood formation, which would entail sections of woody shoot that no longer grow bending towards a light source, does not take place. Nevertheless, the trunks of trees exposed to light on one side can gradually bend towards the light source. This is less a growth response than a product of asymmetrical stresses resulting from the one-sided growth of the crown (→ Fig. 15 b). As such, phototropic and photomorphic adaptive responses often take place at the expense of mechanical efficiency or robustness.

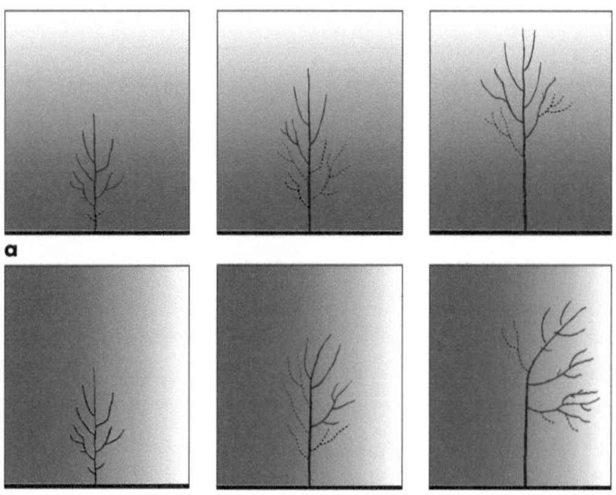

a

b

15 a Tree development in reduced light conditions (shade avoidance).
b Tree development with one-sided exposure.

The significance of light for Baubotanik

How trees respond to different lighting conditions is relevant to Baubotanik in several respects. First of all, one-sided or uneven lighting situations can occur quite easily due to mutual shading, or shade from building structures or building elements, often in conjunction with limited light availability. Phototropic and photomorphic responses must therefore be considered at the design stage and also in the course of development through corresponding maintenance tasks. Ideally, these responses should be considered as form-giving phenomena, i.e. in the sense of co-designing with the tree. Secondly, the shade avoidance response can be exploited to cultivate especially slender and flexible plants that may offer greater design possibilities than trees that have grown more slowly and regularly.

Wound healing

The natural development of a tree is not just characterised by growth, but also by the death of tissue, organs or entire parts of the shoot and root system.[44] Over time, weak or dead branches on the trunk can break off, causing smaller and larger injuries to the tree. To a certain degree, even growth itself causes injury to the plant: for example, the tearing of the epidermis as young shoots grow thicker is essentially a form of injury to the outer tissue, and the resulting periderm can be seen as a wound response inherent to the plant's pattern of development. Over the course of the long life of a tree, external factors can also cause a multitude of other injuries, ranging from superficial damage to the bark resulting from hail to extensive destruction of the bark and the cambium or even serious damage to the body of the wood, as can occur when a strong branch breaks off in a storm. Likewise, tree pruning results in corresponding injuries to the organism, as does the construction, maintenance and use of baubotanical structures.

How trees respond to such injuries is not just important to preserve their vital functions but also to regenerate corresponding shoot or root systems to compensate for losses. Injuries can not only disrupt the function of the affected organs but also represent a gateway for fungi and bacteria to enter the organism, creating more serious damage in the medium and long term. However, only living tissue or tissue that is permeated by living cells can react actively to injuries. Dead tissue, such as the bark and the heartwood, are therefore dependent on passive protective mechanisms such as the storage of tannins. The bast and the living cells of the sapwood, on the other hand, are reactive, and the cambium as the most important secondary growth tissue plays a particularly important role in wound responses.

Wound response mechanisms

If the bark of a tree is injured, the cells of the ground tissue of the bast die in the affected area. The parenchyma cells between the dead and the intact tissue then begin to divide parallel to the wound edge. In a process comparable to the formation of the original periderm, new closure tissue, the wound periderm, develops around the wound. This remodelling of existing tissue can only occur in living tissue and is therefore not possible in the case of deeper injuries to the sapwood, as this consists largely of lignified and dead vessels, tracheids and fibre cells. In such cases, only the cells of the wood rays and the cambium cells between wood and bark can react, with the aim of sealing off intact tissue from areas exposed by the injury. The wound response of the cambium is designed to close an injury as quickly as possible to prevent negative external influences affecting the wood body.

In the first instance, injury to the wood body causes air to penetrate the water channels and interrupt the "water threads" in them, making water transport impossible (air embolism). This can affect several decimetres along the length of a shoot axis, especially in deciduous trees with their relatively long and wide vessel lumens. To prevent air from spreading further into the ducts, the vessels or tracheids are closed off: in deciduous trees this occurs through blister-like protrusions (thyllae) from neighbouring parenchyma cells of the wood rays growing into the vessels or as a result of neighbouring cells pushing mucus plugs into the vessels. Areas of such closure often form a boundary layer, visible as a sharply demarcated line, which can also contain further protective substances. This serves not just to prevent the spread of air, but also averts the ingress of harmful organisms in the still intact wood (compartmentalisation). Nevertheless, in the immediate area of an injury to the wood body, where the cells of the wood rays die, colonisation by wood-decomposing microorganisms is almost always inevitable, and is often visible as a discolouration of the wood.

At the edges of an injury that extends into the wood, the cambium reacts by forming a completely new tissue, the wound callus.[45] A bulge of ground tissue develops (→ Fig. 16 a) with initially disordered, thin-walled, spherical, sparsely lignified and often rather larger cells. These are very reactive and respond to harmful organisms by forming "defence substances" such as tannins. In effect, a barrier zone is created that prevents the advance of wood-decomposing microorganisms into the newly formed tissues. As development of this tissue progresses, the cells of the wound callus differentiate. A cork cambium develops on the surface and further inside, parallel to this, a new cambium (wound cambium). The growth activity of the new cambium results in a bulging overgrowth of the exposed wound (→ Fig. 16 b—d), which has more parenchyma and fewer and shorter vessels or tracheids and fibres compared to normal wood. This bulging overgrowth grows from all sides towards the middle where, in ideal situations, it meets and closes the wound (→ Fig. 16 e). By creating an airtight encapsulation of the wound, it deprives the wood-decomposing microorganisms of their basis for life, stopping their spread and causing them to die. If, however, a tree fails to close a wound, or does so only very slowly, harmful organisms that find conducive living conditions

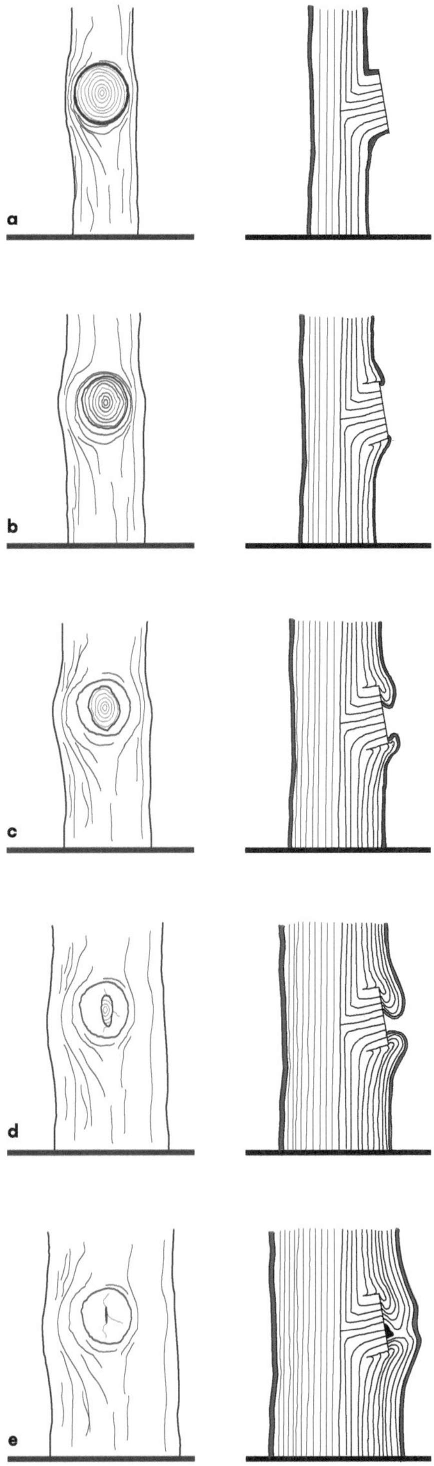

16 a—e Process of wound healing using the example of an injury caused by branch pruning.

may penetrate the boundary layer and continue to spread through the organism. Although the tree tries to counteract this spread by forming new boundary layers, it often suffers ever advancing rot that ultimately even the heartwood is unable to withstand, with the result that the tree becomes hollow, endangering its mechanical stability.

A special form of wound healing occurs when extensive areas of bark are destroyed or removed but living cells capable of division remain on the surface of the wood. In such cases, wound callus can form over a large area of the wood, often starting from the wood rays. The wood or rather the wood rays remain alive under the callus and there is almost no ingress of harmful organisms. All deciduous trees are capable of this wound response, but not conifers, which instead shield against comparable injuries from external influences by intensive resin formation.

Factors influencing wound healing

How quickly a wound closes with wound callus and how effectively the tree seals it off in the wood depends on several factors: the tree species, the vigour or vitality of the tree, and also the size and shape of the wound and the time of the injury over the course of the season.

In terms of the tree species, a basic distinction can be made between weakly compartmentalising species (e.g. birch, poplar, willow, partly ash, fruit trees, spruce, silver maple) and good compartmentalisers (beech, oak, hornbeam, lime, sycamore, pine, plane and field maple). The varying response is largely due to differences in the structure of the wood: effectively partitioning species have more parenchyma, i.e. the proportion of wood rays is higher.

The time at which an injury occurs is relevant in that the more active tissue a tree has, the better it can react to an injury. When wounds occur during dormant periods, more of the adjacent tissue typically dies, overgrowth occurs more slowly and damage to the wood is greater. The period between September and January is considered particularly unfavourable for wound healing (in temperate zones), while the period between April and August is more advantageous.

The deeper the injury, the more it penetrates into the wood, and therefore the older the damaged tissue is, the more difficult it will be to compartmentalise. The capacity of callus tissue to heal a wound is influenced by the shape, size and nature of the wound: the more irregular it is, the harder it will be to heal. In horticulture, a rule of thumb is that wounds caused by branch pruning should not exceed a diameter of 10 cm for well-sealing species, and 5 cm for weakly sealing species to prevent the spread of decay into the wood of the tree. A special form of injury is the drilling of boreholes in arboriculture, which is used to obtain cores for determining the age and growth of a tree. These holes, which penetrate all tissue layers and are several millimetres in diameter, cause only minor damage to the bark and cambium and are usually closed off by tissue within a year. However, they can also lead to discoloration in the wood that can extend axially often for several decimetres. The smaller the diameter and the younger the wood, the smaller the spread of the discoloration. By comparison, the damage caused by alternative tree diagnostics methods such as drilling resistance measurement using drilling needles only a few millimetres thick, which does not require the removal of material, is much less.

The significance of wound response mechanisms for Baubotanik

The entire wound response mechanism including the processes of compartmentalisation, overgrowth and encapsulation of damage is an essential part of modern tree maintenance and is known as CODIT (Compartmentalisation of Damage in Trees).[46] The same basic principles also apply to Baubotanik and therefore represent fundamental knowledge in the field. However, this specific form of using living trees for construction raises new questions and presents special challenges. The first aspect one needs to clarify is the underlying goals and idea behind the baubotanical structure. If the constructive performance of the living structure is paramount, maintaining the health and load-bearing capacity is the primary goal, comparable to ensuring public safety in tree maintenance. If, however, the intention is to create a composite organic-technical structure in which technical components play a key structural role, damage to the tree caused by injuries can certainly be accepted. The interplay of growth and decay then plays a central role in the baubotanical concept. Here, decomposition processes and associated cavities need not necessarily represent a problem but may be regarded as an opportunity to increase biodiversity, as they provide food and a habitat for diverse kinds of fauna.

How different tree species respond to injury is an important criterion in the selection of species for Baubotanik (→ Chapter 3, p. 88). It has implications for their constructive possibilities and thus has a strong influence on the design strategy. Responses of trees to drilling and their compartmentalisation mechanisms are an essential basis for the development of baubotanical jointing techniques. As compartmentalisation depends on the age of the tissue, baubotanical joints should always be created on shoot axes that are as young as possible. To minimise the impact of injuries to the tree, all activities that penetrate the wood or bark, whether pruning or the creation of joints, should be carried out during the growing season when wound healing is most effective. This, however, poses several problems for the baubotanic- al practice because the ideal time for planting is during dormancy, and thus planting, shaping and joining cannot usually be carried out as part of the same work stage.

Overgrowth of non-living elements

As roots develop, they are in constant contact with the soil. After the root has worked its way into the ground as a result of longitudinal growth, secondary growth begins and the root grows thicker, exerting pressure outwards against the surrounding soil, which in turn resists. While loose, fine-grained soil is easily pushed aside by thickness growth, larger stones, rocks or sections of very compact soil do not yield to the pressure of root growth. In such situations, the tree responds locally at the contact point by adapting its growth accordingly, sometimes growing around stones, following their form or even partially enclosing them so that they become part of the tree's structure. The result is a mechanically resilient connection between the roots and solid components within the soil, which helps to anchor the tree. Since branches and trunks grow in the air, they are rarely obstructed by foreign bodies, and these phenomena — which occur frequently below ground — are therefore comparatively rare above ground. In principle, however, branches and stems exhibit the same contact responses as roots. For Baubotanik, these are of particular interest as they make it possible to use growth processes to connect living and technical components.

Contact responses

The growth pressure exerted by the cambium when a plant meets a foreign body can reach values of around 0.7 N/mm^2.[47] That translates to forces in the order of 7 kN for a contact area of 100 cm^2 — i.e. a 10 × 10 cm area of actively grown cambium can push a weight of up to 700 kg. The destruction this can cause is often seen as ripples in pavements or asphalt. These pressure forces can, however, also damage the plant. At the point of contact, the bark tissue can be compressed, obstructing the transport of assimilates, which usually flow downwards. The cambium is then hindered in its growth and smaller, thick-walled cells develop at the contact surface.[48] At the same time, thickness growth increases at the edges, whereby due to the impairment of the phloem, the areas above the contact area are better supplied with assimilates and therefore grow more strongly than below. As a result, the axes appear flattened in cross-section at the contact point and thickened at the edges (→ Fig. 17 a). If we think back to the connection between thickness growth, biomechanics and water transport discussed earlier, this compensatory thickness growth can be explained in different ways. It can either be understood as a response to ensure that sufficient new tissue is formed in the area of a contact point to facilitate water transport. Or it can be explained as a mechanical response to ensure a sufficient mechanically active cross-sectional area that can reduce stress peaks at this point by increasing the contact area.

This first response is often followed by a second developmental step. As a result of strong swelling in the marginal areas, friction or also the fact that sharp objects can literally be pressed into the bark by growth pressure, the outer cork layers and firmer tissue can be damaged. The cork cambium responds by forming wound cork on the outside and secretes smaller, thin-walled cells on the inside. The cambium, too, is stimulated to respond to the wound, creating a bulging section of wound wood that gradually pushes itself over the foreign body. This is — at least initially — usually easy to recognise because it is not covered by species-typical bark, but by thinner, smoother and lighter wound periderm (→ Fig. 17 b, c). Similar to the formation of overgrowth over wounds in the plant stem, this bulge gradually overgrows the surface of the foreign object. If this occurs from several sides, these can join and grow around or even completely enclose the foreign body (→ Fig. 17 d). The tree and foreign body then form a tight-fitting connection and new annual rings with continuous conductive and strengthening tissues enclose the object.

a
b
c
d
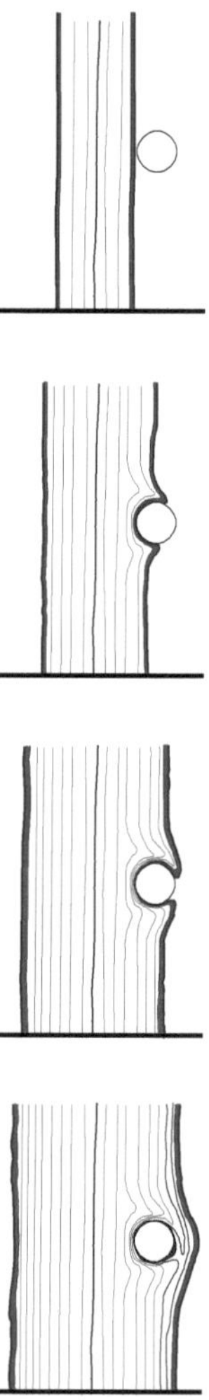

17 a–d Incorporation of a tube (schematic section).

The relevance of overgrowing for Baubotanik

The ability of a tree to grow around or even fully incorporate a foreign body is of fundamental importance for Baubotanik, providing a basis for techniques to connect branches and trunks or even roots with technical components. Although not all baubotanical structures make use of these techniques, they are fundamental to creating composite organic and technical constructions and thus developing new, hybrid building typologies. Nevertheless, the incorporation of foreign bodies is viewed critically in the forestry sector, where it is considered a defect: it is problematic for the later processing of wood and also weakens the plant by interrupting the wood fibres, at least until the foreign body has been fully incorporated. Tree nurseries are therefore careful to prevent cords or wires, etc. from being enclosed by woody plants as they grow. One could argue that this view is at odds with the naturally occurring contact responses of roots with foreign bodies in the soil, which also serve an essential structural function. However, roots are mostly subject to tensile forces, while above ground bending stresses dominate. One way or the other, these considerations highlight how important it is to carefully plan and implement the inclusion or incorporation of technical components in baubotanical structures to as far as possible avoid potential negative effects. Suitable techniques and procedures therefore need to be developed to address these concerns. Three aspects are of key importance here.

Firstly, it is important to clarify how living tissue at the contact area will develop in the long term. Sooner or later, the cambium and the cork cambium, and its corresponding wound cambia, must stop growing in the contact area, as the tissue cannot expand any further. However, because wood and bark tissue renew as the plant organism grows to stay healthy, the question is how they survive in the long term or whether—and then at what point—they die at the contact area. If this happens, it opens up potential points of entry for harmful organisms in the contact area, which over time could lead to rot. Whether a point of inclusion or incorporation remains stable and vital in the long term depends on the extent to which a plant is able to keep the wood and bark tissue alive even with minimal growth, along with its ability to provide an effective barrier to invading harmful organisms through compartmentalisation. These properties vary from species to species and are probably determined by the anatomy of the wood, i.e. the proportion of wood rays in the wood body. Similarly, the rate at which the overgrowth bead grows varies greatly between species. Beech and sycamore trees produce very pronounced overgrowth bulges. Here it seems that the anatomy of the bark (its thickness, fibre content, etc.) plays an important role. As yet, little research has been conducted on the long-term behaviour of points of inclusion and the specific contact responses of different species. More research is necessary to close this gap in knowledge and provide a solid basis for the development of constructive baubotanical joining techniques.

Secondly, the tree's contact response leads to increased growth at the periphery of the inclusion area to compensate for the interrupted growth at the contact surface. This mostly one-sided limitation of growth, however, causes the cross-section to be weakened in one direction. At the same time, the junction between the plant axis and the technical component leads to a stiffening of the tissue that transfers bending stresses into tensile and compressive forces, although the areas above the joint are still exposed to bending. The greatest stresses are expected to occur at the transition between the stiffened and flexible sections, which may be weakened by the one-sided obstruction of growth at the point of inclusion. In the worst case, this could lead to damage or even breakage of a trunk at this point. One possible solution is to effect a gradual transition from the flexible to the stiff, for example by temporarily stabilising the upper section of the axis until the technical component is fully incorporated. Here the design and dimensioning of the included component is also relevant: the smaller the cross-section of the technical element, the more quickly it will be enclosed so that the point of inclusion can stabilise and reinforce itself independently through the formation of continuous tissue.

The third aspect to be considered in the design of inclusion junctions is the obstruction of assimilate transport at the point of contact with foreign bodies. Assimilate congestion can lead to increased growth above the point of contact while the region beneath is undersupplied, exhibits less growth and also weaker development of the overgrowth bead. At the same time, the lower, slower-growing overgrowth bead is vital for absorbing vertical forces. The extent to which this bead, which comprises primarily wound xylem, provides actual, reliable support for the technical component has not yet been conclusively clarified and until then must be viewed critically.[49] If technical components are later to sustain and transfer loads to the tree, it is advisable that these are incorporated as quickly as possible into the fabric of the tree to ensure that the wooden body can enclose and regrow to form a tight-fitting enclosure around the component. Interruptions to assimilate transport are particularly problematic where technical elements cut off a considerable proportion of the assimilate-transporting part of the plant axis. If assimilate transport is completely interrupted, the plant is effectively strangulated and the underlying tissue may die over time. The crown area over such a strangulation site may receive water from the still intact xylem for several years. But once the existing sapwood becomes inactive and any reserve substances in the roots are exhausted, preventing new fine roots from forming and absorbing water and nutrients, the entire tree will die. Ring-porous tree species are particularly sensitive to strangulation as they depend on the annual formation of new sapwood for water transport. Strangulation effects can also occur through the use of tapes, ropes or wires that completely enclose the plant axis (→ Chapter 6, pp. 144—149). In some cases where they quickly cut into the bark and the tissue closes around them again and can restore its transport function, they can grow into a tree without significant consequences. This, however, depends to a large degree on tree species and bark anatomy.

Intergrowth

Alongside overgrowth and the incorporation of non-living elements into living stems, one of the most interesting and most relevant phenomena for Baubotanik is the intergrowth or inosculation of stems, branches and roots. Inosculation is sometimes regarded as a specific botanical curiosity, and sometimes even as an unnatural phenomenon. This is probably because in the vast majority of tree species, inosculaton seldom occurs under normal conditions. To begin with, trees and branches rarely touch each other due to their branching patterns. Only when conditions transpire that branches or trunks become wedged together in such a way that they are firmly pressed together and cannot separate can the situation arise that they start to grow together. Such occurrences are far more common underground. Because roots cannot always spread freely as they grow, and soil constraints may cause them to follow “growth paths” along existing cavities, the probability that they may cross and touch each other is quite high. If ground conditions cause them to be pressed against each other, they can grow together at these contact points. Natural inosculation is therefore more typically found in the root systems of most tree species. This can occur both with roots of the same tree and with the roots of neighbouring trees of the same species.[50] The ecological implications of root inosculations have not been conclusively identified, but most research agrees that this can give tree populations an evolutionary advantage and is more than just a random crossing of roots — even if this occurrence ultimately results from the given soil conditions and, in a sense, is therefore dependent on random external factors. An obvious advantage is that interconnected root systems can give trees better stability.[51] In addition, connected trees can share resources such as water, assimilates or nutrients, maximising their access to resources and increasing tree growth.[53] Intergrowth is therefore a much more frequent occurrence than is commonly assumed; we just don’t see it happening. And rather than being a botanical curiosity, intergrowth fulfils important physiological and mechanical functions in many tree and forest habitats. This is particularly true of the rubber trees (*Ficus elastica*) that the Khasi use for their living bridges, as well as of other fig species, where the growth of aerial roots contributes recognisably to the species’ typical appearance (habitus).

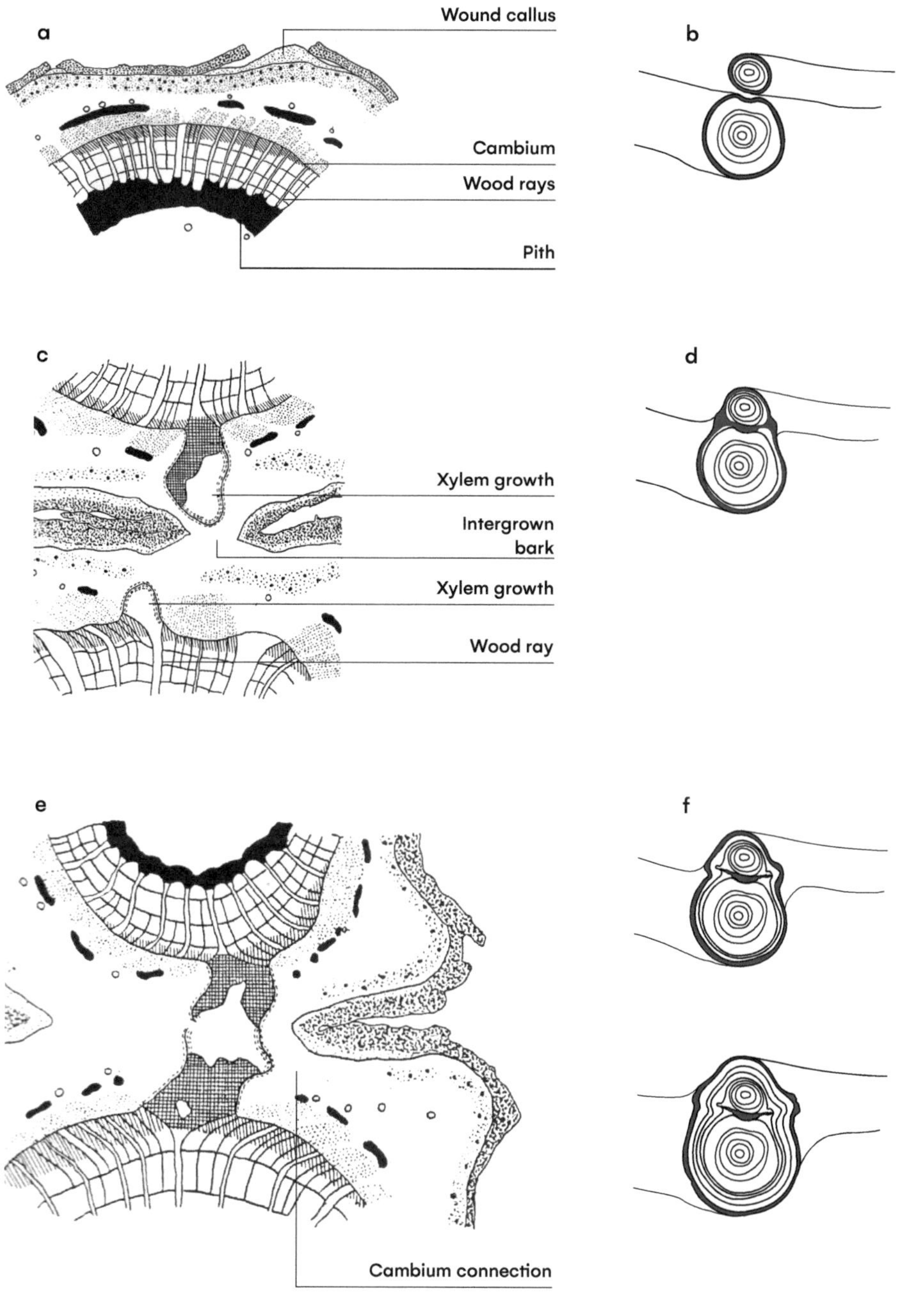

18 The phases of the inosculation process. Left: Representation of the processes at tissue level; right: macroscopic section.
a Contact reaction at the future site of inosculation with an adjoining partner.
b Mutual overgrowth, especially of the stronger-growing inosculation partner.
c Formation of xylem cusps growing towards each other after bark inosculation has taken place.
d Bark fusion.
e Formation of the wood inosculation.
f Formation of common annual rings after wood inosculation has taken place. In this case, the wood bodies are not fused in the middle but in the marginal areas, leaving dead bark tissue inclusions between the fused wood bodies.

The process of inosculation

The process by which trees can grow together naturally[53] — called inosculation and sometimes also (natural) grafting — can be divided into two main phases, in which first the bark and then the wood tissues connect. Only once the second step has happened can one speak of complete, mechanically and physiologically effective inosculation. The actual process of inosculation is preceded by several developmental steps that result directly from pressure at the contact point and are similar to the contact responses to foreign bodies. Here, too, the cambium at the contact point is compressed and produces smaller and thicker-walled cells. At the same time, the width of one or more wood rays in the centre of the contact zone increases significantly, deflecting the other rays outwards, where thickness growth increases significantly. As a result of this, and the compression and deflection of the bark tissue at the point of contact, the bark's outer structural tissue ruptures at the edges of the contact area and wound periderm forms (→ Fig. 18 a, b).

This situation, in which the inosculation partners show initial signs of mutual overgrowth, is the starting point of the first step: at the points where the cork layer has broken open — usually in the area of a thickened wood ray — the thin-walled cells within the cork cambium increase significantly in size, so that the cork cambium bulges outwards. Through further cell divisions of the cork cambium, a kind of growth hump develops, which continues to grow and pushes through the damaged or deformed bark tissue[54] (→ Fig. 18 a). Pushing the already formed, overlying wound cork in front of it, this hump grows towards an opposite hump that arises simultaneously from the cork cambium of the other stem. Once the cusps meet, they break through the separating layers of the wound cork and fuse. An initially thin band of tissue is formed, connecting both stems, which rapidly widens through cell division. The newly formed cells enlarge and take on the shape of ordinary bark cells (ground tissue), with no new strengthening tissue being formed. This growth of the connecting tissue band pushes the old periderm and wound cork outwards. The bark tissues of the two stems are now fused, but the tissues of the xylem are still separated (→ Fig. 18 c, d). At this point, the plants may start to exchange assimilates and also plant hormones transported in the phloem. However, there is not yet any transport of water and nutrients across both individuals and the inosculation does not yet have any significant mechanical strength.

The fusion of the wood bodies, which is still pending, takes place in the second step. Here, in the area of a widened wood ray, increased cell division activity begins in the cambium, causing it to bulge outwards locally. Once again, a kind of hump forms that grows within the previously formed connecting bark tissue towards a comparable hump in the xylem formed by the inosculation partner. The growth of these humps pushes the surrounding tissue aside and compresses it. Once the cusps come into contact with one another, the tissue fuses as the cambium cells of each partner differentiate to form ordinary parenchyma cells (ground tissue) and stop growing (→ Fig. 18 e).
A continuous cambium mantle encompassing both stems then develops and, due to the new growth activity of the cambium, a common annual ring with continuous xylem and phloem tissues develops at the point of intergrowth. The inosculation process is now complete, as all important tissues have grown together to form a continuum. This phase of xylem fusion usually immediately follows the fusion of the bark and both processes normally take place within one growing season.

As the process continues, the cell division activity of the cambium in the area of the fusion is greater than in other areas and the fused wood body begins to gradually assume a uniform, more or less circular contour. The initial existing seam between the fused shoot axes then gradually disappears, although tissue remnants pressed outwards often adhere to this area for years, leaving the fused area recognisable as such (→ Fig. 18 f).

The significance of inosculation for Baubotanik

Gardeners have for a long time exploited the fact that plants can grow together, developing sophisticated techniques for artificially stimulating intergrowth, especially with the aim of plant grafting. These techniques are also used in other areas, for example to "repair" damaged trees by bridging injured bark areas with bypass grafts.[55] In addition, they are used to produce certain growth forms and plant structures (→ Chapter 7, pp. 179—180).

Inosculation plays a central role in Baubotanik because it offers great potential constructively, physiologically and aesthetically: Constructively, because "wood welds" can greatly improve mechanical load-bearing capacity to ensure the constructive resilience of baubotanical structures. Aesthetically, because the interplay of technical joining techniques and plant growth can be seen particularly well at inosculated junctions: the connections are exclusively the result of growth processes, but only come about as a result of technical joining techniques. And physiologically, because they make it possible to combine many small plants into a larger physiological unit and thus into an artificially formed but independently viable overall organism (→ Chapter 3, p. 81).

The fact that intergrowth makes it possible for trees to share nutrients challenges the classical concept of competition for resources. The traditional concepts propagated in forest ecology may therefore need to be revised to account for direct effects between connected trees. Just like natural root inosculations, baubotanical intergrowth can be seen as an intraspecific cooperative behaviour that supports the integrity of existing trees.

As with the incorporation of technical construction elements, there are still many unanswered questions concerning inosculation. These processes have, however, been researched in greater detail than incorporation of foreign bodies. The experiments and tests presented in Chapter 3 build on this knowledge and apply it to the development of baubotanical joining techniques.

3 Techniques and Tree Species

To create structures out of living trees and to establish Baubotanik as a building method, one must translate botanical knowledge into construction methods and techniques. Since 2007, several test series have been undertaken as part of a research programme in the field of Baubotanik, initially at the University of Stuttgart and since 2017 at the Technical University of Munich. Their aim has been to investigate the suitability of different tree species for baubotanical construction as well as techniques for shaping and joining shoots with a view to creating larger and more complex intergrown structures.

As long-term experiments, they involve observing the behaviour and response of plants over many years, and even decades, to arrive at conclusive findings. The results of this to date allow us to draw some preliminary conclusions but are not yet sufficient to make general recommendations. We will therefore present an overview of the different test series followed by a summary of the available findings so far. The intention is to provide practical knowledge for use in baubotanical construction, to help in the selection of suitable tree species in practice and to classify the findings for future research. Based on this we then discuss the choice of tree species in Baubotanik.

Long-term intergrowth studies

Inosculations have traditionally been used in a variety of ways in horticulture, among them grafting. Horticultural grafting is typically used to propagate plants of a certain genotype or to produce plants with specific characteristics by combining different genotypes through inosculation. The method involves cutting and joining smaller plant sections (grafting shoots or scion) and strongly pruned plants (rootstocks) in such a way that their corresponding tissues are brought into alignment and fuse. The plant sections are pressed tightly together using tape, string or staples and the grafting site is sealed airtight, for example using tree wax. The subsequent fusion of tissues in this artificial grafting is much faster than natural grafting processes and ensures the survival of the scion, which would otherwise dry out and die. Nevertheless, most horticultural grafting techniques are of limited use for creating inosculations in Baubotanik. Despite various technical developments in horticulture, grafting is still a time-consuming activity that requires great horticultural skill. In Baubotanik, such rapid grafting is not absolutely necessary as one typically works with plants or larger plant sections that can already grow independently. At such sizes, horticultural grafting techniques are more difficult to implement, as it entails cutting much larger and stiffer plants at several points and then joining them together so that the corresponding tissue meet at exactly the right connecting points. Instead, it is more practicable to join plants in the simplest possible way by bringing them together in such a way that their natural inosculation processes are stimulated. The reason for this is that baubotanical projects of different kinds can be realised in greater numbers only if inosculations are enabled in a practical and affordable way.

The idea of stimulating natural inosculation has been used for thousands of years, not just by the Khasi people for their living bridges but also for cultivating hedges and living fences.[1] In this process, the shoots are intertwined in such a way that they press against each other as they grow thicker and gradually merge. Such techniques have been refined in European horticulture since the Middle Ages to create living garden architecture such as arbours.[2] Thereby, various other techniques have also been used to shape shoots. Typically, young shoots are shaped and fixed to a supporting scaffold while still flexible and then left until they grow thicker and stiffer through secondary growth in thickness and remain in the intended shape.[3] A different variant of this involves not bending but creasing and folding down older shoots, often several years old, to form hedges. In Great Britain, but also elsewhere, the technique of "laying" shoots to create dense, fence-like hedges is still relatively widespread: for this the stems are cut with an axe three quarters of the way through near to the ground so that only a thin strip of sapwood and bark remains to connect the root with the crown; then, without breaking them, the stems are bent horizontally and intertwined. Rather than leveraging a young shoot's natural pliability, these techniques utilise the plant's capacity for wound healing as the primary shaping principle.[4]

At the beginning of the 20th century, the horticulturist Arthur Wiechula developed special joining techniques with the aim of growing living structures. He drove a nail through two intersecting plant axes, onto which a special, self-securing counterplate was pushed on the other side. The patented method pressed the plants against each other to initiate the natural grafting process (→ Chapter 7, pp. 174–176). Wiechula assumed that the fact that the plants were injured, or split, by the nail helped stimulate the inosculation process.[5] Building on Wiechula's approaches, Konstantin Kirsch and Hermann Block adapted this joining technique in the 1980s using first modern wood screws and then later several other techniques to press the plants together such as cords, ribbons, wires, cable ties or stainless steel brackets of the kind used in tree nurseries to fix bamboo poles. According to Block's field report, these alternative fastening methods, unlike nails or screws, must be removed before they grow into the wood, or else the joint is significantly weakened. While in principle the steel bracket could be allowed to grow into the stem, the joints exhibited clear signs of strangulation.[6] Kirsch also experimented with Japanese wooden nails to connect the plants at their crossing points.[7] According to Kirsch and Block, elastic rubber bands can be used to temporarily fix plants at their junction but are unsuitable for creating the conditions for natural grafting.

Bolts are also used in arboriculture, whether as screws inserted in the wood or bolts that pass through the wood and are anchored on the other side with a nut. Typical uses include preventing stems from breaking apart or anchoring steel cables to secure the crown of a tree. Because boring through a stem involves injuring the tree and provides an entry point for organisms and rot, the use of bolts is viewed critically in horticulture today and is avoided where possible.[8] In contrast, the use of steel bolts that are screwed into the trunk are regarded as one of the most reliable and least invasive methods of anchoring heavy loads in tree trunks (for instance, the system by Michael Garnier), for example in tree house architecture.[9]

Shoot shaping techniques have also recently been developed with the aim of creating plantations of ready-grown furniture that can be harvested when complete. Among others, Christopher Cattle and Gavin Munroe in the UK have developed special forms and scaffolds onto which the shoots are attached during growth.[10] In Israel, Golan Ezekiel drew inspiration from the Khasi to develop a way of shaping aerial roots in which the roots are pre-cultivated in a water-nutrient mist and then shaped.[11] Wiechula also investigated horticultural approaches that, much like the laying of hedges, involve the partial cutting of the trunk. These were applied in a similar form by David Nash for his "Ash Dome" (→ Chapter 6, p. 136–137).

The theoretical and particularly the practical findings of these various investigations provided a starting point for a series of experiments documented in the following that aim to explore ways and methods for producing complex intergrown structures.

Test Series 1

Baubotanical joining techniques involve ensuring that plants merge reliably at a desired point. To this end, the shoots must be constantly pressed against each other in such a way that natural grafting processes — known as inosculation — are stimulated. This means of connection must be able to withstand the growth pressure resulting from the growth in thickness or mutual overgrowth until at least a common annual ring has formed and the connection is self-stabilising. At the same time, the fastening method or joining technique should not negatively affect the development of the plant. In particular, the transport functions of the wood and bark may not be permanently interrupted, and injury to the plants should be minimised and where unavoidable not lead to the ingress of bacteria and the subsequent large-scale spread of rot. In addition, there should be no (permanent) mechanical weakening of the joint (→ Chapter 2, p. 52 and pp. 54–58).

With these requirements in mind, a series of tests using different trees was started in 2007 with two main objectives: firstly, to develop practicable connection techniques that meet these requirements; and secondly, to investigate the suitability of these techniques for different tree species with a view to gaining better knowledge of the baubotanical suitability of different tree species. Because intergrowth is such an important aspect, the tests examined species that are known to favourably respond to inosculation achieved by simple means within a short period of time. The tests examined both the immediate reaction of the plant to the joining technique and the inosculation result. The quality criteria for assessing inosculations were whether complete fusion of the wood bodies occurred, ideally without bark inclusion, the rapid formation of a common growth ring and little to no discoloration in the wood, which could indicate the onset of decay.

Procedure and implementation

Ten species of forest or urban trees commonly found in Central Europe, with different wood and bark anatomies and growth rates, were selected for the experiments: White willow (*Salix alba*), black alder (*Alnus glutinosa*), silver birch (*Betula pendula*), black locust (*Robinia pseudoacacia*), London plane tree (*Platanus × hispanica*), Norway maple (*Acer platanoides*), European ash (*Fraxinus excelsior*), English oak (*Quercus robur*), common hornbeam (*Carpinus betulus*) and European beech (*Fagus sylvatica*).[12]

The first test series (→ Fig. 1) started in 2007 with preliminary trials to test the joining techniques. Building on this, the rest of the trials were set up in 2008. 560 plants were used, which were connected to each other at 660 points. Planting took place in March, with joining following in May and June of the same year. In 2009, additional variants and repeat tests were set up for the species willow, plane, ash and birch. Further connection variants followed in 2011, this time exclusively with plane trees. As a rule, one- to three-year-old young plants with shoot lengths of between 0.5 and 1.2 m were used. The birch trees in the 2009 test series were somewhat larger, with shoot lengths of approx. 1.5 and those of the plane trees in 2011 were undertaken with one-year-old shoots of approx. 2 m in length.

The trees were initially planted in containers, and after the first few years many were removed for anatomical studies in winter 2009/10. Of the remaining specimens, 65 pairs of plants of the species willow, black alder, birch, plane and maple that exhibited interesting aspects for further observation (successful growths, but also problem areas), were planted on an experimental

1 Cross-grown plant pairs from Test Series 1 at the Versuchsstation für Gartenbau, Hohenheim.

1

field belonging to the TU Munich in 2017 and further cultivated there. In 2019/20, further samples were again taken for anatomical studies.[13]

Three primary connection techniques were investigated in different variants. In the first technique, the plants were tied together with very thin cords that cut into the bark and then grew in. Fine stainless steel cables and braided Dyneema cord were used. In the second technique, the plants were held together with tapes that yielded to the growth pressure. Fabric adhesive tapes and self-adhesive elastic tapes, as customary in horticultural grafting, were used. In the third technique, the plants were mechanically joined by stainless steel connectors in the form of either wood screws screwed directly into the plant axes, or thin threaded rods or metal bolts (d = 2 mm) with nuts, for which a corresponding hole was pre-drilled in the plants. Starting in 2011, we also started investigating the effect of sealing the screw or hole entry and exit points with tree wax on the development of the joint.

The plants were connected to each other either at individual points or by arranging them parallel to one another over a longer axial section. For the point connections, the shoots were either crossed or bent so that they touched at one point. Usually two plants were connected, but in some cases four to eight plants were connected in bundles to investigate the influence of competition (→ Fig. 2 a, b).

2 a

2 b

2 Overview of the connection techniques and geometries studied (from left to right).
a Parallel connections with wire cord (black locust), grafting tape (willow), adhesive tape (willow) and stainless steel screw (black alder).
b Cross connections with wire cord (ash), wire cord with two plants each (plane) and a stainless steel screw (ash).

The development of the plants and their connections was documented at regular intervals using photos and measurement of the respective diameters. For the anatomical examinations, transverse, longitudinal and serial sections were cut through the junctions to gain insights into the influence of the respective tree species and technique used on the internal structure of the plants. The plants were cut with a mitre saw and scanned at true scale on a flatbed scanner with a resolution of 2400 or 1200 dpi. In some cases, the wood tissue was stained purple with phloroglucinol hydrochloric acid to better assess whether xylem intergrowth had taken place.

In 2020, further macroscopic sections were taken and µ-CT scans produced to assess the inosculations at tissue level. In addition, the resistance to water transport was investigated by experimentally determining the flow rate of coloured water through some of the connections.

Test results and findings

The first set of results from Test Series 1 are shown below for the tree species plane, willow, maple and hornbeam as examples. In the first instance, these focus on the connections of plant pairs, and the results for other species are summarised afterwards.

Plane tree

With plane trees, it proved possible to create inosculations with all joining techniques. The cords usually grew quickly into the bark without serious strangulation occurring. In the connections with yielding tape, bridge-like intergrowth did arise in at least some cases (→ Fig. 3). In cross-section, complete inosculation often appeared very quickly with only minor bark inclusions (→ Fig. 4). The screw connections led to discoloration in the immediate area of the fastener, but this did not spread into the newly formed wood after joining (→ Figs. 5, 6). In some cases, wood screws caused the shoots to split slightly, and in some of these cases the joints broke open again (→ Fig. 7). In the further course of development, successful connections exhibited homogeneous bark surfaces on all sides and, in the case of cross joints, smoothly rounded grooves (→ Fig. 8).

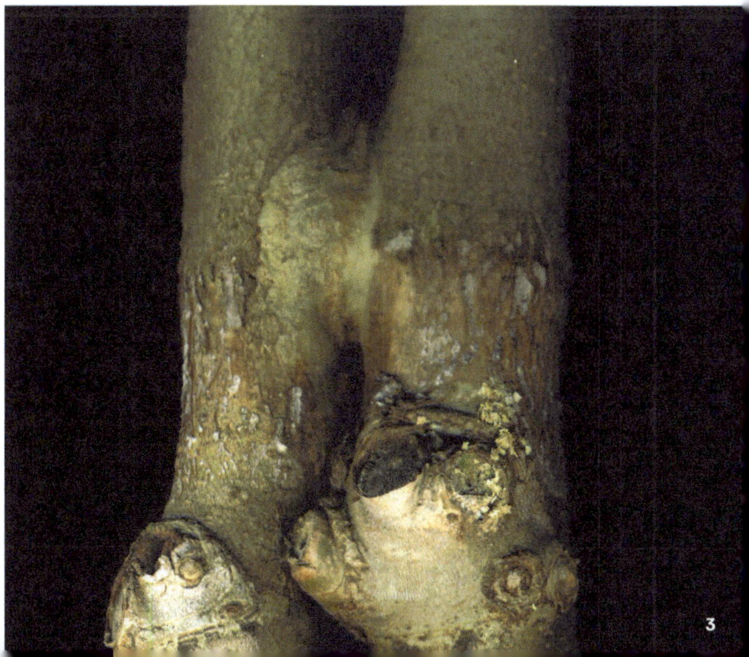

3 Bridge-like intergrowth of two plane trees that were taped together (tape removed for the photo).

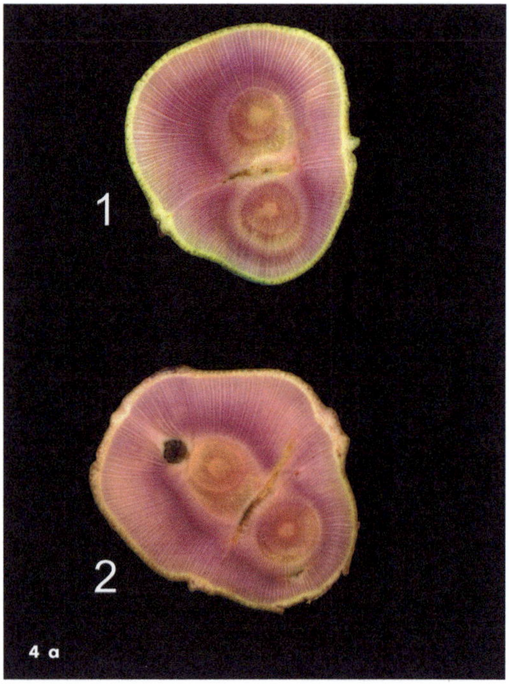

4 a Cross-sections through a complete inosculation of two plane trees with minimal bark inclusions (the entire wood body is coloured).
b View of the same joint. The stainless steel cords used here have been completely incorporated without causing strangulation.

5 After one growing season, wood discoloration in this screwed plane tree connection has spread axially only slightly (by approx. 20 mm upwards and downwards). The numbers indicate the distance upwards (+) or downwards (-) from the joint.

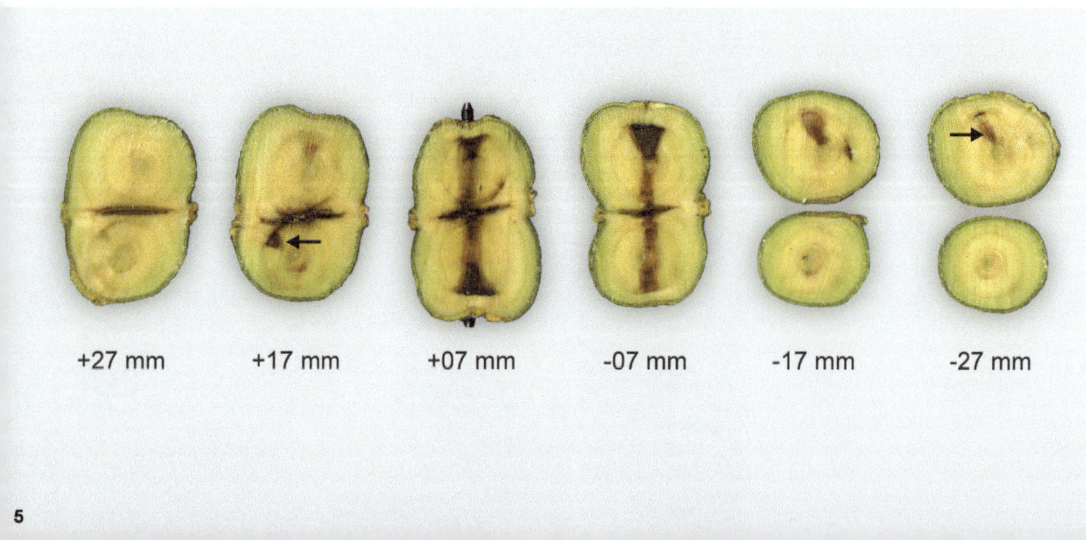

6 Several years later, only local discoloration limited to the directly affected tissues has occurred (the water-conducting sapwood is stained).

7 Rare case of a screw torn out after splitting the wood during screwing.

8 Typical cross-growth in a pair of plane trees with smooth rounding of the join transitions.

Willow

The willow tree likewise proved conducive to forming inosculations using all joining techniques. However, the cords of the tied connections usually caused severe strangulation and frequently snapped as a result of growth in thickness (→ Fig. 9 a, b). Eventually they were incorpor- ated into the stem, but the site was still clearly visible many years later. The connections made with yielding tape were roughly comparable to those of the plane trees. Screw joints created significant extended discoloration of the wood, which often spread over a wide area, especially axially (→ Fig. 10 a, b). Over time and as the joins grew, the crosswise joints often grew significantly thicker in diameter in the area of the intergrowth and resulted in thicker bark deposits at the transitions, as is typical of branch junctions in this species (→ Fig. 11).

9 a Clear obstruction of sap flow (strangulation) in the willow due to ingrown cords.
b In the cross-section, the beginning of a xylem fusion can be seen, at the same time as ingrown bark tissue.

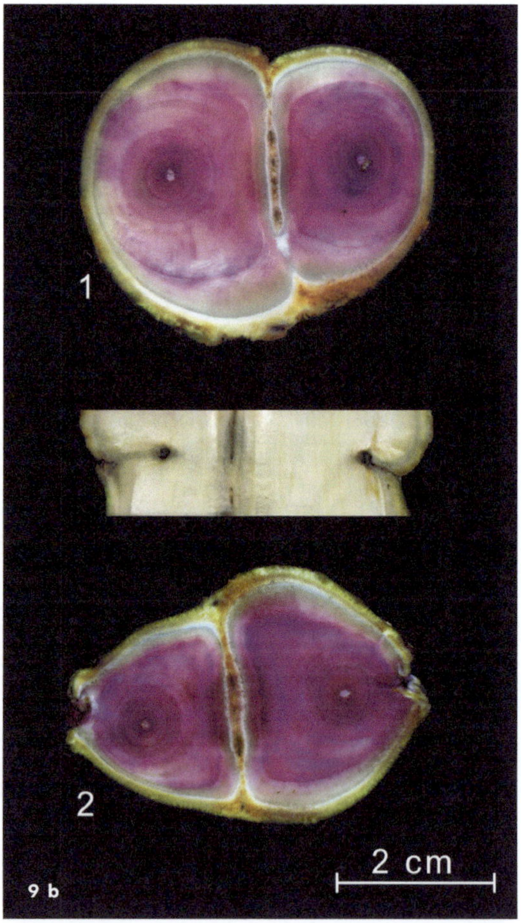

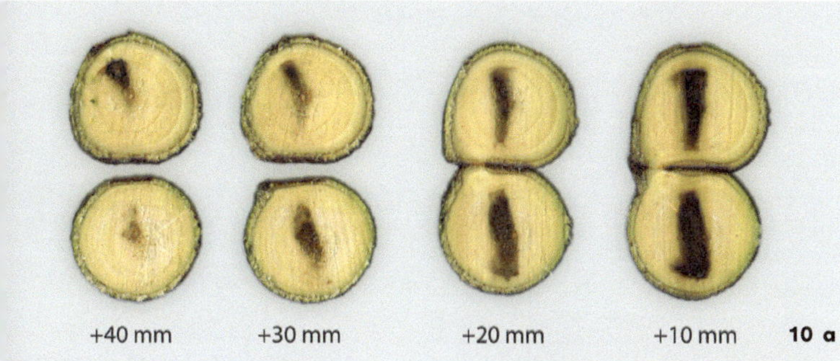

10 a

10 Distinct discoloration in willow stem, **a** spreading axially towards the top and **b** the bottom about twice as far as in plane trees. Also visible is that there has been only partial fusion of the wood bodies.

10 b

11

11 Typical cross-growth in willow with strongly diverging stem diameters.

Maple

In maple, almost no inosculations arose using the tied or taped connections (→ Fig. 12 a). The cords often snapped and also caused strong strangulation of the sap flow (→ Fig. 12 b). The screw connections did result in inosculations in most cases, although these developed somewhat more slowly than, for example, in the plane trees. Wood discoloration was also pronounced, but somewhat less than in willow (→ Fig. 13).

12 a Initial stage of inosculation in a maple sample.
b The tied connections were snapped open by growth in thickness and also caused clear strangulation.

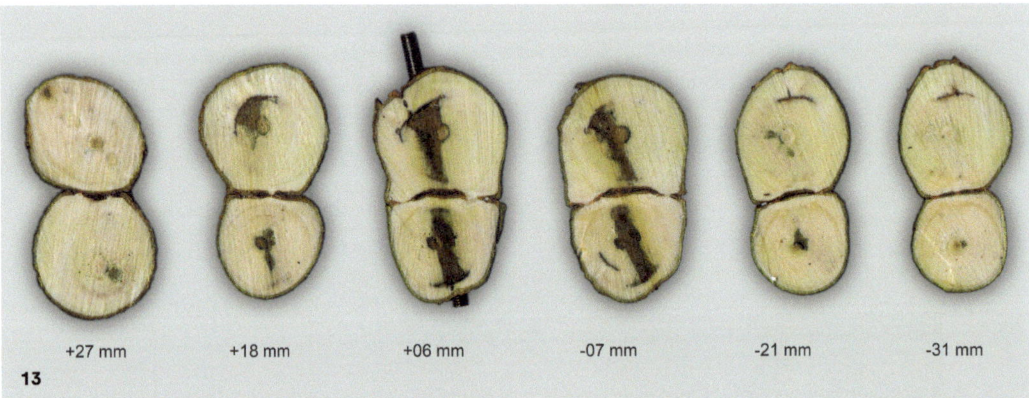

13 Discoloration caused by bolting tended to be slightly more extensive in maple than in plane trees, but less than in willow.

Hornbeam

As is typical for the species, the hornbeam specimens developed more slowly than the other tree species. As with the plane trees, the cords were incorporated by the stems. Inosculations arose in many cases with both the tied and the taped connections. Even when only slight signs of inosculation were visible externally, xylem connections were apparent from early on in the cross-section (→ Fig. 14 a, b). Screw connections were not examined.

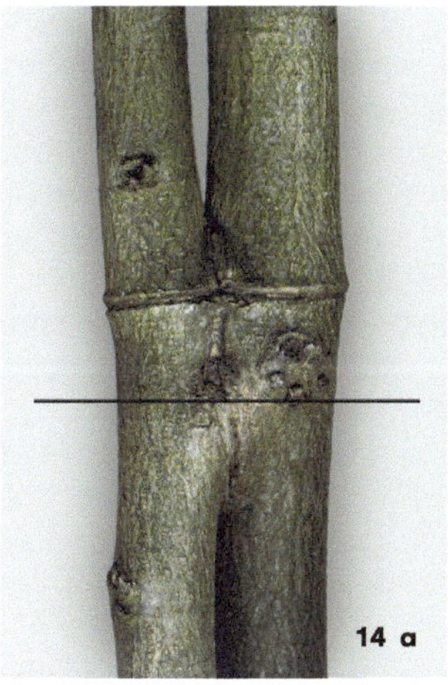

14 a

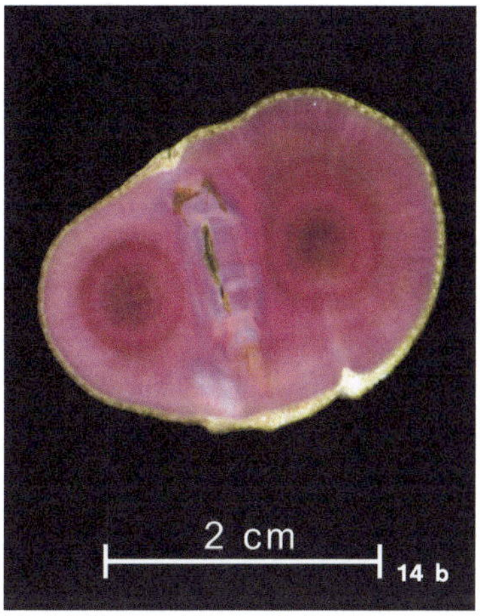

14 b

14 a The cords of the tied connections were incorporated quickly and without complications in the hornbeam samples, and **b** fusion of the wood bodies developed quickly and extensively with only slight bark inclusions.

Other tree species

In the ash tree specimens, the stems swelled markedly, and the cords of the tied connections resulted in very strong strangulation. Otherwise, the results were most comparable to those of the plane trees. Wood discoloration in the screw joints was extremely low.

The results of the trials with birch trees varied considerably. In general, the tied connections grew quickly and well, and in many cases complete inosculations followed quickly. The joins produced by yielding tape were comparable to those of the plane trees. Screwing also quickly produced complete inosculations but was accompanied by marked discoloration of the wood.

The black alder trees grew most vigorously, and here too the cords of the tied connections were quickly incorporated, but also with visible signs of strangulation. The resulting inosculations often exhibited bark inclusion. In the case of the crosswise connections, some plants buckled at the point of connection. The taped connections only rarely resulted in inosculations and screw connections were not examined in detail.

None of the trials conducted with black locust trees and tied or taped connections resulted in any inosculation. Bolted connections were not, however, examined. The tied connections often caused strong swelling and/or buckling of the axis.

In the oak tree specimens, too, the tied connections caused the stems to swell considerably but the cords were rarely incorporated, and when then only very slowly. Intergrowth only properly occurred in some cases, and none were achieved using taped connections. Screw connections were not examined.

The results with beech tree are comparable to those with hornbeam, although overall growth was slightly lower. Screw connections were not examined in detail, but seem to function quite well when judged purely from the outside (→ Fig. 31).

The influence of wood and bark anatomy

These initial qualitative results provide a first indication of the influence of wood and bark anatomy on inosculation processes. Tree species without corky bark (phellem), such as hornbeam and beech, grow together very easily, while the scaly bark of plane trees was also conducive. The longitudinal corky and cracked bark of oak, black locust and partly also maple seemed to hinder inosculation, but this was not seen in willow, alder and ash. The very young shoots used in the trials seem to have very reactive ground tissue in the bark resulting in rapid bark intergrowth. Species with many, longer fibres in the bark (oak, black locust, ash, willow, maple) impede cord ingrowth, while those with low-fibre or short-fibre barks (beech, hornbeam, plane, birch) quickly assimilate the cords. Those ring-porous species (ash, oak, black locust) react to tied connections by swelling strongly, which can be explained by a need to rapidly form a new continuous annual ring. Finally, fusion of the wood bodies appeared to develop faster and more evenly in species with many, finely distributed wood rays (plane, hornbeam, beech) than in species with fewer and coarser wood rays (e.g. oak).

Assessment of joining techniques

The spread of discoloration in the wood body caused by the insertion of screws or bolts seems to largely confirm data in the literature[14] on the compartmentalisation behaviour of the different tree species. However, the young ash shoots exhibited much better compartmentalisation capacity than is observed in older trees. Overall, the fast-growing pioneer tree species such as willow and birch exhibited stronger wood discoloration resulting from bolts or screws. Despite this, mechanical connections through screwing or bolting turned out to be one of the most reliable, practicable and time-saving procedures, though this method should ideally only be used for species with good or very good compartmentalisation. The use of yielding tape to effect connections between plants proved to be particularly gentle on plants, but also not very reliable and difficult to predict in development. In practice, this method works best — if at all — with species with very thin, reactive bark. Tapes proved less suitable for cross connections, as they often had the tendency to grow into the stems in this configuration. Tied connections should likewise only be considered for species with thin or short-fibred bark and their use with ring-porous species should be viewed critically. Stem strangulation can cause temporary weakening and thus mechanical failure, especially in these species.

Assessment of the inosculation trials by tree species

The results suggest that black locust and oak are not, or only rarely suitable for creating intergrown structures due to their combination of long-fibred, thick corky bark and ring-porous, coarsely structured wood. The species where this was most possible are beech and hornbeam, though both these tree species grow very slowly. Plane trees often exhibited the best results with all connection variants and are also relatively fast-growing. In willow and maple, the resulting inosculations are less homogeneous and both screw and tied connections can sometimes cause critical reactions. These are even more pronounced in black alder. Good inosculations in black alder (much like ash) were best achieved using screw connections, and in birch conversely in tied connections rather than screw connections.

Test Series 2

Test Series 1 was conducted using comparatively young plants which are easy to shape and tend to grow faster and better due to their still thin bark. However, such shoots are hardly used in Baubotanik. To create structures of a reasonable size or that have an appreciable leaf mass and spatial presence, it makes much more sense to use plants that are already several years old and have already grown to a height of several metres. The second test series (→ Fig. 15) builds on the interim results of the first tests by examining the growth processes and formability of approx. 4 m high trees. To this end, various species of commercially grown plants from tree nurseries were sourced. This test series also examined how inosculated pairs of plants responded to the removal of a section of their stem (→ plant addition, p. 81). The experiments were designed as exploratory tests to obtain an initial qualitative appraisal for determining the direction of future research and practice.

15 View of Test Series 2 with bent and doubly connected pairs of plants (birch trees in the foreground, hornbeam in the second row behind).

Procedure and implementation

The tree species studied in Test Series 2 were London plane (*Platanus × hispanica*), Norway maple (*Acer platanoides*), hornbeam (*Carpinus betulus*), winter lime or small-leaved lime (*Tilia cordata*), silver birch (*Betula pendula*), parrotia (*Parrotia persica*), Turkish hazel (*Corylus colurna*) and English oak (*Quercus robur*).

This selection aims to identify to what extent the good or very good results of the first test series using young plants can be confirmed with larger plants. The lime tree was also included in this test series due to its widespread use in historical precedents of living architecture, such as the dance linden trees. Parrotia was included because the species is known to be conducive to inosculation, and Turkish hazel due its ability to cope well with the effects of climate change, or at least better than many native species.[15] Despite the comparatively unsuccessful trials in the first series, English oak was also included as it is considered the tree species with the greatest biodiversity potential in Central Europe.[16]

The trials were conducted on a section of Bruns tree nursery in Bad Zwischenahn which was planted with four rows of six pairs of plants each. To produce the "figure of eight" forms, an auxiliary structure made of two rings of steel flats mounted vertically on edge one above the other was used, wrapped with jute fabric to protect the bark of the plants.

Plants were selected that were approx. 4 m high but the smallest possible stem diameter. As a result, the initial diameters of the plants at the lower connection point varied between approx. 1.5 and 3.5 cm. While this breadth of stem sizes limits the comparability of the results, it also reflects the actual commercial availability of slender grown species and thus easily mouldable trees of different species available on the (European) market.

Most of the planting took place in spring 2014, with the connections following in June of the same year. In 2016, gaps that became vacant from unsuccessful attempts were replanted. The plants were connected with stainless steel metal screws (d = 6 mm), nuts and washers or (for very thin shoot diameters) with stainless steel wood screws. For the replanting of specimens that did not exhibit satisfactory inosculations in 2016, the shoot axes were in some cases cut all the way into the wood at their joining point.

The shaping of the trees was achieved by bending the stems, or where they were too thick, by making thin wedge-shape incisions in the stem and bending or kinking the stem using a technique similar to that practised by David Nash (→ Chapter 6, pp. 136–137). When bending, the limits of stem suppleness were first determined by proceeding bit by bit until the first signs of damage became evident as bark cracking or slight buckling. If this was insufficient to create a figure of eight shape, either just one crossing point was created or the technique with partial one-sided incisions was used as described above.

Test results and findings

To provide a more compact overview of the results of Test Series 2, the results of the plane and maple trees are shown in detail, followed by a summary for the remaining species in the test series.

Plane trees (six pairs of plants)

In 2014, we were fortunate to be able to source plane tree shoots that were very slender and easy to shape. They grew well and exhibited vigorous thickness growth (→ Fig. 16 a, b). Most of the bolts or screws used to create the connections were incorporated within the first two vegetation periods and very uniform inosculations with a smooth, homogeneous surface developed (→ Fig. 17). The emergence of extremely strong side shoots in the lower area caused thickness growth in the upper loop to stagnate. In 2020, a section of the stem directly beneath the lower inosculation was cut off. The wood in that area did not exhibit any discoloration and the plant kept growing vigorously in the following vegetation period. For some of the replantings in 2016, stronger plants were used for comparison that could not be bent into a figure of eight and were therefore formed by making wedge-shaped incisions and buckling. The procedure was only partially successful, as the stems often broke off at the kinking point. In such weakened plants, the wound response was slower at the remaining bending points, with the incisions closing off only gradually as wound callus grew (→ Fig. 18 a, b).

16 a Slender plane tree shoots bent into a figure of eight.
b A comparable pair of trees, about six years later after vigorous pruning.

17 The plane trunks have intergrown very evenly at the crossing point.

18 a A thicker plane tree stem bent into shape by making wedge-shaped incisions on one side and then bending or kinking the stem.
b The same spot about four years later. After the shoot broke off at the uppermost bend, the plant exhibited only slight thickness growth and slow wound healing.

Maple (three pairs of plants)

The plants we were able to source were relatively strong and not very flexible. In two of the pairs of plants, therefore, only one cross connection was made, and in one further case, wedge-shaped incisions were made, and the stem bent to a curve as described above. These wounds unfortunately failed to heal, and this trial was unsuccessful. The two remaining pairs of plants grew well and exhibited vigorous growth in thickness (→ Fig. 19 a, b) but their joins developed quite differently. While in one case there was only partial intergrowth and otherwise mutual overgrowth (→ Fig. 20), the other join exhibited very homogeneous development similar to that of the plane trees (→ Fig. 21 a, b). As described above for the plane trees, a section of the stem beneath the inosculation was also severed here. The wood had only minimal discoloration in this area (→ Fig. 22 a, b) and the plants continued to grow vigorously in the following vegetation period.

19 a

19 b

19 a, b The maple plants were much thicker and stiffer than the plane tree specimens and while they could not be formed into a figure of eight, they likewise exhibited very good growth.

20

20 Example of a maple joint where the wood and bark tissues on the lower side have not fused.

21 a, b After about six years, this crossing point between two maple stems shows good inosculation and the bolt has been entirely incorporated into the join.

21 a

21 b

22 a, b Removal of a stem section beneath a maple inosculation. The cross-section directly next to the inosculation shows almost no discoloration.

Hornbeam (four pairs of plants)

Two of the four pairs of plants were thin and bendable enough to be shaped into a figure of eight. The others were much thicker and could not be bent accordingly. Initially only the lower joins were created, with the upper join following in 2016 for one of these two plants, achieved by making wedge-shaped incisions and bending the stem. In this case, no noticeable loss of vitality followed, and by 2020 the cuts and bends had healed well. Most of the bolts were overgrown or completely incorporated by the tree body after four growing seasons. Most of the inosculations developed well, but in some cases the stems exhibited areas with very little thickness growth and no intergrowth at the contact points.

Small-leaved lime (six pairs of plants)

In 2014, three pairs of trees (*Tilia cordata*) were planted that despite their relatively thick trunks could be bent quite easily making it possible to create two connections. In some parts, however, this resulted in a slight buckling of the trunks and after two vegetation periods, two of these three pairs of plants died and the third developed very weakly with practically no inosculations after four vegetation periods. As similar conventional plantings did not exhibit the same behaviour, it is likely that the bending or the joining caused their failure. In 2016, therefore, three new pairs of plants were planted, two of which were shaped as above. These did develop more vigorously but also exhibited very little intergrowth. Instead of callus forming around the bolts, as with the other species, the bolt appeared only to be drawn into the trunk as the stem grew thicker. The third pair of plants were formed using wedge-shaped incisions and bending, and the join was created by cutting the stems into the wood and pressing the two against each other. In this case, callus formed at both the kinks and at the join and the wounds subsequently healed and inosculation developed.

Birch (two pairs of plants)

The comparably thick trunks were relatively easy to bend and indeed were so flexible that they needed additional support above the shaping rings. During bending, some of the stems tore slightly or even snapped. While these wounds took a while to heal, all the plants still thrived, the screws were quickly incorporated by the plant, and the intergrowth points developed quickly and evenly.

Parrotia (two pairs of plants)

The plant stems were already quite thick and virtually unbendable, so only one connection was made at a time. In general, the plants developed vigorously and the bolts were mostly completely incorporated after four vegetation periods. However, the pattern of inosculation was quite different to that of the other species. Intergrowth reactions occurred only in the immediate contact area, but then very evenly.

Hazel (two pairs of plants)

The plants of average stem diameter were easy to bend without any visible damage and continued to thrive well. After four vegetation periods, the bolts were completely incorporated and the inosculations appear to have developed well and evenly, although the thick, corky bark makes it difficult to assess the actual condition within.

Oak (two pairs of plants)

The plants with stems of medium diameter were easy to form, but usually buckled a little in the process. Two connections were made in each case. All plants died within the first two vegetation periods. Such total failures are rare in nursery cultures, and it is therefore likely that the bending or joining was the cause.

Assessment of the results of Test Series 2

In Test Series 2, the best inosculation results were achieved with plane trees, birch, parrotia and hazel. The connections of the hornbeam specimens also developed well in most cases, but not always very evenly. The same applies initially to maple. The sectional cut beneath the inosculation showed that the bolted connection did not cause any negative consequences such as rot in the wood. As such, screwing into or drilling a thin hole through a young stem with a diameter of a few centimetres would seem to be a tolerable intervention, comparable to that of incisions or cuts in similarly strong branches or stems.

Unlike most of the tree species, the oak and lime tree specimens seemed much weakened by the shaping or joining procedures. With the lime trees, inosculations were only achieved by actually cutting the stems. This species has a bark with numerous strong and long bast fibres and a very soft wood, and it seems that the bark hinders the formation and development of intergrowth processes. At the same time, the very soft wood does not seem to adequately resist the growth pressure at the join seam. It is probable that other joining techniques need to be developed when working with lime trees. Exactly why lime and oak trees respond so unfavourably to shaping and joining cannot be ascertained from these tests.

The experience of this test series suggests that the thicker trunks of maple and plane trees cannot be shaped by one-sided incisions and subsequent bending, but that hornbeam and lime respond well to such an approach. Here, too, the findings are not conclusive. Overall, the test series have shown that the trees tolerate bolt connections surprisingly well, and that this represents a reliable joining technique for many species and doesn't involve cutting the bark tissue. This also applies to tree species with relatively thick bark such as birch or hazel but less so to species like lime with very fibrous bark or those with uneven thickness growth, such as hornbeam or maple. In such cases, injuring the joint by sawing can be used to stimulate the formation of wound callus, which then triggers more complete inosculation.

The removal of a root section after complete inosculation did not lead to any noticeable loss of vitality, however it is too early to conclusively say how the plants will develop in the long term, which may depend on how well the cut wound heals.

Test Series 3

A key aim of the research field of Baubotanik is to contribute to making cities more liveable through the fusion of tree and structure. To achieve this, baubotanical structures need to be constructed in dimensions that are relevant for an urban scale. The experiments undertaken so far in the preceding two test series explore the creation of inosculated structures using young plants or trees that are a few metres high, but it will take decades before such structures reach the dimensions of adult trees or multi-storey buildings. Against the background of accelerating urbanisation processes, it is therefore imperative that baubotanical structures reach such dimensions much more quickly. This was the basis for Test Series 3, for which the following hypotheses were formulated.

1. By arranging trees next to and above each other and connecting them so that they fuse, a physiological unit can be created that can transport water from the lowest root to the uppermost leaf.

2. This structure can compensate for the severing of individual root areas by forming new roots on other remaining root areas. This happens where the roots have the best growing conditions.

To investigate the viability of this approach — which we have called "plant addition" (→ Fig. 23 a, b) — the primary research objective of Test Series 3 was to determine if it is possible, once complete fusion has occurred, to then remove the roots of the upper layer of plants in an interconnected, inosculated structure? A secondary objective was to observe the reaction of different tree species to bolted connections as an extension of the first two test series. This test series was likewise conceived as an exploratory investigation, often with only one repetition per tree species. Its intention was to gain experience rather than to provide categorical scientific findings.

23 Schematic representation of the principle of plant addition.
a Arrangement of trees in the ground and on several levels above each other in planters. Connections between plants are established at crossing points to stimulate inosculation.
b Development hypothesis: After successful fusion, the roots of the upper plants can be severed and the planters removed. The plant structure now supplies itself with water and nutrients from the ground.

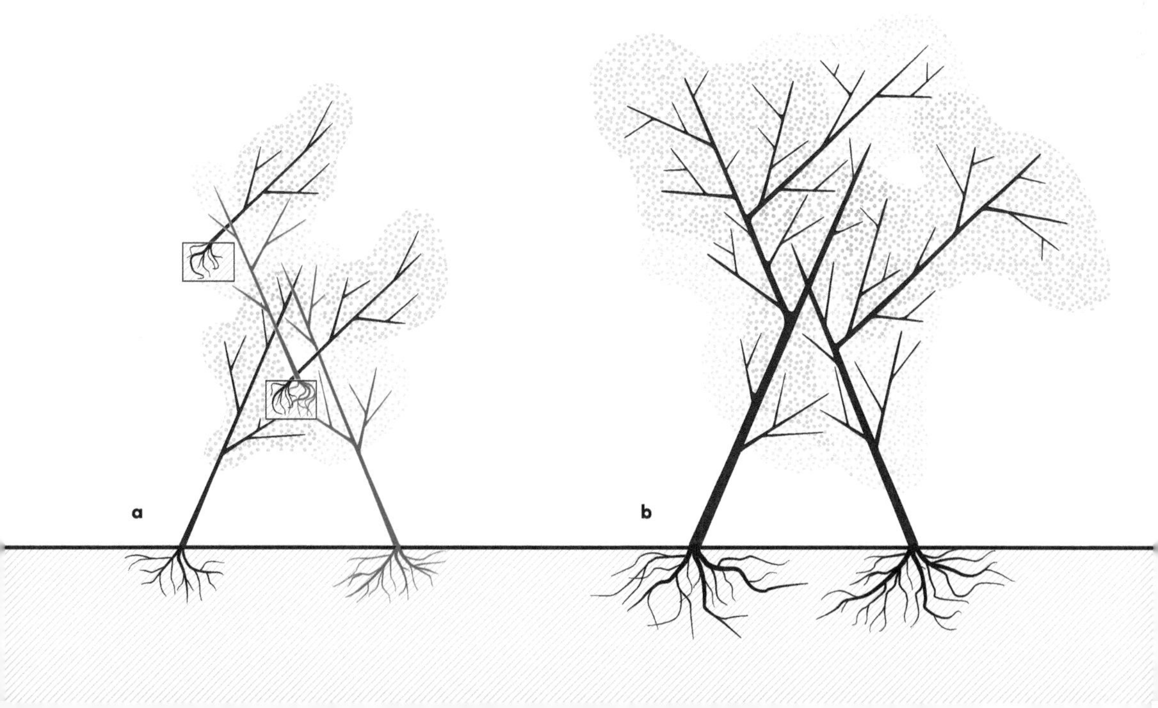

Procedure and implementation

Test Series 3 investigated the following tree species: London plane (*Platanus × hispanica*), hornbeam (*Carpinus betulus*), Norway maple (*Acer platanoides*), silver birch (*Betula pendula*), winter lime or small-leaved lime (*Tilia cordata*), English oak (*Quercus robur*), parrotia (*Parrotia persica*), Turkish hazel (*Corylus colurna*), European beech (*Fagus sylvatica*), European larch (*Larix decidua*), European hop hornbeam (*Ostrya carpinifolia*) and American sweetgum (*Liquidambar styraciflua*). The specific varieties used correspond to those used in Test Series 2 with particular focus on the plane tree and hornbeam. In addition, the European beech variety investigated in Test Series 1 was included along with three other species. Larch is the first coniferous tree species to be included to assess how resin formation, which is typical of conifers, affects inosculation development and wound healing when removing damaged or injured sections of the tree. European hop hornbeam and American sweetgum were included because these species, like Turkish hazel, are reputed to respond well to the consequences of climate change.[17] In addition, American sweetgum has great aesthetic potential due to its impressive autumn colouring.

To plant the trees on two levels, five wooden tower-like structures were erected, each of which can hold eight plants. All the trees were planted in planters, with the lower, significantly larger planters placed directly on the ground and the upper ones on a platform about 2.4 m above the ground.

Three of the towers were used to study four different tree species. Therefore, the lower plants were planted vertically upright while the upper plants were inclined outwards at a shallow angle so that the stems crossed just above the upper planter (→ Fig. 24). The other two towers were planted only with plane trees and hornbeam, with two trunks always connected in parallel from below and trained vertically upwards. The upper plants were again inclined and arranged in such a way that they cross at one point with the vertical plants growing from below, making it possible to always join four trunks at this point.

At the crossing points, the trunks were connected using a similar method to Test Series 2, but this time using 8 mm stainless steel threaded rods and long threaded coupling nuts. The intention here is to prevent the complete overgrowth of the nut by the tree so that the connection point can be connected via the coupling nut to further technical components.

The trees were planted in spring 2013 with the joins following in early summer of the same year. Irrigation was time-controlled via drip irrigation in all of the planters.

The roots of the upper trees were cut off in 2017 and 2019 depending on how well the inosculations at the connection points had developed. The cut was made not directly at the crossing point but approx. 20 cm beneath it. As the trial field was only available for a limited time period, the test series had to be terminated at the end of 2019.

24 Complete and homogenous inosculation of a hornbeam test specimen.

Test results and findings

As with the results of Test Series 2, well-developed and apparently complete inosculatons could be observed within the first three vegetation periods in the plane tree, hornbeam (→ Fig. 25), maple, birch (→ Fig. 26 a, b) and hazel specimens. A comparable pattern was also seen in the beech, larch (→ Fig. 28) and hop hornbeam specimens but the development of the hop hornbeam, maple and some of the hornbeam specimens was not as uniform. Here, the lower areas of the inosculations, furthest away from the assimilate coming from the leaves, flourished less well than the upper parts of the inosculations. In the case of the parrotia plants, intergrowth proceeded more slowly but was ultimately comparable to the samples from Test Series 2. One of the two oaks died in the first growing season and was replaced. In the following vegetation periods, however, they grew much slower than their counterparts from other species. The joins of the lime tree specimens developed similarly to those seen in Test Series 2 (→ Fig. 27) with only mutual overgrowth but no inosculation. In the case of the sweetgum trees, the upper plant developed only weakly and no intergrowth resulted.

During the growing seasons in 2017 and 2018, the irrigation system malfunctioned several times, leading to severe drought damage, especially in the plane trees and partly also in the hornbeams. Two of the plane trees died and the remaining specimens were permanently weakened. As such, these results are given separate consideration in the following breakdown of the outcomes.

25 Trees of different species arranged on two levels and connected to each other as part of Test Series 3.

In July 2017, the roots of the upper specimens where complete intergrowth was observed were cut off (hornbeam, maple, birch, hazel, beech, larch, hop hornbeam). The same procedure was performed in 2019 on species with slower-developing inosculations such as the oak and parrotia specimens. All the plants exhibited good growth in the 2018 and 2019 vegetation periods (→ Fig. 29), although only in the case of the larch (→ Fig. 30) were clear wound reactions visible at the cut surface. In the other species, there was more or less pronounced dieback of the lower trunk sections of the upper trees between the former roots and the inosculation.

As both the sweetgum and lime tree specimens developed no inosculations, the roots of the upper trees were not cut off.

In the remaining plane trees, the roots of the upper plant were removed in one case in 2017. In 2018, these plants exhibited good development, especially considering the prior damage, and first wound reactions at the cut. In spring 2019, however, all plane trees, including those where the root zones had not been removed, were dead. It is therefore unlikely that the removal of the root areas led to the plants' dying; more likely is the influence of drought and/or frost in the planters.

26 a, b Inosculation in the birch trees. The exit points of the long nuts resemble the situation naturally found after a dead branch has been cast off.

28 Uniformly developed inosculation on all sides of the larch specimen.

27 Mutual overgrowth but no visible inosculation of the lime trees.

29 A view of the entire Test Series 3 after most of the stems of the upper plants had been cut off below the inosculation.

30

30 After removal of the upper roots, the larch sample exhibited the clearest wound reactions at the cut surface, combined here with resin formation.

The findings suggest that inosculation of plants arranged one above the other had resulted in the creation of a physiological unit that is able to compensate for the loss of the upper root area. In principle, this seems to be true for all the species studied, provided that complete fusion has occurred and the plants are otherwise healthy. A more significant problem is the cut beneath the inosculation. Given that the stump starts to die back, it seems more sensible to make the cut directly beneath the join. Since in this test series only two plants were arranged one above the other, one cannot conclusively infer how well it performs for several storeys of plants arranged one above the other, but experience from other projects, such as the Green Living Room in Ludwigsburg (→ Chapter 6, pp. 170–173), shows that this too can be successful.

While the removal of the roots of the upper tree sections did not lead to any visible impairment of the tree growth, that does not mean that it has no physiological consequences. On the contrary, one can expect that the tree's growth will respond to the intervention, for example by forming new roots in the remaining root areas, by temporarily slowing down shoot growth and by increasing thickness growth in areas that subsequently need to conduct more water. This needs further investigation in future test series with more repetitions and corresponding measurements.

The very positive results from the experiments with plane trees in the first two test series could not be immediately confirmed in this test series due to the occurrence of drought damage. It is possible that plane trees respond more sensitively to drought stress than other species—particularly given their strong growth and associated greater need for water.

31 Parallel inosculation of two black alder shoots.

Tree species selection in Baubotanik

The results of the test series so far provide an indication of the suitability of different tree species for use in Baubotanik. Nevertheless, these must also be considered in combination with a multitude of other factors that play a role in the selection of tree species for baubotanical projects. Here we discuss how these different factors interact for five of the tree species studied in the experimental series, along with specific further factors from other species and cultivars. These trees represent a cross-section of species with varying characteristics that are common throughout Central Europe and should not be regarded as a pre-selection. Rather, they serve as examples to highlight relevant aspects of tree species selection. An important indicator for the potential suitability of a species for Baubotanik can be seen in historical uses, for example in forestry, parks or streetscapes[18] as well as in their technical properties and the use of their wood. For Baubotanik, however, it is not the dry wood but the properties of green, i.e. fresh wood that is relevant.[19] In the same way, one must also consider their natural occurrence, ecological potential and health effects on humans, not to mention resistance to plant diseases and to possible effects of climate change.

London plane tree

The London plane tree (*Platanus × hispanica*) emerges as one of the "winners" from the test series and is accordingly eminently suitable for Baubotanik. It grows well and quickly, has strong wood and excellent wound-healing capacity. Embedded technical components are quickly incorporated with the wound tissue literally "flowing around" them (→ Chapter 6, p. 167). Many historical examples and traditional horticultural methods testify to the comparative ease with which it can be fashioned into architectural structures. A common example is the horizontal guiding of the branches to create the well-known "roof-trained" canopies. The combination of its good wound healing and regenerative capacities makes it possible to pollard the canopy or alternatively fashion it into geometric forms, as seen in historical parks (→ Fig. 32).

32 Pollarding is a typical horticultural cultivation method used on plane trees.

At the same time, the common plane tree is tolerant of various external factors such as road salt, air pollution and heat, which is why it has been so successful around the world as an urban and street tree.[20] The common plane tree or London plane tree, which is found throughout Central Europe and is discussed here, is thought to have originated in the 17th century from a cross between the Occidental plane tree (*Platanus occidentalis*) and the Oriental plane tree (*Platanus orientalis*). Both these original species are riparian trees in their respective homelands, which suggest that the London plane tree also thrives best on sites with a good water supply (→ Fig. 33). The fact that it can nevertheless cope with heavily sealed, often extremely dry urban sites illustrates its great adaptability. However, when plane trees are grown in planters, they exhibit a certain sensitivity to drought and temperature stress (→ Chapter 3, pp. 83–84).

Plane trees quickly develop strong trunks with wide-spreading crowns, and mature trees can reach heights of more than 45 m and an age of 300 years or more. Some specimens of the Oriental plane tree are even known to be more than 1000 years old. This ability to grow to a large size and age suggests that they can be used to create baubotanical structures on the scale of a multi-storey building and could have a life expectancy exceeding that of a human being and indeed of most conventional buildings.

In terms of appearance, plane trees are easily recognisable due to their scaly bark and thick trunks and branches, as well as the typical maple-like leaves. Otherwise, they are rather inconspicuous, without any dramatic blossoms in spring or particularly striking leaf colouring in autumn. However, the typical spherical fruit clusters are a special ornament in autumn and winter (→ Fig. 34). The fact that these often remain on the tree for months indicates that they are not of great value to fauna, and insects, birds and mammals alike show little interest in consuming the fruit. However, the crowns and especially the hollow trunks of old plane trees are used by various bird species as breeding sites and thus serve an important function as a natural habitat.[21]

33 Originally, plane trees are floodplain woodland trees that thrive in riparian lowlands.

For a long time, plane trees were also considered largely resistant to most tree diseases, but in recent years damage caused by fungal diseases such as leaf blight (*Apiognomonia veneta*) has been observed more frequently. In healthy and well-watered trees, this disease only causes the leaves to be lost prematurely, which the trees quickly compensate for by forming new leaves from replacement buds. Already weakened trees and drought can nevertheless damage entire stands of trees in the long term.[22] A much more serious problem is Massaria disease, in which the harmful fungus (*Splanchnonema platani*) attacks even strong branches and causes intensive decomposition of the wood in a very short time. After just a few months, affected branches, which may often still appear leafy and healthy, can suddenly break off.[23] Given such developments and their possible link to climate change, there has been considerable discussion on whether plane trees can still be regarded as a reliable urban tree species in the context of climate change. Their use in Baubotanik must be assessed accordingly. A further aspect that may limit their suitability is the fact that very fine hairs form on the underside of the leaves and in the fruit that easily become airborne and can cause severe coughing and hay fever when inhaled.[24] People should therefore not spend extended periods in the treetops of plane trees or in the immediate vicinity of the leaves.

Overall, this shows that despite the many advantages that plane trees have for Baubotanik, there are also some very serious disadvantages. It is unclear, for example, how the consequences of climate change will affect the health and mechanical reliability of the trees, either directly or indirectly (e.g. through the increased incidence or new emergence of plant diseases). Equally, the potential negative effect on the well-being of people in the tree canopy must be viewed critically.

34 Autumn colouring and fruit of the plane tree. The fruit often hangs on the tree throughout winter.

White willow

Willow trees (here: *Salix alba*)[25] likewise exhibited good inosculations in the trials, but the tests also revealed that only certain joining techniques led to successful results. Due to its fibrous bark, tied connections could lead to critical strangulation, and the screw connections led to much greater wood discoloration than in, for example, the plane trees. This can be attributed to the fact that willow is less effective at compartmentalising tissue against ingress by bacteria that can lead to decay. Willow wood is generally soft, not very resilient and not very durable—which is typical for such pioneer tree species,[26] to which all willow species belong. Pioneer tree species are able to colonise open spaces very quickly and are not fussy about soil conditions, enabling them to thrive, for example, on relatively barren ground. They are tolerant of climatic extremes and grow very quickly—however, they do not usually live very long. All pioneer species develop best when in light-rich environments and typically have more delicate foliage that produces little shade. They do not, however, thrive in shade, which is why they are frequently displaced by more shade-tolerant species as surrounding woodland grows.

White willow typically occurs naturally in floodplains and alluvial zones that are subject to strongly fluctuating water levels. They survive well in such conditions because they are resistant to flooding but also tolerate temporary drought (→ Fig. 35). They spread easily due to their very light seeds that can be carried many kilometres, but also by the fact that roots or stems that are torn off can take root again and grow into new trees, for example when branches break off and wash downstream during floods. Branches that are several metres long or entire trunks can take root in this way—a property that is used, for example, in soil bioengineering. Willow branches are bundled into fascines or spread on the ground in so-called “spreading layers”. These branches take root in a very short time, stabilising the soil of riverbanks or steep slopes, helping to prevent erosion. [27] In Baubotanik, this phenomenon presents very interesting construction and design possibilities, as structures of a height of several metres can be realised rapidly and simply by using self-rooting cuttings.

White willows can reach a height of 35 m and, in some cases, live up to 200 years—but generally they do not live more than 100 years (→ Fig. 36). Baubotanical structures constructed with willow trees, however, seem to have a much shorter life expectancy, and one should target a design height that is much smaller than their potential growth height. As several projects

35 Typical growth behaviour of a willow on a bank: vigorous new shoots after breaking or capping the main stem.

36 White willows, which can grow up to 35 m tall, form very light canopies.

shown in Chapter 6 reveal, baubotanical structures made of willow tend to be short-lived and ideally self-regenerating. Due to its quick growth and excellent regenerative capacity, growth and incorporation of technical components happens comparatively quickly but at the same time rotting processes often set in, counteracting the increase in stability that comes with growth so that in the medium term this can result in a reduction in load-bearing capacity. In addition, as the plants grow, they compete with one another, which not only leads to the death of individual specimens but also to the weakening of the entire structure, for example due to pest infestation. Alongside various fungal diseases, the so-called "willow borer" is most relevant: The caterpillars of the moth *Cossus cossus* can reach up to 10 cm in size and penetrate deep into the wood, boring feeding tunnels that can cause even healthy trees to die.[28] The threat this poses to the ongoing health and stability of living baubotanical willow structures should not be underestimated.

These aspects significantly limit the possibilities of constructing with willow trees. If, however, one takes into account the specific properties of this species and uses it as a basis for developing a design and construction concept, there are many interesting possibilities for using white willow, and other willow species, for baubotanical projects. Their rapid growth and excellent regenerative capacity mean that projects can be realised quickly and experienced directly. The ability to use cuttings also enables comparatively simple and low-cost construction processes that can even be undertaken by laypeople as community projects.[29] At the same time, willows are an important source of food for bees and other insects due to their early flowering—the well-known catkins (→ Fig. 37). And, although disadvantageous for the construction, when willow structures decay, they not only provide food for wood-degrading microorganisms and insects, but also create an important habitat for cave-dwelling animal species such as bats and owls (→ Fig. 38).

37 Willows are an important source of food for insects in early spring.

38 An old pollarded willow, still sprouting very vigorously, with a completely rotten trunk, providing a habitat for a variety of animals.

Norway maple

After the first series of tests with Norway maple (*Acer platanoides*) failed to produce useful outcomes, the subsequent test series yielded better results with bolted connections that are comparable to those of the willow specimens. They appear to tolerate bolts somewhat better, but not as well as plane trees. The incorporation of the technical components was slower and not as pronounced as with the plane tree, probably due to maple's fibrous bark — a finding that is corroborated by observations of overlapping fences. Norway maple grows rapidly, particularly in its first 20 to 30 years, with annual shoots often exceeding 1 m. It can grow to heights of 20 to 30 m and reach an age of up to 180 years. Its natural habitat is deciduous and mixed forests on moist, humus- and nutrient-rich soils. It thrives best in warm, sunny to semi-shady locations. In Germany, it is used very widely as an urban or street tree due to its robustness and good tolerance of urban climates.[30] It is similarly popular and widespread in gardens and parks, not least because it is a particularly attractive species, of which more than 100 garden forms are known, with diverse leaf shapes and colours as well as different growth forms (e.g. the red-leaved variety *A. platanoides* var. *purpurea*). Characteristic for this tree are its wide, dense crowns, the strong yellow to reddish autumn colours and the yellow flower umbels that appear early in spring. These are also advantageous ecologically as an important food source for bees (→ Figs. 39–42).

The wood of the Norway maple is considered hard, tough and flexible, but also susceptible to insects and fungi, and not very resistant to weathering. Injuries are not quickly resealed by wound callus and can thus lead to microorganism ingress and rot. The ensuing compartmentalisation of the wood varies greatly depending on the age and type of wound.[31] For the same reason, Norway maple is not particularly tolerant of pruning. Depending on the weather and time of year, a heavy discharge of xylem sap (bleeding) can occur at the pruning wound, which can weaken the tree and impede wound healing. Larger pruning wounds should therefore be avoided and the species does not tolerate radical pruning or even pollarding very well. Accordingly, the Norway

39 A young Norway maple in full autumn colour.

40 The flowers of the Norway maple appear before the leaf shoots and are not only attractive but also ecologically valuable.

41 The typical lush green leaves of the Norway maple in summer.

42 In keeping with its natural habit, the Norway maple develops broad, dense crowns with an interesting spatial effect.

maple basically grows most robustly and attractively when it is allowed to develop naturally. This is also reflected by the fact that horticulturally cultivated forms such as roof-trained canopies or geometrically shaped crowns are rarely seen.

Despite its general robustness, Norway maple is more susceptible to powdery mildew (*Uncinula tulasnei*) or maple scab (*Rhytisma acerinum*), both of which usually only result in visual impairments. Much more dangerous is an infestation with Verticillium wilt (*Verticillium dahliae* or *Verticillium albo-atrum*), which also attacks many other plants and is increasingly spreading. This aggressive fungus destroys the water conduits and can only be countered by completely removing infested plant parts — which is problematic given the species' low tolerance of pruning. Such infestations can be brought on by drought stress which means that a good water supply and generally good growing conditions can help prevent infestation. Similar conditions apply to the so-called "sooty bark disease" (*Cryptostroma corticale*).[32]

Norway maple therefore presents an interesting option for Baubotanik when the desired structure does not require extensive shaping of the shoots or excessive pruning. Structural designs should therefore be based on the natural growth form of the tree, and good growth conditions need to be guaranteed over the entire lifetime of the structure. So far, however, there is little practical experience with this species.

Small-leaved lime

The findings of the test series undertaken so far suggest that it is very difficult to initiate inosculations among lime trees (here *Tilia cordata*) and then only by cutting into the bark. As such their applicability for Baubotanik seems questionable, at least at first. At the same time, this species is used widely for various purposes in garden architecture. The dance linden trees and arbours discussed elsewhere (→ Chapter 6, pp. 132—135 and 138—139), are two examples, but their crowns can also be trimmed or shaped into various geometric forms. This can often be seen in historical gardens (→ Fig. 44), but also in contemporary garden and landscape architecture, and tree nurseries offer pre-formed specimens in different varieties. All these variants are made possible by the vigorous growth of the tree combined with the good formability of the shoots.

When growing freely, lime trees can reach heights of 25 to 35 m and can have a life expectancy of several hundred years (→ Fig. 43). Several incidences of specimens that are over 1000 years old have been documented, with trunk diameters of over 5 m.[33] The trunks of these veteran trees are, however, fragments rather than solid wooden trunks, because lime trees achieve such an advanced age not through the longevity of the wood but through its excellent regenerative capacity. Even though they exhibit good compartmentalisation and have a rapid wound-healing capacity due to their vitality, their wood is soft and decomposes quickly once bacteria have got into the wood. In this respect, as well as in terms of their fast growth, lime trees are compar- able to the much shorter-lived willow trees. Lime trees are, however, very shade-tolerant and also produce good shade as a result of their dense foliage (→ Fig. 45). For this reason, they are frequently planted at meeting places in the centre of villages, as well as in parks, urban squares and streets. Lime trees are, however, more susceptible to air pollution and road salts, and the leaves are damaged relatively easily by excessive heat, which limits their applicability for urban situa-

43 The impressive symmetrical crown of a free-standing lime tree.

44 The formability of the shoots and branches and the pruning tolerance of the small-leaved lime make it possible to manipulate the crown shape quite radically, such as the bosquet form shown here.

45 Their dense foliage explains why lime trees are a popular choice for providing shade in public places.

tions, especially in the context of climate change. In principle, however, they are able to adapt to different site conditions.

Apart from Verticillium wilt, mentioned earlier in connection with maple trees, no tree diseases are known that can permanently weaken lime trees under good growing conditions. They are, however, often relatively intensively colonised by scale insects. While these do not damage the trees, they secrete large quantities of honeydew that covers the entire area beneath the tree crown in a sticky layer in summer. This can be unpleasant when in the direct vicinity of living areas, e.g. on façades or balconies. Otherwise, however, lime trees generally have a positive connotation as a tree rooted deeply in cultures and beliefs over the ages. Their small, yellowish-white flowers appear in late June to mid-July and exude a slightly sweet scent that most people find pleasant. At the same time, the small-leaved lime provides a habitat and source of food for over 200 insect species, and is considered one of the species with the highest potential for increasing biodiversity (→ Fig. 46).[34]

For Baubotanik, it can be deduced from this that the species is rather unsuitable for creating inosculated and load-bearing structures. However, the historical techniques of training the shoots, cutting the crown to a particular form or pollarding can be used to create shaded canopies or façades comprised of rows of trees, which offer ecological benefits. Their very dense foliage has both advantages and disadvantages. The problem of honeydew, which seems trivial at first, should also be considered, as it can cause practical problems in everyday use, which may even preclude the use of the species.

46 Lime blossoms produce a pleasant fragrance, but the honeydew also visible in the photo is often perceived as an annoyance.

Hornbeam

In the tests conducted so far, hornbeam (*Carpinus betulus*) has shown itself to be a species that not only grows well and quite easily, but also has great resilience. Neither severe drought stress nor the removal of a section of trunk, or even the most extensive cutting and kinking of the trunk had a lasting effect on the vitality of the specimens. The inherit toughness of this species has been exploited for centuries to similar ends, such as when "laying" hedges or so-called "knicks".[35] Its ability to cope with such drastic interventions can be attributed to its great regenerative capacity as well as its good wound healing and compartmentalisation tendencies, but also to the mechanical or physical properties of the wood. The wood, which was historically used to make machine parts and tools, is particularly heavy, hard and tough—which explains why it does not crack or break when bent, ensuring the conductive vessels continue unbroken. Traditionally, the hornbeam's capacity to produce many new shoots after pruning was used to obtain firewood or foliage for cattle fodder by means of pollarding.[36] This repeated intervention can sometimes result in bizarre, gnarled and often hollow tree shapes that can still be seen in some forests today. By regularly pruning the annual shoots, very dense and compact tree crowns can be formed, which historically played an important role as windbreaks. Their formability also explains their widespread use in different green structures (e.g. pergolas → Fig. 47) and in French garden design (Baroque gardens) and indeed, they are still widely used as hedging plants and topiaries in garden architecture today. Tree nurseries offer a wide selection of pre-cultivated forms such as ready-made hedges or arch elements.

When left to grow freely, hornbeams usually develop into larger shrubs or medium-sized, often multi-stemmed trees with heights of 10 to 20 m (→ Fig. 48). Only in exceptional cases do they reach heights of 25 or 30 m and trunk diameters of up to 1 m. They can grow to an age of 150 to 180 years, but rarely older, and grow comparatively slowly with annual shoot lengths of 20 to 40 cm.[37] The crown is characterised by a multitude of branches and twigs, all of which initially reach upwards and, like the trunks, take on a gnarled, twisted shape as they grow older, their smooth grey bark becoming gradually more apparent with age. The branches also have an irregular cross-section (→ Fig. 49). A key characteristic of hornbeams are their relatively small, elliptical leaves with serrated edges. The foliage, which is deep green in summer, usually turns yellow in autumn and then rapidly brown. It remains on the shoots over the winter, often until new shoots appear in the following spring. As such the trees retain their physical presence and can act as a windbreak even when dormant. The flowers that appear in spring with the leaf shoots are rather inconspicuous (→ Fig. 50). The pollen of the male flowers is carried by the wind to the female inflorescences—often present on the same plant. As wind pollinators, hornbeams are therefore not relevant as a food source for bees and other pollinating insects and their value for fauna is less than that of small-leaved lime, Norway maple and white willow.

47 Due to their formability and pruning tolerance, hornbeams are widely used in garden architecture, as here in a pergola.

48 Typical appearance of a free-standing hornbeam.

Overall, the hornbeam is a relatively competitive forest tree species that tolerates shade well and thrives optimally on nutrient-rich, well-watered soils. Due to its deep-reaching root system, it can survive longer dry spells relatively well and is considered very storm-resistant. Late frosts and prolonged water shortages can, however, cause damage. It tolerates both extremes of climatic conditions, including cold winters with -30 °C frosts and hot summers. Hornbeams are therefore well suited as urban and street trees and are regarded as being highly adaptable to climate change.[38] However, the species is sensitive to soil compaction, salt and flooding. Hornbeam trees are comparatively resistant to pests and tree diseases, and even larger hornbeam forests exhibit hardly any biotic damage. Infestation with fungal diseases usually only leads to minor visual impairments or premature loss of leaves, but not usually to any serious loss of vitality.

Overall, the hornbeam has several qualities that make it attractive for many baubotanical applications. In contrast to the white willow, its comparatively low life expectancy does not have a negative effect on the practical lifespan of baubotanical projects. This is because, due to its robustness, regenerative capacity, shade tolerance and general competitive nature, one can assume that the life expectancy of a living structure made with hornbeam trees will roughly approximate that of the tree species itself—i.e. about 150 years. The mechanical properties of the wood and the potential to create inosculated structures relatively easily suggests that it is suitable for creating load-bearing constructions. However, its relatively slow growth means that many years, or even decades, may pass before the trees reach the desired size and trunk diameter for such a structure. The possible height of such structures is also limited by the natural growth height and habitus of the trees. Due to its strong branching and frequent multi-stem development, the thickness growth of the individual branches is slow. As such, this species is better suited for connecting many branches to form lattice-like structures.

49 The distinctive, irregular and twisted appearance of the hornbeam trunk and the frequently bizarre shape of the crooked trunks and branches become more prominent with age.

50 The flowers of the wind-pollinating species are inconspicuous and do not provide a marked benefit for fauna.

4 Fusion of Trees and Buildings

In Baubotanik, trees and buildings are merged together to form hybrid structures that are at once organic and technical. This interpenetration of the natural and artificial is happening already today at many different scales. In the 19th century, for example, we saw the fusion of city and landscape at an urban scale: parks and boulevards were incorporated into the existing urban fabric and entire urban quarters were designed as green garden cities. Today, the need for greenery in cities is taken for granted and in many European cities trees are an everyday part of the streetscape. At an architectural scale, the connection between trees and buildings is by no means as self-evident. Although we can point to a whole series of historical examples — from the Gardens of Babylon to Le Corbusier's rooftop gardens — such architectural fusions are still not commonplace today. More recently, however, we have been witnessing a revival in the architectural consideration of trees that on the one hand picks up modern approaches from the 20th century and on the other draws on vernacular models. One can identify two principal trends: firstly, the integration of trees into buildings, and secondly, the integration of buildings into trees. As similar as they may sound, these two approaches represent two quite different ways of thinking about trees and architecture, but together they form a contextual and theoretical background within which baubotanical projects are conceived and designed.

Integrating trees in buildings

Every design for a building in the urban realm adopts a standpoint with respect to its surroundings and expresses the architect's attitude towards the city, landscape and nature. This is particularly true for high-rise buildings, which as landmark structures are visible from afar. The "Bosco Verticale" are a pair of skyscrapers in Milan that, like all residential skyscrapers, attempt firstly to efficiently stack living space vertically to make optimal use of the available urban space to address the problems of population growth and urbanisation and to counteract land consumption. What is different in this case is that the two towers, 18 and 27 storeys high, not only contain space for people but also provide a habitat for birds and insects by incorporating 900 trees and over 20,000 shrubs and small plants. So far structures like these that incorporate vegetation to actively promote biodiversity in cities and contribute towards better urban microclimates are an exception in modern urban contexts. Consequently, the two towers not far from Milan's historic city centre stand out from their surroundings as green landmarks (→ Fig. 1). They set an example, showing how future urban landscapes could develop and how plants can be part of not just the architectural concept but also its functionality, for example as a form of natural air conditioning, rather than falling back on purely technical solutions. The residents of these vertical gardens experience greenery in very concrete terms: up to a height of 100 m, their view of the surroundings is mediated by a living façade. Instead of looking out onto greenery, they look through greenery at the city and experience a proximity to nature in the city centre that one usually only has in the more outlying and less densely built-up districts.[1]

The Bosco Verticale is without doubt an elitist project with flats designed for a wealthy clientele, who not only buy an impressive view over Milan, but also a piece of nature in the city (→ Fig. 2). Strictly speaking, the latter is not quite correct, because although the flats are sold as private property, the plants belong to the house man-

1 Completed in 2014, the Bosco Verticale in Milan (Stefano Boeri) represents a new architectural typology in which trees act as ambassadors for a new relationship between city and nature.

2 Bosco Verticale. Between the branches and twigs, the tree-covered balconies allow a view over the city.

agement, who are also responsible for organising their maintenance. During the annual pruning, which is undertaken by professional gardeners who abseil down from the roof of the high-rise building, the residents are therefore only onlookers. For Stefano Boeri, who conceived and designed the project with his architectural firm, the Bosco Verticale are not a one-off project but rather represent a prototype that shows how architecture can adopt a more responsible attitude to the future: What we build today is part of the city of tomorrow.[2] The logical extension of this principle is a "Forest City", which Boeri envisions as a compact and green city formed by dozens of large and medium-sized buildings in the style of the Bosco Verticale. This vision may even become reality as part of a master plan the office is drawing up for an urban extension to the Chinese city of Shijiazhuang which will house 100,000 inhabitants. If this is successful it could serve as a forward-looking model for rapid urban growth in China.[3]

With its lush planting, the appearance of the Bosco Verticale changes constantly. The leaves move and rustle in the wind, change colour in autumn and finally sail to the ground — sometimes more than 100 m deep — down into the city below. The presence of nature adds diversity to people's immediate surroundings and arouses emotions — emotions of the kind we don't usually associate with architecture. The French architect Edouard François sees such architecture as an answer to the desires and longings of a society that is gradually turning away from materialistic profit-seeking and relentless progress and towards inner values and needs.[4] It is no surprise, therefore, that François reappraises whether and how he can use vegetation in each new project. The façade of the Tower Flower apartment building in Paris, for example, consists of uniform rows of concrete tubs planted with bamboo. Together they form a green wall that on the one hand defines an urban space by demarcating the edge of the block, and on the other softens its linearity. It blends into its surroundings and at the same time expresses the complexity of the city. The relationship between building, plant and context is quite different in François' project The building that grows in Montpellier from 2000. Here, balconies of different sizes and shapes project out irregularly at different heights into the crowns of trees planted close to the building (→ Fig. 3). By responding to tree

3 The building that grows, Montpellier, Edouard François, 2000: Complex interactions between trees and buildings are used to create a multitude of different visual relationships and spaces (photo: 2011).

4 Edouard François envisions his Tower of Biodiversity from 2016 in the city skyline of Paris not as a building but as a green cloud — an ephemeral phenomenon constantly interacting with the environment.

5 Tree House in Darmstadt, Ot Hoffmann, 1970. The terraced structure appears like a modern-day Hanging Gardens of Babylon. Unlike other prestigious but elitist examples, Hoffmann wanted to show how such approaches could be applied to more typical dense housing schemes (photo: 2006).

6 Today one can no longer tell which terraces of Hoffmann's own home, built in 1970, were originally planted and which have since been colonised by plants (photo: 2006).

growth, it creates a range of diverse spaces for both private retreat and communal interaction without defining them precisely beforehand.[5]

A very similar approach was taken some 30 years earlier in Ot Hoffmann's designs for the Tree House in Darmstadt, which was completed in 1970. Here, the architect created natural spaces on the roof terraces, balconies and eaves that today look rather wild and unkempt (→ Figs. 5, 6). Some of the plants were specifically selected, but otherwise the entire site was deliberately given over to natural colonisation. Similar to Edouard François' concept for the Tower of Biodiversity which contains planters with native plants that can distribute their seeds via the wind to the wider urban surroundings (→ Fig. 4), the Tree House in Darmstadt communicates with its surroundings through generative reproduction. The roof terrace is thus not only a small wilderness, but also a research field. Ot Hoffmann meticulously noted, analysed and mapped the uncontrolled processes over decades in order to learn from them for future designs. Knowing how to adapt construction principles to support green architecture more practically, he argued, is critical to both prevent structural damage and enable plants to grow healthily.[6] The architect saw his work very much in the tradition of classical modern architecture and Le Corbusier's roof gardens. It is precisely this interplay of underlying technical knowledge, attention to detail but also an awareness that designing with nature is often simply about making spaces of possibility that characterises Ot Hoffmann's work — spaces in which plants can develop freely and in which people are able to contribute to the design.

The ability to contribute to, influence and take personal responsibility for one's own surroundings gives residents a strong sense of identity. This requires, however, that architects relinquish their traditional role as the sole designer and instead design processes in which cultural and social aspects also play a crucial role alongside aesthetic questions. The active participation of numerous different people in a design process can significantly change the appearance of a building. This was a central principle in the work of Friedensreich Hundertwasser, who, unlike Ot Hoffmann, saw his work as an oppositional response to the "smooth, sterile and cold" architecture of modernism in post-war Europe. According to Hundertwasser, making buildings for people is resolutely opposed to standardisation and conformity, and should instead respond to the creative urge of the inhabitants and make it visible to the outside world. An example of this was his concept of window rights, according to which every resident should have the right to lean out of their window and alter the façade as far their arm can reach. In the Hundertwasserhaus in Vienna, this right is anchored in the rental contract and has resulted in a colourful, varied façade that reflects the diversity of the users. However, by carrying out this work himself, or having workmen do it on his behalf, not all of his projects quite live up to his own participatory principles. In the end, what remained was a superficial decoration that quickly became his visual trademark. Unsurprisingly, much of Hundertwasser's work met with considerable resistance in architectural circles. Aside from the criticism of formalism, however, the conceptual and experimental aspects of his work, which includes the use of plants, deserve consideration. The 250 trees and shrubs that moved into the building together with the inhabitants in 1985 similarly contribute to the diversity and individual personalisation of the building. Hundertwasser was an active protagonist of the ecology movement of the 1970s and 1980s, and as a sign of reconciliation with nature, he conceived of so-called "tree tenants" for the flats inaccessible to humans. The trees, which are planted in flats filled with soil and look out of the windows like residents, lend the vertical façades a new spatial presence and actively signify the coexistence of humans and nature (→ Fig. 7). They have their own place in the house and in return provide fresh, cool air for their human neighbours. In conceptual sketches, Hundertwasser also showed how tree tenants could be integrated into the water and nutrient cycle of the house. While these ideas seemed utopian or even bizarre at the time, they are now being intensively researched as blue-green infrastructure or blue-green architecture (→ Chapter 5, p. 119).[8]

While the Hundertwasserhaus was intended as a critique of post-war modernism and the functionalism of the construction sector, only a few kilometres away — also in Vienna — another housing complex very much in the modernist vein was attempting to enrich the utilitarian nature of multi-storey housing by incorporating vegetation. Harry Glück's stepped terrace housing for the Wohnpark Alt-Erlaa was built between 1973 and 1985 as an answer to the housing shortages at that time. Through standardisation and repetition, and through their height and mass, they were an attempt at cost-effective architecture and provided 3180 residential units. Motivated by a desire to create personal outdoor space adjoining the apartments, the lower part of the buildings terrace outwards to create balconies, resulting in an enormous building depth at the base of the buildings. The ensuing dark spaces in the interior

7 Hundertwasserhaus, Vienna, Friedensreich Hundertwasser, 1985. The "tree tenants" in Hundertwasser's houses have their own room in the house in which they take root, while the crown looks out of the window. As tenants alongside the residents, Hundertwasser highlights the coexistence of humans and nature.

are used productively to house swimming pools, cinemas, community spaces, gymnasiums and ball courts.[9]

The housing estate at Alt-Erlaa is a successful example of how industrial construction methods can be employed to create affordable but also qualitative housing for a large number of people while also incorporating a variety of leisure and communal facilities. These social facilities are unusual for social housing, as are the large balconies for the lower flats that feature 4 m² large, plantable concrete troughs (→ Fig. 8). Like Stefano Boeri's Bosco Verticale some 40 years later, the terracing principle at Alt-Erlaa is based on the idea of stacking single-family houses. However, Harry Glück's Alt-Erlaa is not the reserve of affluent urban residents but was expressly designed to be accessible to lower-income sections of the population. This is made possible in part by the low construction costs, but also by the fact that the maintenance of the vegetation is left entirely to the residents. To this day, the satisfaction levels of the residents are above average and the lush and often meticulously maintained vegetation on many terraces show that this concept has succeeded.

8 The Wohnpark Alt-Erlaa, Vienna (Harry Glück, 1973—1985) is a vast social housing estate that shows that green architecture is possible using functionalist construction methods. The residents are responsible for planting trees and bushes on the balconies.

Integrating buildings in trees

Forests have served and continue to serve as a habitat for many indigenous peoples: their flora and fauna are a source of food and provide material for making everyday objects and dwellings. In the forests of New Guinea, the Korowai people still live largely according to this principle: they dwell in tree houses made exclusively from tree trunks, lianas, sections of bark and leaves of the sago palms. Each house is a communal project built by the members of a family clan that together share a clearing for better visibility. This "plot" comprises a group of several elevated tree houses, used by the families, that surround a lower communal building. Most of the structures are located at a height of 5 to 15 m—high enough to provide shelter from wild animals and flooding. Their comparatively low durability, a factor of the humid climate, means that the houses are renewed every three to five years, allowing the builders to adapt their design to changing conditions. This tradition of building highly adaptable constructions also makes it possible for the Korowai to retreat up to 50 m into the treetops in times of tribal conflict.[10]

The Korowai live in trees for largely pragmatic reasons. And they are similarly pragmatic about using them: when erecting a new tree house, the first thing they usually do is cut off the main trunk to create a support and use the remainder then as building material (→ Fig. 9). Nevertheless, the Korowai with their tree houses can be regarded as an example of living simply in harmony with nature. Today, living in the canopies of primeval forests is a romantic notion that is largely unattainable for most of the world's population now that nearly half of all forests on earth have been cleared or irretrievably destroyed. This is even more devastating when one considers that the canopies of primeval forests probably harbour three quarters of all insect species and some 10,000 as yet unclassified species of plants.[11] Forest canopies are therefore of extreme interest to scientists. To access them for research purposes, fixed lattice towers or cranes are usually erected, but constructing these in remote locations is not only time-consuming and expensive but also provides access to only a particular point in the canopy and usually at the cost of damaging the forest floor and sometimes also the canopy in question. To overcome these limitations, the pilot Cleyet-Marrel, the botanist Francis Hallé and the architect Gilles Ebersold came together in the 1980s and jointly designed an ultra-light, inflatable structure for the Radeau des Cimes Expedition that can be transported by airship and lowered where required directly onto the canopy of the Amazon rainforest.

This "canopy raft" comprises sections of inflatable tubes joined to form a hexagon that can be laid on the treetops from above and distribute their weight over a large area via the twigs and branches of several trees. A net spanning between the tubes adapts flexibly to the shape of the underlying branches and leaves and serves as the researchers' "working platform" (→ Fig. 10). As a temporary structure, it can be moved very easily without having to change its construction. Although the project was developed to serve a scientific purpose, and is a work of engineering art, the project participants describe their expedition in poetic terms as an intense experience of nature. This initially science-driven motivation ultimately led to the development of a completely new type of "tree house".[12]

The sensual experiences that so captivated the researchers on the Radeau des Cimes Expedition along with the romantic notion of living in

9 When building a new tree house, the Korowai in New Guinea cut off the trunk to create a support and use the remainder as building material.

10 The inflatable structure of the Radeau des Cimes Expedition can "land" directly on the canopy of the tropical rainforest, giving researchers direct access to the treetops.

the treetop are probably the strongest drivers for a veritable tree house boom that has emerged in recent years across the world. Until recently, tree houses were mostly built by and for children, but increasingly architects, carpenters and architectonically ambitious individuals have ventured to build larger constructions in trees. As a building task, tree houses are particularly challenging as tree crowns present a difficult and complex terrain for anchoring a building. One cannot simply transfer a conventional design from the ground to the air. In addition, anything that is more than a simple gazebo and is intended for living in, whether temporarily as a holiday home or for year-round living, must fulfil a range of design and technical requirements. The architecture of tree houses can make more or less of the varying ambience and spatial qualities of tree canopies. The degree of interaction a structure has with the tree informs its appearance and atmosphere. A structure that is conceived as a capsule strung between several trees consciously separates itself from its context, creating a contrast between inside and outside and between the natural and the artificial: the architectural intervention is a foreign body in natural surroundings (→ Fig. 11). The interior is more introverted and the views from its openings are of the treetops of the surrounding trees, rather than the trees themselves. When, on the other hand, a structure is conceived to actually sit in a tree, the branches and trunks may pass through it, influencing its interior. The resulting interweaving of natural and artificial elements creates an environment in which the tree is not just physically present in the architecture but can also be experienced directly and haptically. If these interiors are largely open to their surroundings, the border between indoors and outdoors blurs. The grown and the built, and the natural and the artificial overlap at many different levels, and looking out of the house is simultaneously looking out of the treetop (→ Fig. 12).

In Germany, one of the first protagonists to recognise this not just as a design challenge but

11 The Eryn Sphere tree house (Free Spirit Spheres, Qualicum Beach, British Columbia, 2007) is a tiny house suspended between tall trees on the west coast of Canada. While not actually in a treetop, it provides a comfortable interior from which to appreciate a view of the surrounding forest.

also as a business model was the Bremen-based architect Andreas Wenning, who now specialises in the professional design and construction of tree houses. As a child, he harboured the desire to design and build a small room high in a tree, but it wasn't until after his architectural studies that he put it into practice. His goal is to free the tree house from its niche existence and develop models for users who appreciate the experience of living in the treetops but do not want to sacrifice the comforts and forms of modern architecture. With his designs for purist tree houses, which are almost always constructed of wood, Wenning produces contemporary interpretations of tree houses that are intended as a counter-model to the nostalgic appearance of traditional tree houses (→ Fig. 13).[13]

Through his exploration of increasingly sophisticated solutions, Andreas Wenning has pioneered the development of a construction theory of tree house building. His focus is first and foremost on how a structure can be anchored in a living organism and how the growth and pronounced movements of a tree, such as occur during a storm, can be accommodated in the design of tree houses.[14] The intention is always to interfere as little as possible with the tree's development, to avoid unnecessary injury to the tree and not to weaken it mechanically. Unlike the tree houses of the Korowai, who as semi-nomads use a tree for only a few years for their temporary tree house and then move on, these modern tree houses are designed to last for decades and guarantee safe living in the tree crown.

Wenning's answer here is to avoid any structural connection between the tree and the structure and to completely dispense with screws and bolts for fastening. Instead, he uses steel cables attached to strong branches or the trunk with the help of heavy-duty textile belts of the kind used in tree maintenance. This avoids injury to the three while allowing it to move freely and to grow with minimal constraints. The use of steel cables allows the tree house construction to be erected quickly and easily adjusted.[15] Working together with structural engineers and arborists, Wenning has in some cases been able to satisfy structural proofs, and in turn gain approval from the building authorities. In other cases, Wenning resorts to external structural supports that relieve the tree of excess weight or even support the entire tree house. This is mostly necessary when the tree is unsuitable, for example due to its species, or when the client has specific requirements with regard to size or technical services. Such examples of multi-storey structures built

12 The prototypical tree house designed by the architects Schneider + Schumacher (Solingen, 2009) epitomises the idea of lightness and the blurring of the interior and the treetops.

13 Andreas Wenning's tree houses are modern wooden structures whose construction has been developed in collaboration with arborists and engineers. The platform on the left is suspended from the tree, while the actual house stands on thin steel supports next to the tree (Djuren tree house, Groß Ippener, 2008).

as low-energy constructions fully equipped with the latest technical niceties certainly provide a comfortable living environment, but it is doubtful whether the experience of living in a treetop is still the primary focus.

Wenning's American counterpart Pete Nelson remains a little truer to the original idea of the tree house. His designs for tree houses, although formally more traditional-looking, are almost always supported exclusively by trees. The impressive redwoods (*Sequoia sempervirens*) that Nelsen often uses as the supports for his designs are typically of a considerable size and have a strong load-bearing capacity. Nevertheless, the same basic constructional conditions apply here too. Nelson's answer to anchoring the tree house most sensitively to the tree differs from Wenning's in that he uses special threaded bolts, originally developed by the tree house specialist Michael Garnier, with which locally arising high forces can be transferred into the trunk (→ Chapter 3, p. 64). The tree house then rests on these supports in a sliding fashion so that tree growth and wind vibration can occur freely.

Baubotanik — a fusion of building and tree

Whether one is integrating trees into buildings or buildings into trees, both have the potential to create spaces with special architectural qualities and both present specific design and construction challenges. When trees are incorporated into buildings, the main questions are how to deal constructively with the high loads of planters and necessary soil volumes, and how to solve the technical aspects of sealing the root space, irrigation, fertilisation and maintenance. With tree houses, on the other hand, the loads of the structure have to be transferred via the trees to the ground: here it is necessary to find plant-friendly solutions that can accommodate the dynamics of growth and wind vibrations. In the case of the tree house, the starting point is always a found, given natural object around which one works, while the planting of trees in structures always has an inherently horticultural aspect and questions of growth and change must be addressed through the project's conceptual design. Very similar questions also arise when designing baubotanical projects using the approach of plant addition.

As different as the aspects of growth, care and participation may be, all of the examples mentioned above where trees have been integrated into buildings have one thing in common: they were conceived as pioneering projects or prototypes.[16] The end result is an urban vision in which trees and buildings are combined at an architectural level to create a new form of urban landscape. The declared aim is to present solutions that can benefit society as a whole by offering liveable, healthy environments in which nature can be experienced directly where one lives — i.e. as part of everyday life.

Tree houses are built with a very different motivation. Invariably they provide a means of escape from everyday life rather than a way of experiencing nature in everyday life. Consequently, most tree houses are located far from any city and usually isolated within a forest or woodland. The aim is to experience undisturbed nature as closely as possible, i.e. to be alone in nature. Unsurprisingly, the most popular type of tree house is the holiday home. Tree houses cannot and do not want to be a solution to the questions of housing broad sections of the population. Similarly, they do not address the social and ecological questions of global urban expansion. Despite this, modern tree house architects such as Andreas Wenning have made a vital contribution to architecture using trees because their specific inquiry into designing, constructing and building in treetops have focused attention on the tree as a medium of architecture. New typological structures such as treetop walkways have likewise enriched the public's appreciation of trees by extending an ordinary walk in the woods into the treetops, making it possible to experience the vertical layers of trees and woodland from the shady undergrowth to the sunny canopies.

By merging — or fusing — trees and structures into a single entity (→ Fig. 14 and → Arbor Kitchen, Chapter 8, pp. 192—195), baubotanical projects exhibit aspects of both categories of architecture with trees discussed above: where the technical component predominates and interiors are created, baubotanical projects are more comparable to the first category where trees are incorporated into buildings (→ House of the Future, Chapter 8, pp. 206—209). Where the plant component predominates and an open, freely evolving structure is formed, baubotanical projects are more akin to integrating buildings in trees (→ Baubotanik Footbridge, Chapter 6, pp. 144—149). Due to this ambivalence, Baubotanik cannot be attributed to one or the other architectural typology but should rather be seen as part of a vision for rethinking cities through green architecture. At an architectural level, the challenge is always to constantly re-examine, based on the given context and programme, the relationship between indoor and outdoor space, the experience of nature and comfort, of plants and technology, and of control and free growth.

14 The fusion of house and tree in Baubotanik is illustrated by the Arbor Kitchen experimental pavilion, where the trees not only support a roof, but also grow below it and out of the ridge.

5 How Living Structures Interact with Their Environment

Buildings are linked to natural material cycles through their processes of production, use and disposal. They also interact directly with their environment, for example, through energy flows, although modern-day construction typically limits the extent of such interactions through technical means such as insulation and sealing.[1] Baubotanical projects, by contrast, interact constantly and actively with their environment, and many processes normally attributed to the "natural environment" are integral to the construction itself. Instead of the usual dichotomy between the natural and the artificial, the interaction between technical and biological systems is multi-faceted and characterised by a relationship of mutual "give and take". Understanding this interdependency between technical and biological systems and how one can shape their diverse relationships is essential to establishing a synthesis of the two and developing synergies in baubotanical projects.

Human-nature relationships in Baubotanik

The term "ecosystem services" is widely used in environmental research and design and expresses how natural systems are understood as serving humans. Inherent to this notion is that humans are thought of as being distinct from the environment or the ecosystems that make human life possible in the first place through the "services" they deliver, such as the provision of drinking water or clean air.[2] Here, the initial assumption is that the prerequisites for the emergence, development and continuing availability of such ecosystems are naturally given. The role of humans is to ensure these conditions are not impaired by environmental damage, climate change or pollution. However, given that almost all ecosystems have been changed or degraded to a greater or lesser degree by humans, the focus has shifted from preserving existing ecosystems to reactivating disturbed systems or creating new ones.[3] If this is done against the background of a value system that not just recognises the utilitarian value — the ecosystem services — but also ascribes nature a value in itself,[4] the relationship of "give and take" is reversed: it is now humans who serve nature — without necessarily drawing direct benefit from it — by creating conditions in which more complex systems and diverse forms of life can develop or regenerate.

In densely populated urban areas dominated by buildings and technical infrastructure, considerable effort is often needed to create the conditions in which "natural" systems can emerge and develop. This does not necessarily have to entail the creation of complex systems such as urban woodland but can include selective interventions such as planting street trees or greening a roof. Most of these, however, are not self-sustaining but rather subsystems that are dependent on a constant and artificial supply of matter (e.g. water and nutrients) and/or energy (also in the form of labour).[5] Despite this, such green interventions are still of great value to humans, as well as to "nature itself", especially in a space that is otherwise predominantly technical and artificial.[6] One must, however, be mindful of the technical effort required to create and maintain the conditions to ensure their upkeep. The material and energy input they require consumes natural resources elsewhere, or places demands on already stretched ecosystems, or causes environmental damage. It is often difficult, and sometimes even impossible, to reliably assess these costs because one has to weigh up often quite different categories — energy, biodiversity, beauty — against one another. That said, ecological life cycle assessments of green roofs, for example, have shown that they usually have a positive overall balance.[7]

In Baubotanik, too, nature — here specifically trees — is placed in the service of humans: baubotanical structures shade and cool the local environment, purify the air and also serve technical functions such as bearing loads or providing partial air conditioning. At the same time, they can become valuable natural habitats and contribute to local biodiversity. While one could see this as a further "service" to humans who enjoy birds and butterflies or benefit from the pollination of its flowers, it also ascribes value to the tree itself, and in turn to nature. But, as with other green interventions in the built environment, baubotanical projects also require the creation and ongoing provision of suitable growing conditions using technical means. Here it is humans, or the technology they develop and provide, that serve the tree, and thus also nature. In addition, baubotanical projects require suitable "living building material": pre-cultivated trees that themselves are the product of an often years-long, labour- and sometimes material- and energy-intensive "production process". To understand these complex relationships and their respective influences so that we may design with them in mind, let us consider two examples of the ecosystem services of Baubotanik — "microclimate and air quality" and "water balance and material cycles" — in relation to the technical and constructive measures required to ensure the growth of the plants.

Microclimate

Fully developed forests with mature trees have a particularly beneficial effect on the local climate. Their extensive, largely closed canopy limits how much sun reaches the ground, reducing the degree to which it heats up compared to open areas without vegetation. At night, the canopy also limits the degree to which heat escapes, so that the temperature is often a little higher than in open areas. At the same time, wind speeds in forests are much lower as the foliage layers of the treetop and the forest edge deflect or slow down the winds (→ Fig. 1).[8] Urban areas, by contrast, are often subject to microclimatic extremes. Sealed surfaces and buildings exposed directly to the sun heat up considerably during the day and retain that thermal energy due to their high mass. Although this heat is partially radiated back at night, in densely built-up areas heat does not just escape into the atmosphere but radiates onto and reflects back from neighbouring buildings. Heat levels may be further exacerbated by exhaust heat from motor vehicles and air-conditioning units, especially at night. The resulting warmth can produce a "heat island effect", in particular when the placement of buildings hinders wind flows and cross ventilation that could bring an inflow of cooler air from the surroundings. In densely built-up areas, the air temperature can, therefore, often be to 10 °C higher than the surrounding countryside.[9] For humans, the resulting heat stress is not just a factor of the air temperature, but also of heat radiation (through direct solar radiation or radiation from heated surfaces), air movement and air humidity.[10] Continuing climate change will bring not just a general rise in mean temperatures but also longer and more extreme periods of sustained high temperatures in many parts of the world, which in turn will intensify the problem of urban heat islands. That the consequences of this can be fatal became dramatically apparent in the heatwave summer of 2003, which until recently was one of the most severe natural disasters on the European continent to date with an estimated 45,000 to 70,000 heat-related fatalities.[11]

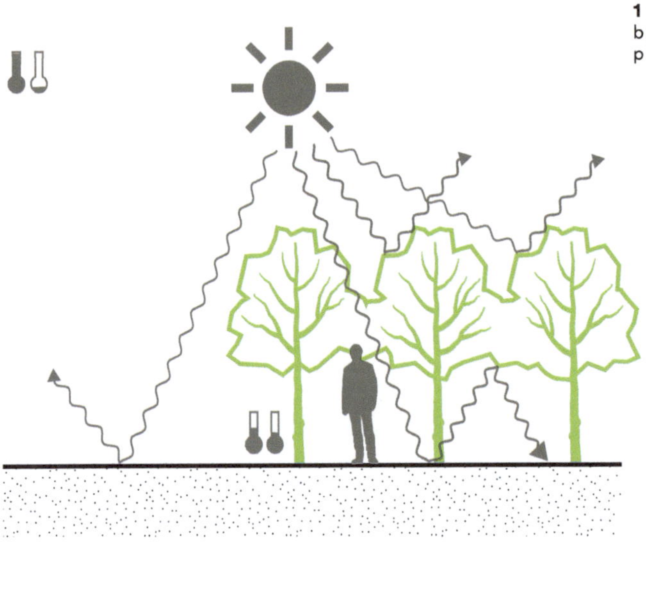

1 Forests generally produce a balanced microclimate that is pleasant for humans.

The climatic potential of Baubotanik

Trees have a significant influence on the air temperature of urban areas through the shade they provide and the transpiration capacity of their leaves. This counteracts the build-up of heat and improves the thermal well-being of local residents. But to achieve this on a scale that can reduce the urban heat island effect, the planting of individual trees is not enough. By way of example, a third of the urban area of Hong Kong would need to be planted with trees to reduce the air temperature by an average of 1 °C.[12] The resulting competition for land can only be resolved by greening buildings. The fusion of trees and structures in Baubotanik offers great potential, as trees can contribute significantly more to local cooling than, for example, extensive greening with climbing plants. For example, measurements show that trees can cool the outside air locally by up to 3.5 °C due to the shade they provide and high transpiration levels, while façade greening can only reduce air temperatures by a maximum of 1.3 °C.[13]

Various studies[14] also indicate that trees planted in the immediate vicinity of houses effectively contribute to reducing the energy demand for cooling buildings as a result of localised cooling through shading and transpiration. According to a study,[15] the cooling effect increases with the size of the tree and its proximity to the building. This suggests that the best possible cooling effect can probably be achieved by integrating trees directly into the building envelope, while at the same time avoiding or at least mitigating the competition for space between trees and buildings. Although concrete studies and measurements are still lacking, it is likely that Baubotanik can contribute not only to helping cities adapt to climate change by improving local microclimates, but also to lessening impact on the climate by reducing the energy required for artificial cooling and thus reducing CO_2 emissions.[16] One should also note in this context that urban heat islands are not just a localised problem but also contribute to between 2 and 4 % of global warming.[17] While this value may at first seem low, it is of the same order of magnitude as the effect of all air traffic on climate change (approx. 3.5 %).[18] This means that measures to reduce the heat island effect with the help of Baubotanik and other forms of urban greenery are at least as relevant from a global perspective as measures to reduce air traffic.

One should, however, also be aware that not all effects of trees in urban contexts are automatically positive for human well-being or energy consumption. For example, extended areas of woodland in cities, like buildings, can impede air flow and wind speeds. As a consequence, the influx of fresh air from the surroundings and the corresponding outflow of hot, polluted air may be slowed.[19] This can be addressed through the astute choice and placement of design measures to maximise the effective provision of tree canopies and shade while ensuring the best possible air exchange. For example, baubotanical building typologies that incorporate trees into building structures as “tree façades” can provide a similar or even larger amount of green foliage without planting trees in the street space, thus ensuring a ventilation corridor is kept free to allow night-time cooling during hot periods.

Protective effects and protection needs of trees

As important as night-time cooling and adequate air exchange are, the problem of ventilating cities to counteract heat island effects does not apply all over the world, nor at all times of the year. In some cities, the qualities of outdoor spaces are impaired by the very opposite: too strong winds. Here too, trees can be used to protect against strong winds. The protective hedges of the "Monschau Hedge Land" in the Eifel region of Germany are an impressive testimony to this tradition. These up to 10 m high hedge constructions are elaborately woven and trimmed over decades to protect houses and gardens from cold winds, driving snow and heavy rain. The hedges not only make being in the garden adjoining the house more tolerable, but also reduce the energy demand for heating the houses (→ Fig. 2).[20] Similar hedges erected as windbreaks in the open countryside improve crop yields in the fields. To this end, wind-resistant, specially pruned trees were planted to protect more sensitive plants, people or buildings from extreme weather conditions.

Other historical and current examples show that the opposite relationship between trees and structures also exists: in particularly windy regions, technical structures such as walls are often erected to provide protection against the wind for gardens, fields or trees worthy of protection (→ Fig. 3). An example of this are the "giardini panteschi" on the Italian island of Pantelleria, which are enclosed by high dry stone walls that shelter a single citrus tree which would otherwise not thrive on the island. The massive walls not only protect against the wind, but also balance out diurnal temperature fluctuations and reduce evapotranspiration.[21] Comparable approaches can be found in many European countries. In Great Britain and France, for example, there are numerous traditional forms of walled gardens, or wall constructions designed especially for growing espalier fruit crops. One such type is the so-called "Talut wall", which has a small projecting roof to protect the espalier trees. Sometimes glass panes were mounted in front of the plants for additional protection, resulting in a minimal form of architectural enclosure that regulates the natural climatic conditions. Further technical advancements led to the development of the so-called "hot wall", in which a system of chimneys or hot water pipes in the wall could keep the temperatures high enough in winter to shield frost-sensitive tree species from freezing and to increase their yield.[22]

In the context of sustainable, ecologically-driven architecture, the level of technical input and energy required just to create suitable growth

2 Particularly wind-resistant and specially pruned trees are traditionally used as windbreaks to shelter outdoor spaces or protect buildings or crops from extreme weather conditions.

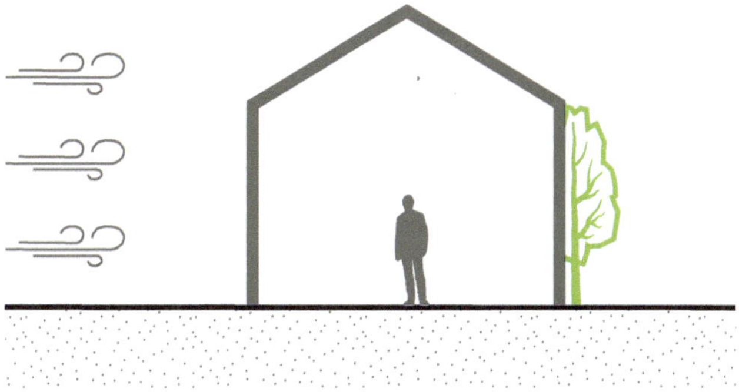

3 Structures such as houses or even specially built walls provide protection against inclement weather and strong winds, so that more sensitive tree species can thrive.

conditions for particularly sensitive plants seems absurd — but in the field of industrialised horticulture, this is precisely what happens and is standard practice (→ Fig. 4). Similarly, in tree nurseries, it is common to construct simple technical or structural enclosures to protect young trees and woody plants against unfavourable climatic conditions or extreme weather events. This is because young or freshly transplanted trees often respond negatively to changes in growing conditions. For example, sudden prolonged exposure to direct sunlight can cause their bark to partially die, which is why the trunks of young plants are protected by reed mats, jute fabric or white paint. The trees used in baubotanical structures may often be strongly exposed to sunlight due to their inclined position, and for this reason, appropriate technical protection may be advisable. In a similar way, continuing climate change is expected to lead to more frequent and more extreme weather events, which will make it increasingly important to devise corresponding structures to protect trees and baubotanical constructions against potential damage, especially during critical phases of development. Given that with continuing climate change the problem of urban heat islands is likely to intensify, and with it the need for more urban greenery, it appears increasingly clear that the answer lies in the interaction of technical and natural systems.

4 In tree nurseries, considerable technical effort is invested in creating optimal conditions for growing sensitive trees and woody plants.

Designing symbioses between tree and structure

The desired symbiosis between a tree and a structure can be exemplified by the interplay between tree crowns and building façades: where trees are arranged as a second, baubotanical layer in front of glass façades, for example, they effectively replace mechanical shading devices and parts of the air-conditioning technology in summer, by preventing the interior from overheating. The environmental benefit is twofold because, not only is heat reflected back and the air cooled through evaporation but also air-conditioning units within the building emit less or no waste heat into the environment. In winter in temperate latitudes, when the trees have shed their leaves, sunlight can penetrate deep into the building, creating bright interiors in darker seasons and making the most of solar heat gain (→ Chapter 8, pp. 208–209). In summer, however, the degree of shading through leaves can in some cases reduce light levels indoors significantly. A common criticism is that large trees with voluminous and dense crowns negatively impact on the interiors and adjoining outdoor spaces by excessive shading or blocking views. This poses both a baubotanical design problem and raises research questions. As with trees in general, the growth of leaves, and with it the degree of shading, is a factor of its growth pattern and cannot be precisely planned. At the same time, baubotanical solutions must also be designed in conjunction with their environment, especially when they are part of a sophisticated building concept. Aspects that are relevant to indoor lighting levels at a building level, such as room height, building depth or the number and size of openings must be planned in conjunction with the arrangement and design of a botanical structure and the choice of tree species.

Air quality

Alongside comfortable temperatures and good lighting conditions, the quality of the air we breathe is of vital importance for human health and well-being. Air pollution is considered to be the most significant environmental cause of illness and premature death worldwide.[23] The contribution that trees can make is made apparent by the fact that urban trees across cities in the USA filter a total of more than 700,000 tonnes of pollutants out of the air each year.[24] As large as this number sounds, it is only a small percentage of the total emission of air pollutants in urban areas. At a local scale, however, urban trees still make a significant contribution to improving air quality—and in this context, baubotanical projects with large, active filtering tree canopies likewise have a similar beneficial effect.

One of the most serious air pollutants in modern urban areas is nitrogen dioxide (NO_2), which results from many combustion processes. As an irritant gas, it can lead to inflammation of the respiratory tract, breathing difficulties and (chronic) bronchitis, as well as cause allergies. It also contributes to fine particular matter, and is a precursor for ground level ozone.[25] The latter affects humans as an irritant for mucous membranes, the respiratory tract and eyes, as well as plants and ecosystems. As such, it affects the very trees—and by extension also baubotanical structures—that help filter pollutants from the air. Air quality that is healthy for humans and conducive to the development of urban ecosystems can therefore ultimately only be achieved by drastically reducing the sources of emission, such as motorised private transport and combustion processes. As such, although urban greenery and baubotanical projects can help mitigate the negative consequences of air pollution, they are not an answer in themselves, and should not be used as an argument against more intensive attempts to reduce or eliminate emissions of pollutants that are in principle avoidable.

As discussed earlier, trees themselves can also be a source of substances that when airborne are harmful to human health. Pollen from blossoms or fine hairs from leaves (→ plane tree, Chapter 3, p. 89), for example, can cause allergic reactions, as can the volatile organic compounds (VOCs) that some tree species emit in considerable quantities. When these react with nitrogen oxides, they contribute to the formation of particulate matter and ozone.[26] While this may seem paradoxical, it is the combination of substances from trees with nitrogen oxides caused by road traffic that is responsible for this effect. In the design of baubotanical projects, one should therefore strive, through the choice of suitable species, to minimise or avoid negative effects while maximising the positive effects on human health and air quality that the trees provide. Evergreen conifers, for example, are better at binding fine dust due to their larger surface area and year-round greenery, while deciduous trees are better at breaking down nitrogen oxides and typically have a greater cooling effect.[27]

Water balance and material cycles

Forests not only balance out climatic effects, they can also help regulate the water balance. A simple example is that, as a rule, wooded areas retain a far greater proportion of precipitation than surfaces not covered by vegetation or that are sealed, where rainwater run-off can be considerable. The canopy catches part of the rain, which either evaporates again shortly afterwards, drips off after a short delay or runs down the trunks into the ground. The rate of precipitation is thus slowed down and somewhat reduced before it passes in a similar way through shrub and herb layers to the ground, where some of it evaporates while the remainder seeps into and is absorbed by the living, open-pored topsoil, which acts like a sponge. From there, it is either absorbed by the roots of trees and shrubs and returned to the atmosphere through transpiration, or seeps gradually deeper, filtered and purified by the soil, into the groundwater layer.[28] This process of absorbing precipitation and returning it to the atmosphere as water vapour after a time lag, contributes to the formation of clouds, and thus ultimately to more precipitation. Studies have

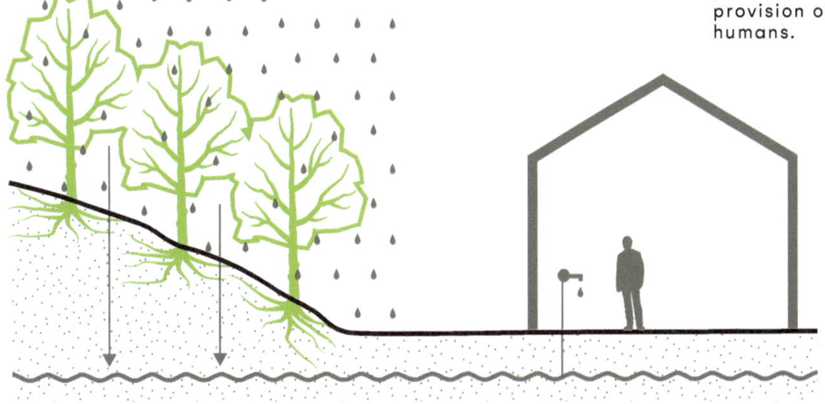

5 Forests contribute significantly to the formation of groundwater and the distribution of precipitation, and thus to the provision of drinking water for humans.

shown that air moving over tropical forests for ten days produces at least twice as much rainfall as air moving over non-forested areas.[29] Comparable effects can also be observed for European forests, which contribute to cloud formation and further precipitation, and in turn to water transport from coastal regions over long distances deep into the interior of the continent. Here one sees, on the one hand, how important forests are for the local provision of clean drinking water through their contribution to groundwater formation (→ Fig. 5), while on the other hand they contribute to the water distribution on a larger scale through their role in atmospheric processes, which also mitigate flooding, among other things.[30]

Increasing drought conditions around the world are, however, impacting on the health of forests, causing trees to wither or die, or else creating conditions conducive to pest infestation or forest fires.[31] Trees in excessively hot, heavily sealed areas—such as in urban contexts—are particularly susceptible to drought. The effect of cooling through evapotranspiration through the leaves—especially valuable during hot spells—depends on the availability of sufficient water reserves in the soil. While trees can respond to short-term water shortages by closing the stomata of the leaves, this also causes evapotranspiration and photosynthesis to decrease accordingly. To ensure the continued health and climatic benefit of trees in urban contexts, technical measures are therefore increasingly needed to provide them with sufficient water. A simple approach is to improve water storage in the root zone, but where this is inadequate or not possible for structural reasons, there is little alternative but to provide artificial irrigation. Where drinking water is used for plant watering, the situation arises that the tree—which in forest contexts is part of a system that filters and provides water—becomes the consumer of a scarce resource, often artificially purified at great cost. Rainwater collected in cisterns is a plausible and, in many cases sustainable, alternative (→ Fig. 6). But to be able to cover water needs over increasingly long dry periods, large storage tanks are required. These are not always feasible due to their size and the cost of their construction, and upwards of a certain size, the resource requirements needed for their construction can exceed their ecological benefit.

6 In urban contexts, trees often become consumers of a scarce resource — water — that has to be supplied by technical means.

Baubotanik as blue-green architecture

An alternative approach here is to integrate the irrigation of trees or baubotanical projects into the technical water flows of buildings and cities. There are typically numerous underutilised sources of water in cities that could potentially be activated for irrigation purposes. For example, water from drains or groundwater management measures that divert groundwater away from underground infrastructures, to keep them dry, is typically fed directly into the sewer system.[32] Here there is great potential, although the suitability of such water for irrigation purposes and the technical feasibility of utilising it must be assessed on a case by case basis. Another source is grey water, i.e. lightly soiled wastewater from kitchens, showers, washing machines, and so on. A key advantage here is that, unlike rainwater, there is a relatively constant supply and flow, obviating the need for storage tanks. Unlike rainwater, however, grey water generally requires treatment before it can be used for irrigation purposes as it frequently contains contaminants in the form of soaps, cleaning agents, fats or salts that can damage trees and the environment. Such treatment can be by technical means or also using natural systems such as plant and soil filters or special variants of roof and façade greening. Other problematic issues that must also be considered are the possibility of odours or hygiene aspects.[33]

This shows how important it is to consider and record possible water resources from the outset when conceiving a baubotanical project. First one must ensure that the needs of the plants can be met, both quantitatively and qualitatively. However, one must "start from the perspective of water" when considering and developing baubotanical projects and strategies. That means, in turn, that the need for irrigation water is often paralleled by a "disposal problem" on the other side, to which a baubotanical project can make a crucial contribution. In many built-up areas, the capacity of the sewer systems is quickly exceeded in the event of heavy rainfall. Streets and basements may flood, sewage treatment plants may overflow, polluting downstream waterways and consecutively leading to further flooding. To counter this, large quantities of rainfall must be temporarily buffered, for example in swales or other suitable water-retaining terrain modulations.[34] This can then gradually infiltrate the ground to replenish natural reservoirs, such as the soil and groundwater reserves, or be fed into technical reservoirs specially conceived for irrigation. The ultimate "disposal" of the water takes place after a significant time delay via the evapotranspiration capacity of the leaves of urban trees. This two-sided approach — addressing the need for irrigation and the problem of coping with sudden excesses of water — not only makes an active contribution to flood protection but also transforms a problem into a microclimatic benefit. At a city-wide level, what results is a blue-green network in which technical systems for water storage and treatment interact with nature-based solutions. Baubotanical projects can play an important role in this network as "blue-green architecture" that helps cities become "green sponges" so that they (re)acquire many of the functions of natural forests and are better able to manage their water balance.[35] By incorporating technical systems such as large buffer tanks, treatment plants or pumps for water distribution, such networks may be able to ensure the supply of water in prolonged dry periods even better than natural forest ecosystems can. Aside from the corresponding investments these require, one must also be aware that the more sophisticated such systems become, the more one is dependent on their continuing operation. This is particularly obvious in the case of trees in planters, where the failure of an irrigation system can lead to irreversible drought damage after only a few days. Nevertheless, as the technique of baubotanical plant addition shows, the use of technically supported vegetation systems can offer a plausible approach to establishing vegetation structures in a comparatively short space of time that in the long term become increasingly robust by being able to tap into water reserves in a larger volume of soil (→ Chapter 3, p. 81).

Activating nutrients in baubotanical projects

In addition to a supply of water, trees also need sufficient essential nutrients to thrive and develop. The needs of baubotanical projects are in essence no different to that of trees, but the plants should be as vital and healthy as possible so that they can adequately compensate for the interventions resulting from pruning, forming and connecting of their shoots. In natural habitats, trees are part of a complex system of material cycles that supplies necessary nutrients: leaves, dead twigs, branches and sometimes entire trees fall to the ground where they are decomposed by animals and microorganisms. These decomposition processes release important nutrients that in turn supply new trees. At the same time, organisms in the soil convert the energy once stored in the wood, releasing most of the stored carbon back into the atmosphere as CO_2. A smaller proportion remains in the soil for the long term as permanent humus, over time increasing the fertility of the soil by enriching its ability to store nutrients and water. Humans benefit directly from the improvement of the soil and function of the forest through their use of products of the forest, and indirectly by utilising the fertility of formerly forested areas for agriculture (→ Fig. 7).

In many urban or baubotanical situations, however, the trees are largely disconnected from these cycles. The area beneath the tree crown is often sealed and serves other functions so that falling leaves and branches do not remain where they are but are “disposed of” elsewhere, depriving the site of potential nutrients and soil organisms and many insects of natural biomass. Instead of soil fertility's building up and improving as it does in forests, the soil’s stock of nutrients is successively depleted. In many urban situations, trees can often nevertheless survive for decades without artificial nutrient supply,[36] but their vitality often suffers. A variety of ways have been developed to improve growth conditions through fertilisation, but also through the introduction of beneficial bacteria and vitality-enhancing substances such as amino acids and vitamins.[37] While this closes the gap in the natural nutrient cycle using practicable and ecologically acceptable measures, these somewhat selective technical means do not establish synergies but only ongoing costs. As with water cycles, robust and self-replenishing nutrient cycles need to be created by linking natural and technical cycles. Experiments have demonstrated how this can be done by using domestic wastewater to irrigate plantations of willow trees, whereby the nutrients contained in the water are absorbed by the trees and thus also removed from the water and therefore from the environment.[38] Such approaches have not yet been systematically applied in Baubotanik or in urban contexts in general, but the fact that tree roots often penetrate sewer pipes to benefit from nutrients in wastewater show that untapped synergies are possible (→ Fig. 8) that in some senses recall Hundertwasser’s concept of “tree tenants” (→ Chapter 4, p. 102).[39] Up to now, however, the unplanned and predominantly destructive penetration of technical infrastructure by trees represents more of a conflict than it does a synergetic potential.[40]

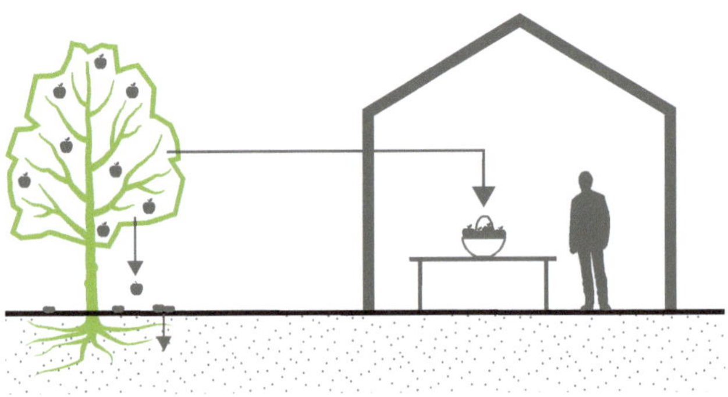

7 The leaves the forest sheds in autumn form a warming blanket on the forest floor before decomposing. Humans benefit from the resulting improved soil fertility, for example, by eating the fruits of the trees.

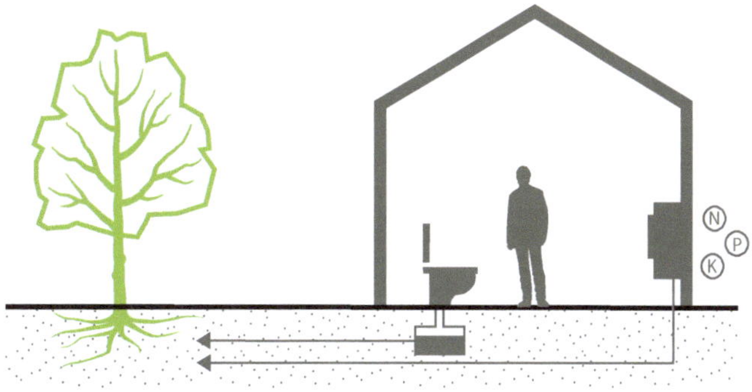

8 If the natural nutrient cycle is not self-sustaining, the supply of nutrients can be solved by technical means. Synergies can be created by interlinking technical nutrient flows such as the wastewater system with natural cycles.

Soil composition and consumption

Through the build-up of humus, trees contribute not only to developing fertile topsoil but also to protecting the soil against erosion, in turn securing riverbanks and steep slopes. This phenomenon is exploited, for example in soil bioengineering (→ Chapter 3, p. 90). However, when topsoil is removed to obtain planting substrate for growing new trees, the principle is reversed, causing ecological degradation. Tree nurseries, for example, commonly use peat to grow trees in planters. The harvesting of peat not only depletes ecologically valuable peatlands, but also causes significant quantities of CO_2 to be released.[41] Here we see that the production of the "living building material" of a baubotanical project can, in some circumstances, be quite harmful to the climate, even though CO_2 is sequestered during growth. In fact, however, it is possible to store the carbon absorbed by the plant during growth permanently in the soil by converting wood and green cuttings that are trimmed during the maintenance of baubotanical projects into charcoal or plant carbon and working it into the soil. This process, which in principle dates back thousands of years, is an important basis for the formation of anthropogenic soils such as terra preta de indio in the Amazon Basin. Here, plant carbon contributes significantly to soil fertility by improving water and nutrient storage as a kind of permanent humus.[42] Today, this approach is being developed further, in particular with the aim of removing CO_2 from the atmosphere by storing carbon in the soil, thus mitigating or even reversing the greenhouse effect. If such approaches are combined with baubotanical projects, they can have a positive CO_2 balance not only during their growth, but also beyond their lifetime.[43]

Designing baubotanical projects as integral components of ecosystems ultimately means considering not only the build-up but also the decomposition of biomass. This entails seeing foliage, dead wood or green waste as a valuable asset that can be activated for multiple purposes in the nutrient and carbon cycle. Only then will we create projects that become more robust in the long term, where growing conditions over time improve and which, at the end of their lifespan, not only have a positive climatic balance but also pass on soil that is more fertile and ecosystems that are more diverse. In urban conditions, however, this may mean using technical means to close interrupted cycles or sensibly interlinking natural and technical cycles.

6 Designing with Trees and Time

Throughout their entire lifetime, baubotanical structures are characterised by the interplay of two quite different poles which are embodied in the word "Baubotanik"—building and botany. At one pole are trees, their growth processes and diverse responses to environmental influences, ranging from adaptations of their form to the death or shedding of plant parts. At the other are humans, who intervene in these processes to create living structures according to their own designs. The preceding chapters have discussed the growth and response patterns of trees and thus devoted considerable attention to botanical aspects.

Design strategies

The design of living architecture must accordingly consider the processual character of buildings that grow as part of its concept. Alongside typical design questions—what is the purpose and goal of the project, and with which means and materials can this best be achieved?—one must also consider when these goals should occur and how the path to realising them should be designed. Is the beginning of a project an act of planting or an act of building? Can important goals be realised at the beginning, or only after years or even decades? Will functions that trees will eventually fulfil be initially provided by supporting technical structures or architectural means? Do goals develop or change over time?

1 Developmental steps of the horticultural strategy: from initially small plants, a baubotanical structure develops in a continuous process of upkeep and training.

1

Horticultural strategy

The project examples in this chapter illustrate a variety of possible answers to such questions. They also reveal a range of different design approaches to expressing the relationship between growing and building. These can be broadly categorised into three basic strategies. The first of these is the horticultural strategy — the planting of relatively small trees which are continuously controlled in their development in order to create living structures primarily through growth (→ Fig. 1). When working with young and flexible shoots, one can in principle produce all conceivable shapes that the tree's growth pattern will tolerate (→ Fig. 2). Aside from this comparative design freedom, what characterises these projects is the often long period of time between the start of the project and when the projected goal is reached. A central concern here is how to ensure the project is kept alive over many years or even decades so that the planned horticultural measures are carried out at the necessary intervals. In the case of the Khasi living bridges already described in the introduction, this is primarily anchored in their social system, in that responsibility is passed down through generations in a traditional society (→ Chapter 6, pp. 128—131). That such systems can fail as soon as social structures change is documented by the eventful history of the dance linden tree at Peesten (→ Chapter 6, pp. 132—135), which we only have the good fortune to experience today because the idea of the project survived even the death of the tree due to the presence of architectural insertions.[1] A completely different and highly individual approach can be seen in the work of the artist David Nash and his living Ash Dome (→ Chapter 6, pp. 136—137) which is directly linked to his own biography. Other projects such as the Torre Verde (→ Chapter 6, pp. 142—143) or the Cattedrale Vegetale (→ Chapter 6, pp. 140—141) attempt to anticipate the future geometry and spatial appearance of the project by means of a non-living structure that disappears over the course of time.

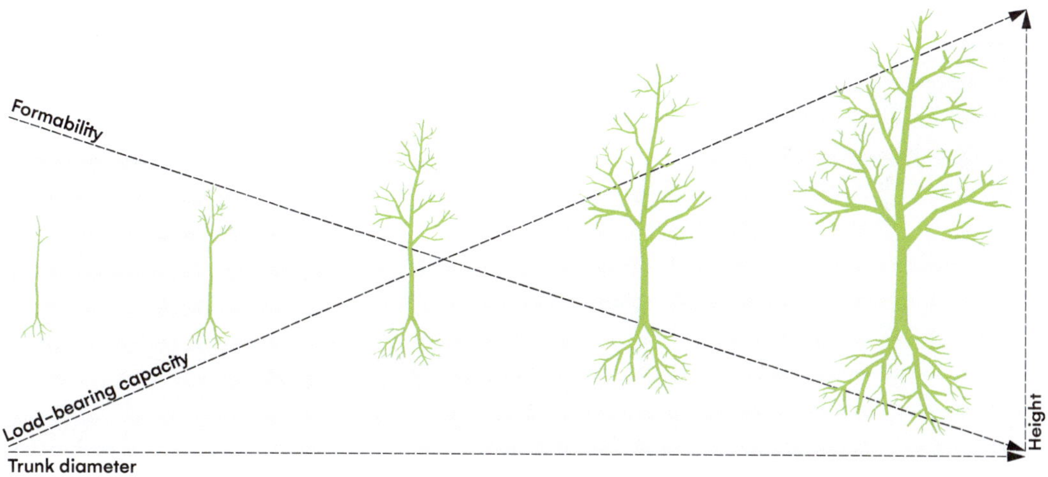

2

2 Trees in different stages of development and their structural potential: while young trees are flexible and formable but not capable of bearing loads, older trees can immediately serve structural functions but are difficult to shape and connect. This results in different approaches to deal with the factor of time in Baubotanik.

Constructional strategy

The constructional strategy entails creating living structures by assembling larger trees into configurations that are already of the desired size with respect to their basic geometry. While this approach is suitable for creating living structures that can be used immediately, the size of these structures is limited by the size of the available plants and the design freedom is mostly limited by the shape of the trees, which are harder to form the more mature they are[2] (→ Figs. 2, 3). This can be seen in projects such as the Baubotanik Footbridge (→ Chapter 6, pp. 144—149) or the Waldkirchen Bird Watching Station (→ Chapter 6, pp. 150—151) which have simple geometric forms formed mostly of straight elements.

Where larger plant structures also need to be load-bearing alongside being immediately usable, the solution invariably entails planting numerous plants in close proximity to one another. In such cases, however, the plants may compete with and crowd each other out (→ Chapter 2, pp. 40—41). Possible solutions include using temporary artificial supporting structures to reduce the density of plants, as seen, for example, in the Steveraue Platform (→ Chapter 6, pp. 152—153), or elevating the process of competition and displacement to a theme of the design concept, as seen in the example of Village de Gîtes les Tropes where a tree façade has been planted with different tree species (→ Chapter 6, pp. 154—157).

3

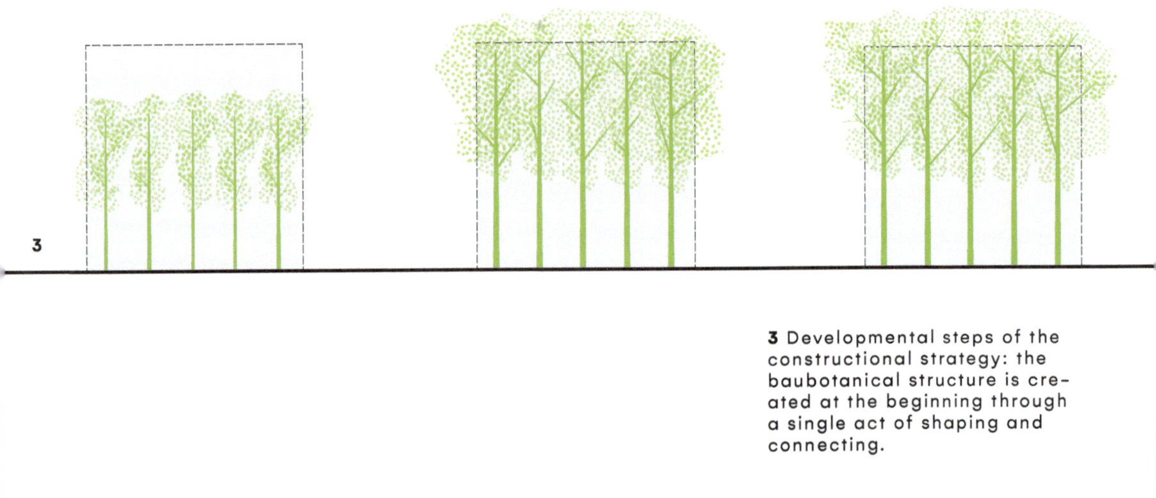

3 Developmental steps of the constructional strategy: the baubotanical structure is created at the beginning through a single act of shaping and connecting.

Constructional-horticultural strategy

The third strategy combines aspects of the two previous approaches and therefore can be best described as constructional-horticultural strategy (→ Fig. 4). This approach employs the technique of plant addition in which living structures of the desired size are created directly using a large number of smaller plants that grow and join together. Young plants, their roots planted in special containers, are arranged in three-dimensional space, often with the help of a supporting scaffold, and joined together in such a way that over time they fuse to form an interconnected system (→ Chapter 3, p. 81). With time, a self-supporting plant structure grows that receives water from the ground and no longer needs the interim roots so that the supporting scaffolding, planters and irrigation systems can be dismantled. This method leverages the regenerative capacity of plants in combination with growth processes to transfer the additive principle of architectural construction—forming large structures from a multitude of smaller elements—to living structures. The relationship of this approach to time is somewhat ambivalent as it is both fast and slow. On the one hand, the living structure has its intended dimensions almost from the very beginning, but on the other it takes years for the plants to merge into a self-sustaining unit and acquire a corresponding load-bearing capacity. Such projects have comparatively high construction and vegetation requirements at the outset of the project. For example, the necessary planters and substrates produce high static loads and the supply of the plants in their containers with water and nutrients requires sophisticated technical facilities and a reliable source of good-quality irrigation water (→ Chapter 5, pp. 117—119). Because the approach is comparatively new, only a few experimental projects have been realised so far, such as the Baubotanik Tower (→ Chapter 6, pp. 158—161) and the Plane Tree Cube in Nagold (→ Chapter 6, pp. 162—169). The Green Living Room in Ludwigsburg (→ Chapter 6, pp. 170—173) makes a virtue of the necessary planters by using them to create a green wall that serves further spatial and ecological functions.

4

4 Developmental steps of a constructional-horticultural strategy: the baubotanical structure is formed from a multitude of young plants arranged above and next to each other that are joined together by means of plant addition.

Design examples

The projects presented here represent a wide variety of objectives and motivations, ranging from artistic and conceptual to horticultural and landscape architectural approaches as well as technically motivated experiments. Aside from this, they also differ in terms of how, if at all, the processual character of the projects is addressed by the designers and whether this is documented or presented in their plans or conceptual drawings. For example, in the case of the Cattedrale Vegetale (→ pp. 140–141), drawings only exist for the starting point, and the development is mentioned only as an open process subject to a few pruning instructions. By contrast, projects such as the Wacholderpark Pergola (→ pp. 138–139) focus on a desired end state and disregard the initial situation in the design and drawings. In fact, only very few projects include descriptions of the process of development. For easier comparison of the different approaches, we have therefore prepared drawings showing the temporal development of each of the projects, typically in the form of four to five sequential elevations or sections. As the various projects differ greatly in terms of how advanced they are, some of the sequential drawings necessarily show projected future states that may come to pass as shown or in a similar form, while others show a developmental stage in the past. These older projects are particularly interesting in that they show how unplanned events have shaped their ongoing development. We have opted not to state a year alongside the developmental stages as for both the historical reconstructions of projects and the projections of future development stages, one cannot pinpoint an exact date at which a stage was or will be reached. Instead, they illustrate the pattern of development.

Living root bridge, Wah Thyllong → pp. 128–131

Dance linden tree, Peesten → pp. 132–135

Ash Dome → pp. 136–137

Wacholderpark Pergolas → pp. 138–139

Cattedrale Vegetale → pp. 140–141

Torre Verde → pp. 142–143

Baubotanik Footbridge
→ pp. 144–149

Waldkirchen Bird Watching Station
→ pp. 150–151

Steveraue Platform → pp. 152–153

Village de Gîtes les Tropes → pp. 154–157

Baubotanik Tower
→ pp. 158–161

Plane Tree Cube, Nagold → pp. 162–169

Green Living Room, Ludwigsburg
→ pp. 170–173

Living root bridge, Wah Thyllong

Design and realisation: Khasi People (ethnic group in north-eastern India)

Maintenance: Several generations of Khasi

Strategy: Horticultural

Location: Mawlynnong, Nowhet, Riwai, Meghalaya, India

Tree species: Rubber tree (*Ficus elastica*)

Technical components: Stone slabs, supporting structures made of bamboo and betel nut trunks

Techniques: Shaping and interweaving of aerial roots

Botanical phenomena: Overgrowth and intergrowth (inosculation)

The root bridge spanning the Thyllong River near the villages of Mawlynnong, Nowhet and Riwai (→ Figs. 5–9) has a length of about 13 m. It is one of a total of 75 living root bridges in India that were documented as part of extensive mapping work by the Baubotanik Research Group, among others.[3] This particular bridge has stone slabs embedded as the walking surface and excellent load-bearing capacity: it can support dozens of people crossing at once and has withstood enormous hydraulic loads in the past when the river has swollen to a raging torrent in the rainy season, which has very high rainfall. In fact, the ongoing vitality and survival of the bridge is less endangered by this than by increasingly intensive tourism and the associated constructions built for these visitors.

The aerial roots that constitute the fabric of the living construction have grown from the trunks and branches of rubber trees (*Ficus elastica*). Usually, they hang freely downwards like dangling strings and initially exhibit virtually only longitudinal growth and barely any geotropic responses (→ Chapter 2, p. 50). They are therefore extremely slender and flexible and can be trained and shaped very easily in almost any direction. The Khasi utilise this specific growth pattern by guiding the roots across the river in hollowed-out betel nut trunks and, with the help of temporary bamboo supporting constructions, knotting them together to form complex, network-like structures. When the root tips reach the ground on the opposite bank, the first thing that happens is that they anchor themselves, producing a tension that causes the roots to tighten and presses them tightly together at the nodes. Secondary thickness growth then sets in, and the root network grows into a horizontally spanning, truss-like load-bearing structure.

The bridge is estimated to be just under 200 years old, although it is hard to categorically determine the age of such structures due to a lack of historical records.[4] As such, one can only speculatively reconstruct the history of the Wah Thyllong Bridge. In principle, the process of creating the living bridges has no fixed plan. Instead, the Khasi respond to developments and to unexpected events, such as damage caused by floods, landslides or fires, as they happen. The timeline in → Fig. 7 is therefore an approximation of a possible development process. It is not known, for example, whether trees were planted on both sides of the river, or whether growth started on one side only and new saplings emerged later on the other side from the roots, which over time developed into a second tree crown. Unlike many of the remoter bridges, which are now rarely used or have been replaced by technical constructions, the Wah Thyllong Bridge is regularly maintained due to its value for tourism. New aerial roots that form on the underside of the bridge are threaded back into the structure to stabilise it and compensate for weak areas. Traditionally, the knowledge required for this was passed on orally from generation to generation.[5]

5 The Wah Thyllong root bridge ca. 2015. One can clearly see the woven supporting structure of the lateral trusses, which are also the railings, and of the basic structure of the walking surface. The bridge is anchored by the roots growing into the very rocky soil at the banks on each side.

6 The Wah Thyllong Bridge in 2019 showing the bamboo poles used to guide the roots. On the right of the picture are new retaining walls built to improve access for tourists.

7 Development of Wah Thyllong Bridge over the past 200 years.

8 A detail of another bridge showing how the aerial roots are guided along a hollowed-out betel nut trunk. The use of wires to connect the two banks does not correspond to the traditional technique.

9 Intertwined roots after several years of growth, also on another bridge. The completely intergrown aerial roots form a walking surface and a handrail structure.

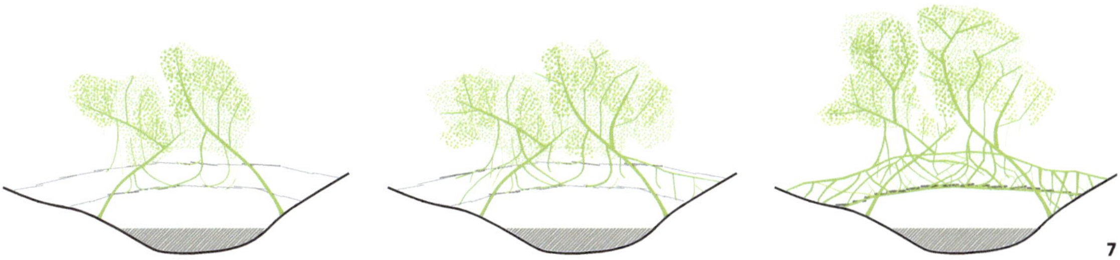

7

Dance linden tree, Peesten

Design and realisation: Diverse owners and groups

Maintenance: Varying, currently Förderverein Tanzlinde Peesten

Strategy: Horticultural

Location: Peesten, Germany

Tree species: Large-leaved lime (*Tilia platyphyllos*)

Technical components: Wooden construction, stone staircase, stone columns

Techniques: Directing the shoots, topiary

Botanical phenomena: Geotropic and geomorphic responses (→ Chapter 2, Fig. 14)

The dance linden tree in Peesten (German name: Tanzlinde Peesten) in the German-Bavarian region of Franconian Switzerland is one of the most emblematic examples of the fusion of tree and building (→ Figs. 10—16). It is noteworthy not just for its design but also for the well-documented history of its development over several centuries in which the relationship between the living and non-living elements of its architecture has changed fundamentally several times over.

First planted in the 16th century, the tree initially served as a meeting place and space for holding court in the locality. To increase its cover, the branches were trained horizontally outwards, assisted by supporting structures of wood. The reshaping of the tree corresponds well to the species' own growth pattern in which the lower branches are already more or less horizontal, so that the direction of reshaping essentially made the tree's natural direction of growth geometrically more precise.

It was only after some 200 years that work began on converting the space in the treetop into an elevated dance hall. In the 19th century, the construction was comprehensively renewed and given its present form. A semi-circular brick spiral staircase was constructed to reach the upper level, and the wooden supporting posts were replaced by stone columns. These were not only more durable and stable, but also underlined the architectural pretensions of the building. A floor comprising two layers of beams rests on the columns. The lower layer supports the branches, the upper the actual dance floor. The dance hall was given open lattice walls along which the lower branches are drawn with window-like openings and an implied roof structure supporting the branches above. It is an impressive room in the treetop in which living and non-living elements interplay in many ways.

10 The development from the end of the 16th to the end of the 19th centuries is characterised by vital growth and the gradual expansion of the wooden construction. In the 19th century, the wooden supports were replaced by stone columns and a stone staircase was added.

10

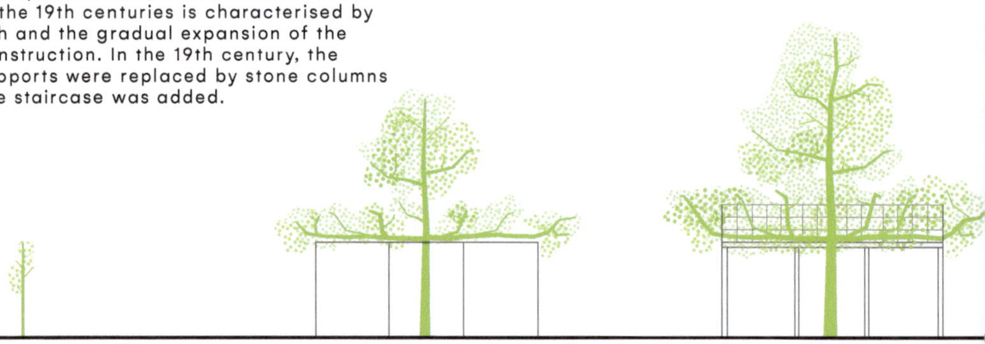

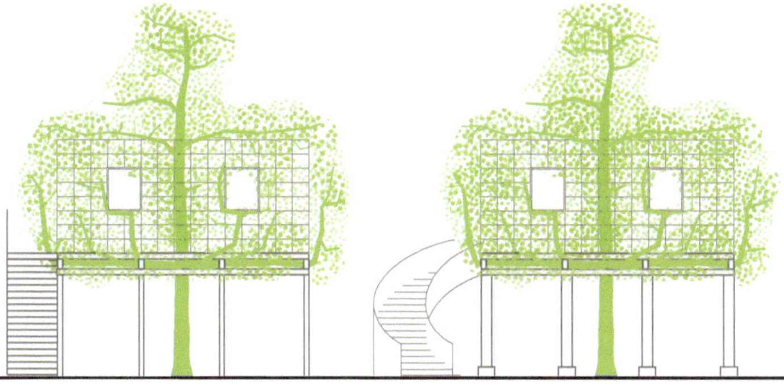

11 The dance linden tree in Peesten with the new tree planted in the 1950s and the reconstructed wooden structure (photo: 2014).

The entire process of development, in which the growth of the tree, its shaping and maintenance and the addition and later conversion of non-living architectural elements go hand in hand, is characteristic of dance linden trees in general. The lime tree in Peesten had its heyday in the middle of the 19th century, after which it gradually fell into neglect, as was the case with many dance linden trees. By 1920 it was already so dilapidated that it could no longer be used and by 1947 at the latest, the tree had died completely and the wooden structure was demolished. All that remained were the stone spiral staircase and the columns as a testimony to happier times in the past. As early as 1950, a new tree was planted, and when it failed to grow, another more successful attempt was made the following year. As the tree grew, so did the hope that the structure could one day be used again as a dance linden tree. The branches were once gain trained horizontally outwards and thanks to the commitment of the citizens of Peesten, the wooden construction was reconstructed 50 years after the new planting and the dance linden tree reopened in 2001. Today, the living structure is used for traditional festivals, but also for readings and concerts.[6]

12 View of the River Main valley through the hybrid wall of the oak wood lattice structure and the living lime branches (photo: 2018).

13

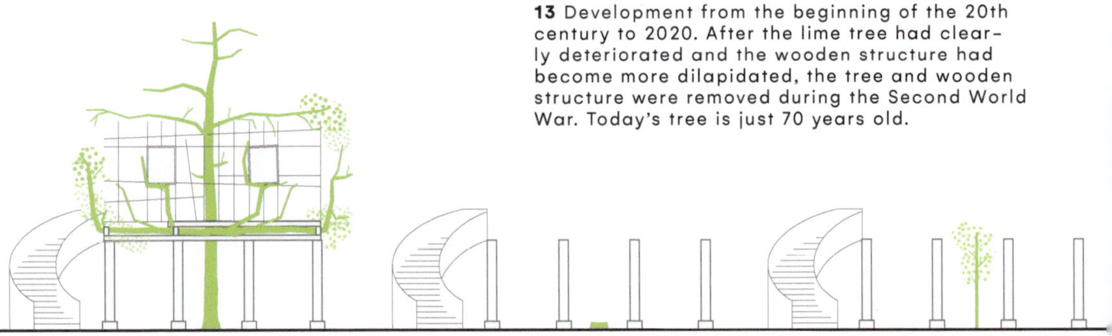

13 Development from the beginning of the 20th century to 2020. After the lime tree had clearly deteriorated and the wooden structure had become more dilapidated, the tree and wooden structure were removed during the Second World War. Today's tree is just 70 years old.

14 The main trunk penetrates the dance floor. It does not sustain any vertical loads but contributes to stiffening the structure. Horizontal forces are taken up by the trunk through the threaded rods visible in the picture (photo: 2018).

15 The branches of the central trunk are guided outwards between two sets of beams resting on the stone columns (photo: 2018).

16 A lithograph by Carl August Lebschée showing the condition of the dance linden tree in the mid-19th century. In the depiction, the tree looks like it was flourishing and was obviously pruned regularly.

Ash Dome

Design and realisation: David Nash (artist)

Maintenance: David Nash

Strategy: Horticultural

Location: Cae'n-y-coed, Wales, Great Britain

Tree species: European ash (*Fraxinus excelsior*)

Technical components: Wooden posts (temporary)

Techniques: Kinking by sawing, pruning of lower branches

Botanical phenomena: Intergrowth (inosculation), wound healing at kinks, competition

The Ash Dome in north Wales (→ Figs. 17—20) consists of 22 ash trees arranged in a circle, planted in 1977 by the artist David Nash. The sculpture, which can be walked into at ground level, is conceived as a processual work of art, the form of which was precisely planned in drawings by the artist. One of the most important aspects of the project is the artist's promise to devote 30 to 40 years to it. In the process, he guided the shoots successively inwards in a spiral, creating a space that becomes gradually more enclosed towards the top. To achieve this, he developed his own technique for shaping the trunks which involves making wedge-shaped incisions in one side of the shoot and then kinking the shoots to reconnect the cut surfaces. The shoots grow together again, often forming thick bulges around the incisions. The result is a striking twisting form in which sections of often gnarled trunk zigzag upwards. Over a period of more than 40 years, the artist documented the ongoing upkeep and horticultural work in photos that record not just the growth of the plant structure but also the artist's own aging process, placing the life story of the structure in relation to that of its creator.[7] The future of the project is, however, uncertain due to the spread of ash dieback.

17 The distinctive twist of the trunks was achieved by making multiple wedge-shaped incisions

18 In the following, the shoot was kinked and then subsequent wound healing occurred.

20

19 David Nash in his living spatial sculpture, which he has shaped and maintained himself over decades (photo: 2009).

20 Development between 1977 and 2015.

Wacholderpark Pergolas

Design: Leberecht Migge (landscape architect)

Realisation: Jacob Ochs Gardening Contractors

Maintenance: City of Hamburg

Strategy: Horticultural

Location: Hamburg, Germany

Tree species: Small-leaved lime (*Tilia cordata*)

Technical components: Temporary trellis (steel)

Techniques: Training shoots, pollarding

Botanical phenomena: Head formation (wound healing and reiteration)

The two pergolas, 70 and 80 m long respectively, are part of the Public Gardens at Hamburg-Fuhlsbüttel designed in 1911 by the landscape architect Leberecht Migge in Hamburg (→ Figs. 21–23). Today, it is known as the Wacholderpark. As a member of the Werkbund and representative of the reform garden movement, Migge favoured the architectural use of plants in which trees in particular were used to define space and were strictly geometrically shaped. Much like the green architecture of the Baroque garden, which are comparable in many respects, no mention is made of growth processes.[8] Instead, a clearly defined goal was sketched that should be quickly reached and then maintained in that state for as long as possible. In the case of the Wacholderpark, young lime trees were trained along a temporary trellis for several years until each side had acquired the shape of half of an arch and thus their intended final form and size as well as an inherent stability so that the auxiliary structures could be removed. Subsequently, the shoots of these shaped trees were pollarded (i.e. cut back to the trunk) every year (→ Chapter 2, p. 42). By repeating this process over many decades, the heads grew out into long, bulging and knobbly structures. Otherwise, however, the structure hardly changed: by trimming the leaf mass to consistently low levels, there was little competition between the individual trees and the trunks exhibited only minimal thickness growth.

21 In summer, the foliage cover provides shade and creates an area clearly delineated from the open space.

23

22 The shaped lime trees of the pergola are characterised by the knobbly heads resulting from annual pruning (pollarding) (photo: 2015).

23 Reconstruction of the pergolas' development since their planting in 1911 shows that the lime trees have hardly grown in thickness due to the pollarding and the relatively high density of plants (see the dance linden tree planted 40 years later in Peesten (→ Chapter 6, pp. 132–135).

Cattedrale Vegetale

Design: Giuliano Mauri (Artist)

Realisation: Giuliano Mauri/Arte Sella

Maintenance: Arte Sella

Strategy: Horticultural

Location: Trento, Italy

Tree species: Hornbeam (*Carpinus betulus*)

Technical components: Temporary construction of round timber and dead branches

Techniques: Topiary

The Cattedrale Vegetale (→ Figs. 24—26) was built in 2001 by the land-art artist Giuliano Mauri. It consists of four approx. 28 m long rows of "columns", reminiscent of the nave and aisles of a cathedral. The columns are simple roundwood constructions to which slightly curved branches are attached at the top, suggesting a vaulted ceiling. A young hornbeam has been planted in each column. The trees gradually grow upwards inside the columns, filling them with foliage. Any branches growing out of the columns are regularly trimmed. The artist precisely planned the initial state in his drawings, but otherwise the development of the project is left largely open. The wooden construction of the columns is deliberately exposed to natural weathering processes and will disappear over time, leaving only the trees standing. Eventually, when the treetops above the columns have joined together, the living plants will create a spatial effect that will echo the atmosphere and subdued lighting of a church interior through the filtering effect of the leaves. Ultimately, this piece of living architecture is nothing more than a grove of geometrically planted and regularly pruned trees in four rows. The temporary wooden construction provides a basic idea of the final spatial effect and at the same time serves as a scaffold for maintenance.[9]

24 The Cattedrale Vegetale in winter 2014/15.

26

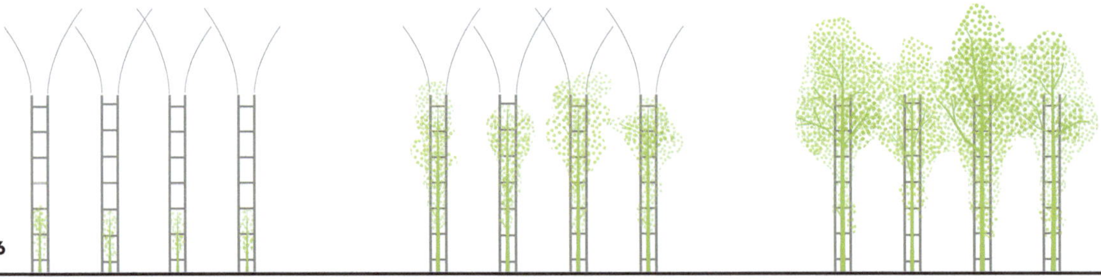

25 The Cattedrale Vegetale in autumn 2013, about 12 years after planting.

26 The first three drawings in the sequential series show the development since planting in 2001; the last two show the possible development from 2020 to 2040.

Torre Verde

Design and realisation: Ferdinand Ludwig with Master students (MMLU University of Alghero), Ente Foreste Sardegna

Maintenance: Staff at Porto Conte National Park

Strategy: Horticultural

Location: Porto Conte, Sardinia, Italy

Tree species: Carob tree (*Ceratonia siliqua*)

Technical components: Reed, iron wire (temporary)

Techniques: Shaping and connecting shoots

Botanical phenomena: Intergrowth (inosculation)

The Torre Verde (→ Figs. 27–29) was built in summer 2014 under the direction of Ferdinand Ludwig in a "Design and Build" workshop with students on the grounds of the Porto Conte National Park in Sardinia (project management: Annacaterina Piras, Stefan Tischer). The aim of the workshop was to design and realise a baubotanical project in just three days, using only materials and young plants available on site. The design of the approx. 6 m high tower draws inspiration from the fortified towers in the vicinity as well as the possibilities offered by the found materials. It comprises eight almost vertical and 14 diagonally arranged bundles of reed, which are held together by four horizontal rings of the same material. Young carob trees, about 2 m tall, were planted at the base of each bundle and will be trained as they grow and joined where they intersect. The reed construction is intended only as a temporary supporting framework and will rot and disintegrate over time, but it helps visualise the extent of the intended tower, a little like a built sketch of the future living structure. It soon became clear after a year that the supporting structure, held together with just wire, was too fragile, and most of it collapsed during a storm. The plants, however, survived the collapse virtually unharmed and were re-erected and attached to wooden stakes. They continue to grow and are being shaped, maintained and connected as best possible without the help of a supporting framework.

27 Re-attachment of the shoots after the premature collapse of the temporary structure (photo: 2015).

29

28 The Torre Verde immediately after planting and completion of the temporary structure (photo: 2014).

29 The sequential series shows the originally intended development over 20 years.

Baubotanik Footbridge

Design and realisation: Ferdinand Ludwig, Oliver Storz, Cornelius Hackenbracht

Maintenance: Neue Kunst am Ried Sculpture Park

Scientific monitoring: Baubotanik Research Group (University of Stuttgart/TU Munich)

Strategy: Constructional

Location: Wald-Ruhestetten, Germany

Tree species: Basket willow (*Salix viminalis*)

Technical components: Steel grating, stainless steel tube

Techniques: Bundling willow rods

Botanical phenomena: Adventitious root formation, overgrowth, intergrowth (inosculation), competition

The Baubotanik Footbridge (original name: Baubotanischer Steg) was designed in 2005 by Ferdinand Ludwig and Oliver Storz and realised together with the sculptor Cornelius Hackenbracht at the "Neue Kunst am Ried Sculpture Park" in Wald-Ruhestetten near Lake Constance (→ Figs. 30—38). It is the first experimental and demonstration building by the Baubotanik Research Group and illustrates the conceptual and constructional approach of Baubotanik by means of a simple hybrid vegetal-technical structure. Its development was monitored and documented on an ongoing basis to gain more knowledge about the construction and maintenance of baubotanical structures.

The structure was originally formed of 64 vertical bundle supports, each consisting of 12 to 15 plants. This supports a footbridge walkway at a height of about 2.5 m above ground along with a stainless steel tube that serves as a handrail. Another 16 diagonally arranged bundles stiffen the construction. The regularly spaced plant supports, and the 22 m long platform made of sections of steel grating create an elevated walkway that can be accessed via two lateral sections of walkway with ladders. The living plant structure was constructed from up to 4.5 m long willow rods (*Salix viminalis*) which were buried approx. 80 cm deep in the ground where they took root independently as a product of their good regenerative capacity (→ Chapter 2, pp. 41—43). Consequently, there is no foundation in a conventional sense; the bundles transfer all building loads into the subsoil and the roots anchor the construction in the soil.

The bundle supports were sufficiently dimensioned from the outset to be able to sustain the expected loads once the initial phase of construction was complete.[10] To transfer the live

30 First sprouting in spring 2005.

31 The Baubotanik Footbridge in autumn 2010 after about five years of growth.

loads of the walkway, some of the rods were cut below the level of the walkway as a bearing surface for the beams supporting the walkway. The handrail was clamped or pressed between clusters of willow rods and held in place with polyester tape.[11]

The site is a sunny wetland meadow, providing excellent growing conditions for the willow rods—an essential basis for the vital growth of the structure. The first leaves sprouted only a few weeks after initial "completion" in spring 2005, vividly demonstrating the idea and vitality of the living structure. That same summer, more than 1 m long shoots developed and a lush canopy emerged, turning the footbridge into a dense green wall. At the same time many plants exhibited clear growth in thickness, with the rods growing from initially the thickness of a thumb to strong trunks, their grey-green stems turning into a gnarled bark. Over time, the stainless steel tube of the handrail was completely incorporated into the bundles in many places. The intention was that the polyester tape holding the bundles together would also be incorporated by the plant, but this only happened in isolated cases and often resulted in strangulation. The tape was therefore successively removed and replaced with screws (→ Chapter 2, p. 58).

Due to the large number of plants needed to ensure the structure had sufficient initial strength, there was significant competition between the willow shoots within as well as between the bundles. Over time, some plants lagged far behind in development and died, especially in the diagonal bundles and within the vertical bundles those plants that were cut to serve as a bearing for the walkway. This development can be explained by poor exposure to sunlight in the inward-lying rods and geomorphic reactions in the diagonally arranged bundles (→ Chapter 2, pp. 49–50).

In winter, once the willow has shed its leaves and the technical character of the construction becomes more apparent, the footbridge structure undergoes regular maintenance pruning. The maintenance concept was continuously adapted based on the experience gained with each new year. Initially all the shoots beneath the walkway were removed and shoots with strong growth were cut back to expose the weaker rods to more sunlight. From 2010 onwards, new shoots were cultivated at the base to replace those that were potentially failing, and then later incorporated into the supporting bundles in subsequent years. In addition, further rods were planted in the immediate vicinity to grow stronger saplings to replace bundles that had grown particularly weak or had even died completely. However, after these did not develop as well as expected due to competition from neighbouring, fully developed plants, a new maintenance strategy was implemented from 2016 onwards. In 2017, a supporting steel scaffold was erected underneath about a third

35

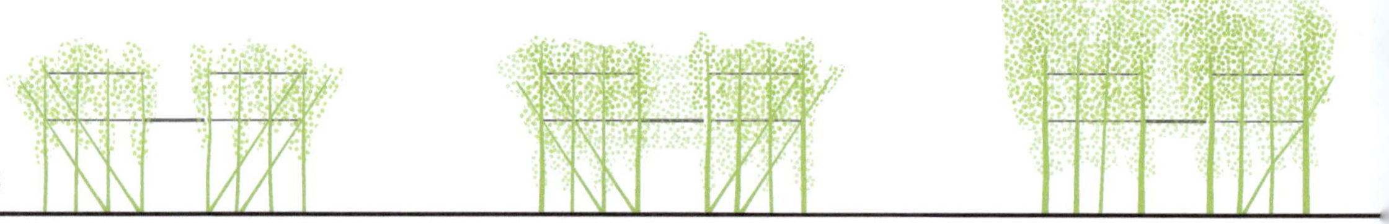

32 After seven years the handrail was completely incorporated by the vertical columns which had grown evenly around them.

34 As part of the restoration work, partially dead plant bundles were left suspended in the structure as insect habitats (photo: 2015).

33 Connection between a diagonal bracing bundle and vertical column bundle. Rods with vigorous growth have inosculated while weaker rods have already partly died (photo: 2010).

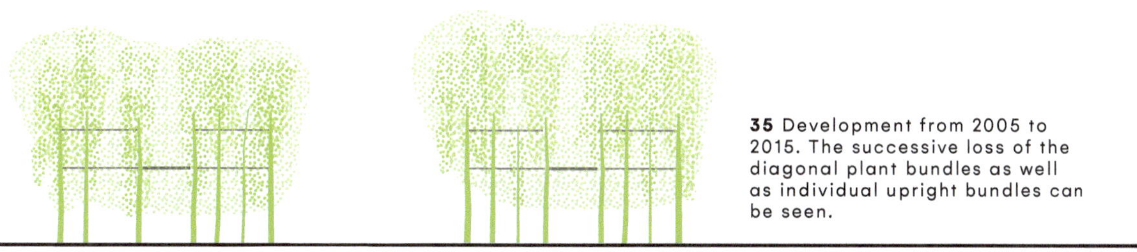

35 Development from 2005 to 2015. The successive loss of the diagonal plant bundles as well as individual upright bundles can be seen.

36 In winter, the technical components are much more visible and the underlying structure is clearly legible (photo: 2006).

of the walkway and handrail, and all the bundles were cut down to just above ground level. Of the shoots that then emerged at the base, the two strongest were selected and routed parallel upwards and around the crossbeam of the walkway and the handrail. As part of this, the two shoots were connected with screws approx. every 25 cm and thereby pressed against the non-living technical components. After just three years, the plants regained their original height and had almost completely fused at the lower

38 The first stage shows the introduction of partial supporting scaffolding in 2017 and the capping of the bundle supports close to the ground. The second stage shows the regenerated state after about three years. The remaining stages show the planned next steps for the following ten years.

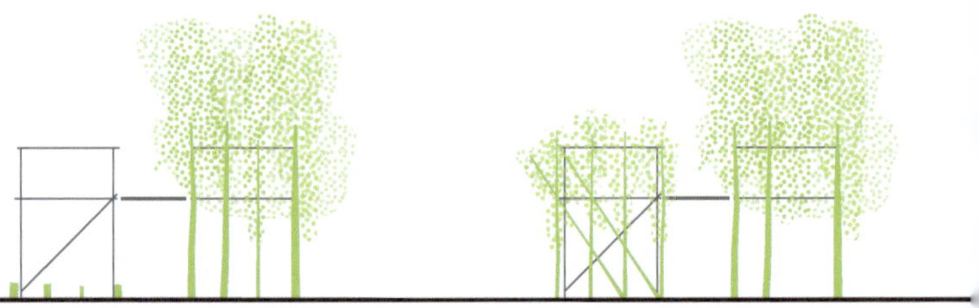

sections. Once these had sufficient load-bearing capacity due to ongoing thickness growth and incorporation of technical components, the scaffolding was dismantled and the same procedure undertaken step by step for the remaining stretch of walkway. This process both sustainably rectified the problems of the initial project design (strangulation tendency, excessive plant density causing competition) and also showed how plant regeneration processes can be used in Baubotanik to repair living structures.

37 In summer, the technical components are almost completely obscured by plant growth and the footbridge looks more like a hedge in the landscape (photo: 2007).

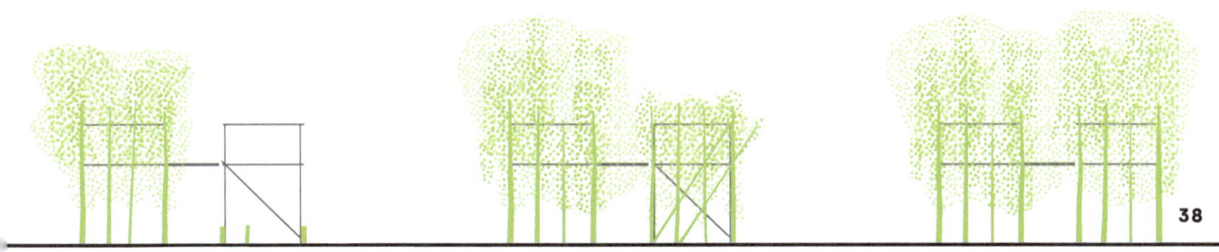

38

Waldkirchen Bird Watching Station

Design: Ferdinand Ludwig, Oliver Storz, Hannes Schwertfeger

Realisation: Weidenart Freitag

Maintenance: BUND/Municipality of Waldkirchen

Strategy: Constructional

Location: Waldkirchen, Germany

Tree species: White willow (*Salix alba*)

Technical components: Steel elements, textile membrane roof, wooden platform

Techniques: Bundling willow rods

Botanical phenomena: Adventitious root formation, overgrowth, intergrowth (inosculation), competition

Waldkirchen Bird Watching Station (original name: Vogelbeobachtungsstation Waldkirchen) in the Bavarian Forest, Germany, was created in 2007 as part of a small horticultural show (→ Figs. 39—40). Built on an elliptical ground plan of approx. 3 × 6 m, a living structure made of willow rods was formed that supported a viewing platform spanned by a funnel-shaped membrane roof. The platform was reached via rungs incorporated into the baubotanical construction. The plant structure, more than 6 m high in total, was formed directly from willow rods up to 9 m long and 12 cm in diameter using a construction principle similar to that of the Baubotanik Footbridge (→ pp. 144—149). The dimensions of the living supporting structure were determined by the connection detail of the plants and the platform. Pairs of plants were pressed against the surrounding U-profile of the platform without penetrating the plant shoots. To ensure full load-bearing capacity on "completion" of the structure, a large number of plants needed to be used. As with the footbridge, the grouping of many shoots into bundles resulted in strong competition between the plants, causing some to eventually die and others to grow very slowly. Within a few years, the load-bearing capacity of the construction decreased, and the structure had to be partially dismantled. The impressive feat of constructing an immediately usable two-storey living structure was therefore only made possible using a form of construction that was unable to survive or develop in the long term.

40

39 The bird watching station in the year of completion and planting (photo: 2007).

40 The development from planting (2007) to 2013 documents the partial deconstruction of the technical components. Due to the fact that dying processes eventually outweighed the growth processes, the load-bearing capacity of the living structure decreased over time.

Steveraue Platform

Design: Oliver Storz, Hannes Schwertfeger

Realisation: Bureau Baubotanik

Maintenance: Bureau Baubotanik, Municipality of Olfen

Strategy: Constructional

Location: Olfen, Germany

Tree species: Basket willow (*Salix viminalis*)

Technical components: Steel and wooden elements

Techniques: Bundling willow rods in pairs

Botanical phenomena: Adventitious root formation, overgrowth, intergrowth (inosculation), competition

The Steveraue Platform (→ Figs. 41—42) by Bureau Baubotanik was created in 2010 as part of the renaturation of the river Stever and its flood meadows in the north of the town of Olfen. Willow rods arranged in pairs were connected here to form a lattice-like structure into which a staircase, a viewing platform, railings and "window frames" were incorporated, as well as a crowning steel tube at a height of about 6 m. In the long term, the intention was that the plant structure would take over the load-bearing function and absorb the dead weight of the technical components as well as all live loads. To be able to use the structure from the beginning, a temporary supporting structure made of yellow steel pipes was erected, which could then be successively dismantled after the willow rods had taken root in the ground and acquired sufficient stability through incorporation of the steel elements, inosculation of the plant shoots and growth in thickness. Compared to the approach used for Waldkirchen Bird Watching Station (→ pp. 150—151), this process permitted a much lower plant density so that the plants can develop more vigorously in the medium term. Nevertheless, here too competition between shoots led to the decline of some plants and slow growth among the remainder. As a consequence, the supporting structural elements have not yet been dismantled. Conceptually, the planned shift from an initially predominantly technical to a later predominantly baubotanical load-bearing structure also reflects the long-term processes of the floodplain landscape as it changes as a result of renaturation.

42

41 The platform in the Steveraue about one year after planting.

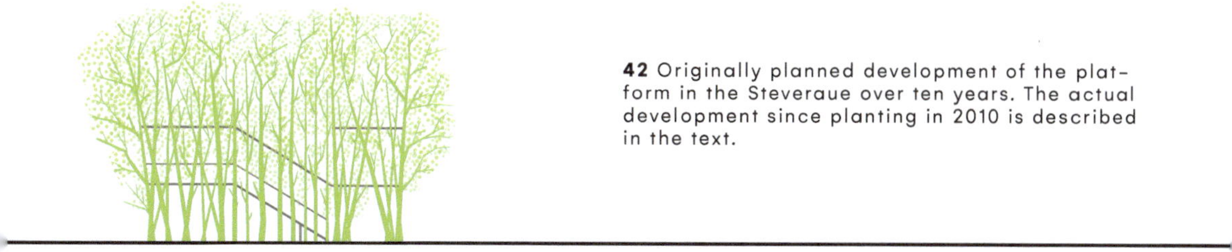

42 Originally planned development of the platform in the Steveraue over ten years. The actual development since planting in 2010 is described in the text.

Village de Gîtes les Tropes

Design: Edouard François (architect) with Duncan Lewis

Realisation: SOCAMIP (contractor)

Maintenance: Gardener specialising in topiary

Strategy: Constructional

Location: Jupilles, France

Tree species: Various maple, thuja and cherry species

Technical components: Conventional building, wooden slats, wire mesh

Techniques: Topiary

Botanical phenomena: Competition

The Village de Gîtes les Tropes (→ Figs. 43–48), designed by the architect Edouard François in 1996 in the village of Jupilles near the Forêt de Bercé, merges conventionally constructed buildings with trees to form an architectural whole. Three simple, rectilinear structures containing holiday apartments are enveloped by a "tree façade" that is planted directly in front of the two-storey "technical façade" of the buildings. A range of different deciduous and evergreen as well as red-leaved species were used, arranged in random order at slightly varying spacings of approx. 2 m. A lightweight slat construction placed in front of the buildings that is covered with wire mesh in the area of the upper storey defines the growth space of the tree crowns: any branches growing out of this space are regularly cut back to stay in the plane of the wire mesh. Over the course of time, this has resulted in a strictly geometric crown form that runs like a ribbon around the outside of the upper storey. To begin with there were large gaps between the individual trees which have since closed. The rigour of the geometry is broken down using different tree species to create a dynamic pattern of varying leaf colours and transparencies that changes constantly with the seasons. In addition, the proportions of the individual trees change over time, as more dominant species displace weaker ones.

On the ground floor, the architecture is clad with interchanging sections of untreated wooden planks and floor-to-ceiling windows, echoing the pattern of the bare trunks of the trees. On the upper floor projecting framed windows pierce the tree façade, ending flush with the plane of the wire mesh. At the ends, the "tree façades" detach from the buildings and continue as elevated hedges that enclose courtyard-like open spaces. The sum of these different architectural devices results in a closely intertwined combination of trees, buildings and outdoor spaces achieved using comparatively simple horticultural means.

44

43 Entrance to one of the units at Village de Gîtes les Tropes. Over time, the rigorously pruned trees of different species form a dynamically changing façade on the first floor (photo ca. 2016).

44 The timeline of approx. 20 years of development showing how the trees planted in the size of the structure compete for limited crown space. This desired effect was already anticipated by the designer when the project was built in 1996.

45

45 Conceptual drawing illustrating how the different tree species gradually populate the canopy space. Top: winter view; bottom: summer view.

46

46 Initial situation shortly after planting.

47 The trimmed tree canopies not only act as the façade of the upper floor of the buildings, but also frame adjoining open spaces (photo: ca. 2016).

48 Approx. 20 years after planting, the evergreen conifers have proven to be more dominant than the deciduous tree species. Only a few branches of the maple in the centre of the picture can still hold their own.

Baubotanik Tower

Design and realisation: Ferdinand Ludwig, Cornelius Hackenbracht

Maintenance: Neue Kunst am Ried Sculpture Park

Scientific monitoring: Baubotanik Research Group (University of Stuttgart/TU Munich)

Strategy: Constructional-horticultural

Location: Wald-Ruhestetten, Germany

Tree species: White willow (*Salix alba*), downy birch (*Betula pubescens*)

Technical components: Steel elements, planters, irrigation system

Techniques: Plant addition (shaping and connecting shoots)

Botanical phenomena: Intergrowth (inosculation), overgrowth, competition

The Baubotanik Tower (→ Figs. 49–53; original name: Baubotanischer Turm) was conceived as an experimental and demonstration structure of the Baubotanik Research Group, created in 2009 by Ferdinand Ludwig and Cornelius Hackenbracht in cooperation with BaStHo (structural engineering), Helix Pflanzen (precultivated plants), GaLaTech (foundation construction) and Christoph Blattmacher (steel construction). Its purpose is to investigate baubotanical design principles and showcase the possibilities of plant addition, which was trialled here for the first time on an actual structure (→ Chapter 3, p. 81). The tower, which is just under 8 m high, has three square platforms made of galvanised steel that can be accessed via ladders for maintenance and plant care. Planters with young, approx. 2 m tall white willows were arranged on these and four intermediate levels so that the plants intersect and can gradually fuse to form an interconnected physiological and structural unit that is rooted in the ground. In the long term, a self-supporting botanical structure should result that can sustain all relevant loads. Until then, the structure and its loads are borne by a supporting scaffold.

The design of the baubotanical structure aims to align architectural and constructional objectives as far as possible with the growth patterns of the plants. The result of these considerations is a diamond-shaped arrangement of intersecting plants that are anchored at their nodal points to horizontal, technical components. From a botanical standpoint, this arrangement is advantageous because all plants are equally strong and only slightly inclined, thus minimising the geomorphic response of the trees. Simultaneously, it should favour uniform development of the entire project (→ Chapter 2, pp. 49–50). By anchoring the plants to the technical structure at their intersections, triangular structural forms are created that lend the tower better rigidity. At the same time, the structure is designed with redundance in mind so that it can tolerate the failure of individual plants or sections: two plants are connected to form

50

49 Baubotanik Tower in the fourth year after planting.

50 Originally forecast development over a period of approx. 35 years. Due to the replacement of the plants seven years after planting, the actual development lags behind this forecast. However, the set targets seem achievable.

pairs that cross above and below the connecting points to the technical framework so that they are each enclosed by four shoots (→ Fig. 53). Should an individual plant or pair of plants die, the remaining ones are still structurally linked to each other and the connecting point. In addition, each main and intermediate level has 12 such connection points, and in the worst case up to eight could potentially fail without the structure's becoming unstable, provided the remaining connections are sufficiently strong.

The plants were fixed to a bamboo trellis and connected in parallel at short intervals of approx. 20 cm and at the crossing points with small stainless steel screws. The roots are held in wire mesh baskets filled with plant substrate that is kept moist by means of a simple drip-feed irrigation system. The temporary supporting framework is mounted on screw foundations that can also be removed at a later date. The entire system is conceived so that the pipe connections or the diagonal bracing can be successively loosened as the load-bearing capacity of the botanical structure allows.

An important part of the research project was to create simple growth models for predicting the development of the baubotanical structure. In a multi-step process the overall increase in biomass was first calculated so that the thickness growth of the individual plants and stem sections could be estimated based on exposure to the sun and competition with neighbouring plants. Parallel to this, the self-thinning rule (→ Chapter 2, pp. 40—41) was applied to determine how many plants or stems may die off as the total biomass increases. In a final step, these idealised development trends were then subject to random influences and linked to possible development scenarios. The calculations revealed that right from the outset, the plant density was already so high that most plants would have slow growth in thickness and casualties resulting from plant competition would be likely. The plants that would thrive best were at the corners and uppermost levels, where there was most exposure to sunlight, space was least constricting and competition lowest (→ Fig. 52). The model did not, however, show when the tower will reach a self-supporting stage, which will be determined during the project using load tests.

The actual development of the plants in the first three vegetation periods corresponded quite accurately to this forecast. In particular, the observed differences in thickness growth were consistent with the calculations. As per the concept of plant addition, it was also possible to separate the plants from their roots in the planters at the lowest and the highest level without any visible impairment of development. However, as growth progressed, increased fungal infestation in the plants appeared which impacted seriously on the plants' overall vitality. Development therefore remained well behind the forecast and even various technical adjustments, treatment of damaged plants and replacement of dead plants were unable to resolve the problem entirely. In the end, it seems that the selected tree species is susceptible to fungal infestation at the particular site, and that the problem was exacerbated by dense planting, mutual shading and high humidity in the tower. In Spring 2016, therefore, all the plants were removed and replaced by downy birch (*Betula pubescens*), which had previously proved suitable in test plantings at the site (→ Fig. 51 b). A new planting pattern was tested and the plant density significantly reduced in order to lower competition effects in future development. Since the replanting, all plants show a much more vital development, which is why the objective of the original goals seems achievable in principle even though there was a time delay due to the replanting.

51 a Situation after planning in 2009.
b Condition in 2021, four years after replacing the plants.
c Structural model that simulates the originally forecast development.

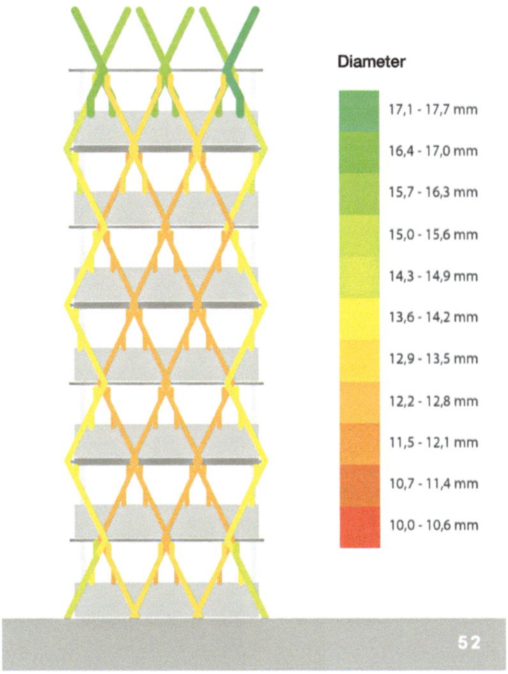

52 Calculation of expected stem diameter growth. Due to better exposure and the larger potential crown space at the top and at the corners, stronger growth was deemed likely in these areas. This prognosis coincided with the actual development in the first few years.

53 Junction with crossed shoots growing in pairs and incorporated technical components. Condition approx. two years after planting.

Plane Tree Cube, Nagold

Design: Office for Living Architecture (OLA)

Realisation: Helix Pflanzen, Gartenbau Walker, Stahlbau Stadler

Maintenance: Helix Pflanzen

Scientific monitoring: Baubotanik Research Group (University of Stuttgart/TU Munich)

Strategy: Constructional-horticultural

Location: Nagold, Germany

Tree species: London plane tree (*Platanus × hispanica*)

Technical components: Steel construction (partly temporary), planters, irrigation system

Techniques: Plant addition (shaping and connecting shoots)

Botanical phenomena: Overgrowth, intergrowth (inosculation), competition

The Plane Tree Cube in Nagold (→ Figs. 54—64; original name: Platanenkubus) by the Office for Living Architecture (OLA), realised together with Ingenieurbüro Brocke (structural design) and SecOp (horticultural consulting), takes the approaches explored in the Baubotanik Tower and continues them at a larger scale to extend them into the urban context. The project was realised as part of the Regional Horticultural Show at Nagold in 2012 and is conceived as a long-term urban-baubotanical experiment. With the help of plant addition, the 10 × 10 × 10 m cube is a completely green structure that, once erected, already has the equivalent green volume of a fully grown tree. In the initial stage, plane trees were arranged in planters on six levels to form green walls that enclose an inner space open to the sky. Inside, maintenance walkways for gardeners are arranged on three levels around the perimeter with visitor platforms on the west side, accessed via straight flights of steel stairs. In a manner similar to the Baubotanik Tower (→ pp. 158—161), the plants are arranged in a diamond-shaped pattern and interconnected in such a way that they will fuse to form a single organism that can supply itself with water and nutrients from the ground in the long term, allowing the planters and irrigation system to be dismantled at a later date, along with no longer needed maintenance walkways. The entire structure is initially supported by vertical steel columns that will be removed when the plant structure is strong enough to bear all occurring loads. If growing conditions are good, it is estimated that this will take between 15 and 20 years.[12]

The platforms are attached to steel trusses around the perimeter that transfer loads to the plant structure at numerous points to accommodate locally varying structural strength resulting

55

54 The Plane Tree Cube in 2021: a green volume between the viaduct, a local landmark, and the newly built child day care centre on the left.

55 Timeline showing the project's development from planting and opening (2012) over approx. 30 years. Its condition after ten years growth lies somewhere between the second and third drawing.

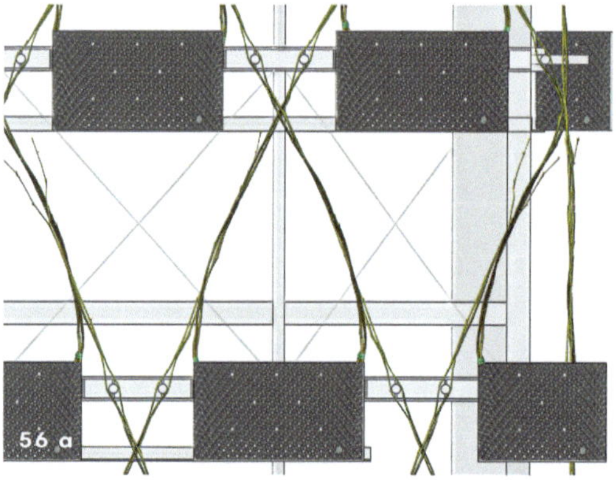

56 a

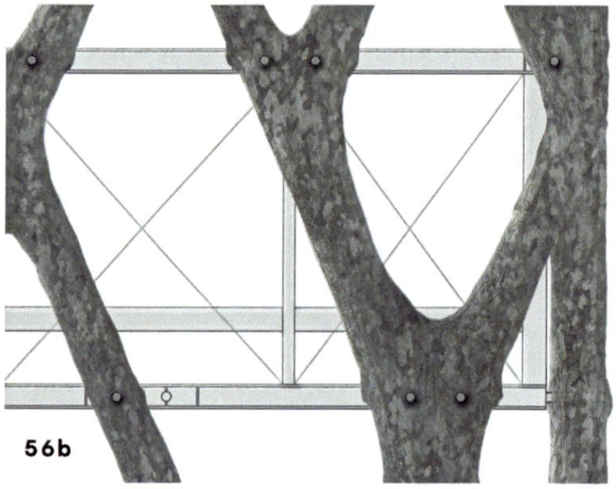

56b

56 Detail of the construction and vegetation technique.
a Situation immediately after initial completion. The young plane trees grow out of the planters attached to the steel structure. They are trained around the connection points so that they can incorporate them.
b Possible state of development after 20 to 30 years. The planters and vertical steel columns have been dismantled, and the inosculated tree trunks now serve the primary load-bearing function.

57 Prediction of the cube's spatial development.
a To begin with, the cube is enclosed on all sides by green walls and open at the top.
b Over time the canopy grows mainly at the top while the trunks emerge at its base.

57 a

from irregular stem growth or the potential death of plants or stem sections.

Over time, the upper section will become gradually more enclosed as the plant canopy grows, while the lower areas will acquire a stronger presence as the trunks grow thicker and more gnarled. After the horticultural show, during which the cube served as a lookout point and shady retreat, the show grounds were redeveloped into a new urban district. Originally, the plan was that the Plane Tree Cube would become a baubotanical town square serving a variety of possible uses, due to its multiple levels. After changes to the urban development plan, the Plane Tree Cube was incorporated into the outdoor landscaping of a child day care centre in 2021.

In its first five years, the project's development was determined by ongoing adaptations and refinement of the technical facilities, which had to withstand the extreme demands of public use and the harsh weather conditions at the edge of the mountainous Black Forest region. Since then, the plants have developed well, exhibiting strong growth in thickness and good development at the baubotanical connections.

57 b

58 Cross-growth with ingrown screw (photo: 2019).

59 Condition immediately after completion of construction (photo: 2011).

60 Visualisation of the interior 20 to 30 years after planting.

61 Autumnal view of the interior (photo: 2019).

62 Four plants that have fused to form a single trunk at one base point (photo: 2021).

63 Connection point showing early (left) and advanced (right) overgrowth (photo: 2021).

64 The "living façade" of the Plane Tree Cube in autumn 2019.

Green Living Room, Ludwigsburg

Design: Office for Living Architecture (OLA)

Realisation: Helix Pflanzen/GaLa-Tech

Strategy: Constructional-horticultural

Location: Rathausplatz Ludwigsburg, Germany

Tree species: London plane tree (*Platanus × hispanica*)

Technical components: Wire mesh baskets, bamboo canes

Techniques: Plant addition (shaping and connecting shoots)

Botanical phenomena: Intergrowth (inosculation), competition

The Green Living Room in Ludwigsburg (→ Figs. 65–68; original name: Grünes Zimmer) demonstrates the possibilities of Baubotanik and plant addition as a sustainable contribution to urban design. Built in 2013, the project employs a custom-designed modular system of self-supporting wire mesh baskets that can be stacked in different configurations to create the planters required for plant addition. These basic modules were used to form three green walls planted with various perennials and ground cover species that in their arrangement define different spatial situations — a "green living room". Along two sections, additional overhead baubotanical structures were installed that extend horizontally beyond the end of the walls creating plant canopies that provide shade in the otherwise treeless space. Sections of these plane tree roofs project almost 3 m outwards and were initially supported by bamboo canes. Over time, they are to become self-supporting. To this end, they need regular pruning and forming in order to develop horizontally, i.e. against their natural direction of growth. Here the planter-walls will remain as a permanent part of the design. The Green Living Room was erected as part of the EU research project TURAS to serve as a demonstration building and open-air laboratory to monitor the contribution of baubotanical structures to local urban climates.[13] The plants are watered using rainwater collected from the roof of an adjacent administrative building and stored in cisterns, demonstrating how Baubotanik can be integrated into the water management systems of innovative green infrastructure (→ Chapter 5, p. 119). Due to the good supply of water and the mild climate of the wine-growing region, the plants grew well and vigorously and inosculations took place rapidly.

66

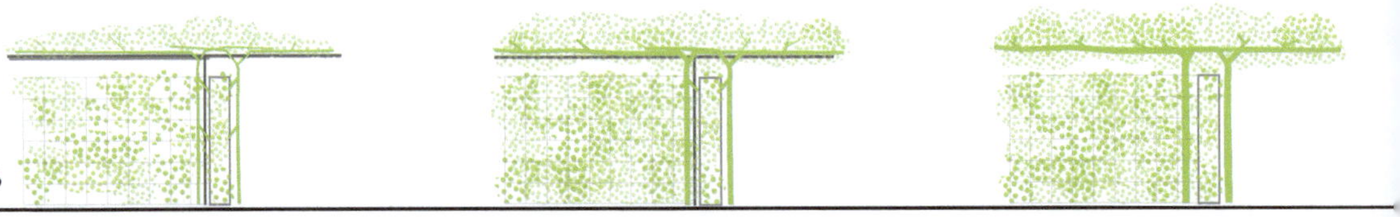

65 The Green Living Room at Rathausplatz in Ludwigsburg showing the planted walls and the baubotanical shading canopies in the year after initial completion (photo: 2013).

66 Projected development over approx. 30 years. The actual growth (especially the annual sprouting after pollarding) has been even more vigorous than shown here.

67 Development of the vegetation (photos: **a** spring 2014, **b** summer 2014, **c** 2015, **d** 2018).

68

68 Inosculation after about eight years of development. In some places, the stems have reached diameters of up to 12 cm (photo: 2021).

7 Utopias and Visions: Living Architecture between Science and Fiction

As a new architectural practice and research discipline, Baubotanik builds on historical, built examples such as the dance linden trees or the living root bridges of the Khasi people. At the same time, like many new forms of architecture, it is also shaped by utopian approaches, speculative designs and visionary concepts.

Arthur Wiechula's "living wooden houses"

An early pioneer in designing with living plants was the gardener Arthur Wiechula (1867—1941), who in the early 20th century began to develop a concrete vision for growing complete residential and commercial buildings from "living wood". In his book *Wachsende Häuser aus lebenden Bäumen entstehend* (Growing Houses from Living Trees), published in 1926, he describes his "natural building method" as follows: "Here it is not a question of forming buildings out of foliage, but of letting the wood itself grow into such forms where it constitutes structural enclosures, structures that have solid walls, doors and windows, and which, like any other house, can be used for purposes of all kinds without fear of snow, rain, wind, cold or heat getting in."[1] To achieve this, he planted trees at close intervals, arranging them like a grid so that he could connect them at the crossing points using specially developed horticultural techniques, procedures and tools similar to those described in → Chapter 3, p. 63, most of which he also patented. Rather than just enabling inosculation where the parts of the tree were interconnected, his method envisaged that the thickness growth would make the individual shoots and trunks gradually merge into a continuous wooden surface clad with bark, resulting not just in walls but also roof surfaces and intermediate floor levels (→ Fig. 1). To create openings, Wiechula suggested simply leaving large openings in the grid into which frames for windows or doors would be inserted at an early stage and subsequently incorporated by the growing structure.

Absolutely sure of his approach, Wiechula was convinced that his techniques made practical and economic sense, shortcutting, as he saw it, the "diversion of planting trees, cutting them down, sawing them into boards and putting them back together again", since the wood would have the right shape from the start. During use, too, his approach had inherent advantages over other building methods, because, he argued, his buildings were "structures with a very long service life but also a low cost which, moreover, gain in value as they continually produce more wood."[2] Surprisingly, the only disadvantage he saw concerned the aesthetics of the building interiors which, in his estimation, could only be used for residential purposes if the inside of the walls were covered with wood or plaster, "so that the home furnishings have a familiar background, and do not offend the eye of the cultured person, which would happen in most cases with natural walls covered with living bark".[3] Alongside their use for residential buildings, he was (unsurprisingly) equally convinced of his method's suitability for garden houses, but also, for example, for railway platform roofs or agricultural buildings (→ Figs. 2, 3).

In view of such fantastic promises, it is hardly surprising that the publication of his book immediately provoked controversy. On the one hand, his approach was celebrated as visionary and forward-looking, while on the other, critics were sceptical, not least because Wiechula was obviously unable to deliver on his promises even in simple projects, such as the planting of a lattice-like snow fence for the Deutsche Reichsbahn. He himself always claimed that his method had

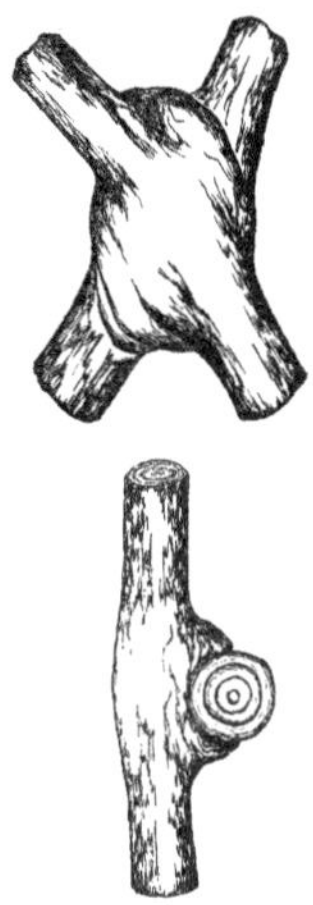

1 a

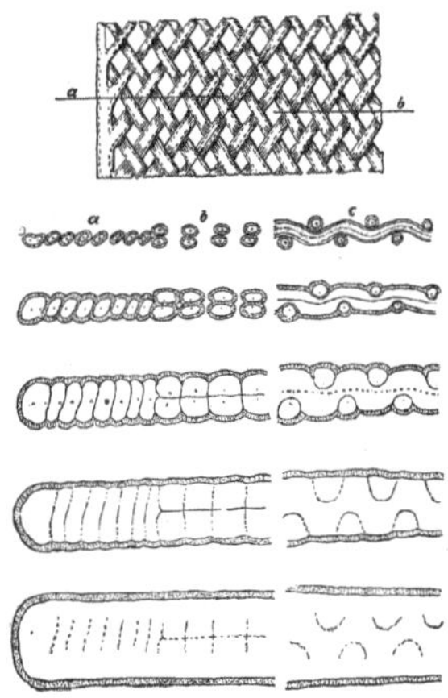

1 b

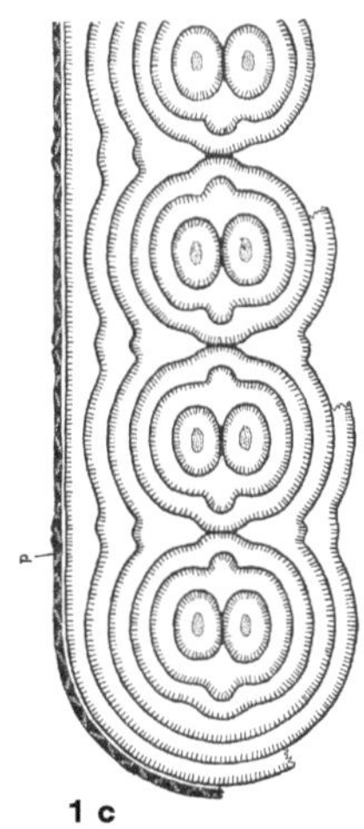

1 c

1 a Elevation and section of inosculated shoots without bark.
b Schematic drawing of how the cross-connected shoots could fuse to form a closed wall.
c Detailed cross-section through such a wall.

proven itself in practice in a series of successfully realised projects. However, evidence of these or even remnants thereof were never found.[4] Even his contemporaries had their doubts: "In his advertisements, Wiechula still produces drawings of living houses and living walls as he did many years ago, although he has not yet been able to produce any such structures. There has been no lack of commissions. But hear for yourselves what the people got for their money!"[5] This critical portrayal coincided with the fact that Wiechula's apparently economical approach soon failed and the business he founded had to file for bankruptcy as early as 1929. It was therefore hard to take the gardener seriously as the rationally reasoned and pragmatic "natural construction engineer" he held himself to be. However, his fantastical drawings have since become icons of plant architecture, although (or precisely because?) they remained unbuilt architectural visions and in all probability could never be realised, as they fundamentally contradict the laws of botany and overestimate the growth potential of trees many times over (→ Chapter 2, p. 28).[6] In the following years and decades, his approach gradually fell into oblivion, although some of his patents for connecting plants were still used for a while by a tree nursery for the production of weaving hedges. Ultimately, it was his techniques for connecting plants that were most innovative and practicable, and in principle they form the basis for today's baubotanical connection techniques with stainless steel screws.

2

2 Arthur Wiechula, Design for a hunters' lookout, replete with a convenient, grown staircase, 1925.

3 Arthur Wiechula, Design for a farm building in which the living wooden wall was to be grown triple-skinned for better thermal insulation, 1925.

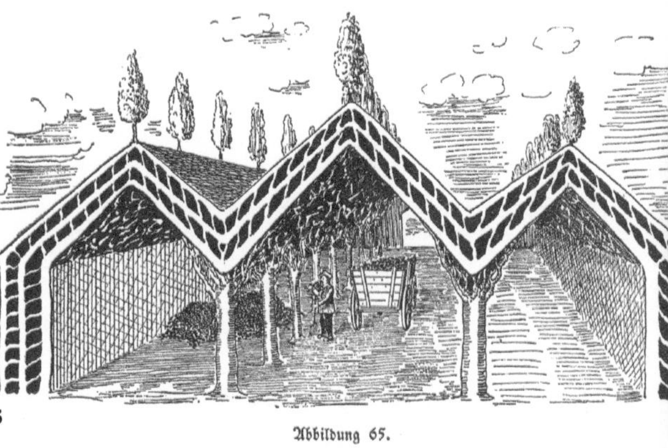

3

The Forest Garden Village by Konstantin Kirsch

Arthur Wiechula's work was rediscovered in the 1980s — more or less simultaneously and independently of each other — by the then architecture student Konstantin Kirsch and the master gardener Herrmann Fritz Block. Taking Wiechula more or less at his word, they started a large number of buildings, also developing their own plant connection techniques based on Wiechula's patents. Some of the structures created by Kirsch (partly together with Block) have meanwhile become the basis of a site near Kassel known as the "forest garden village" (original name: Waldgartendorf), where various living structures in different stages of development can be viewed. Particularly worthy of mention here are a "lime house" in the form of three intersecting domes, as well as an "ash house" consisting of several rooms with a round ground plan[7] and a "beech house". Thanks to years of horticultural upkeep, they have grown into quite impressive structures over the years, often with hundreds of inosculations. In many buildings, the plants are now so large that not only lattice-like wall structures, but also similarly formed roof structures have grown. The structures created by Block in 2001 at the teaching garden at the Hohen Schloss of the Unterallgäu district (Bad Grönenbach, Germany) have also reached a comparable stage of development, including an arbour made of Norway maple (*Acer platanoides*) and one of hornbeam (*Carpinus betulus*).[8] Overall, however, the degree of growth is much lower than Wiechula's original predictions and many plants exhibit only minimal growth in thickness due to the enormous degree of competition between the plants (→ Fig. 4). Wiechela's notion of the closed wall surface has therefore not come to pass, even if Kirsch has in some places achieved something approaching that by repeatedly weaving shoots into the gaps of a lattice wall (→ Fig. 5 a, b).

One should note in this context that Kirsch closely links his vision of a living architecture with a highly problematic right-wing esoteric vision of society. In Germany, he is considered one of the protagonists of the so-called "Anastasia Movement" which advocates, among other things, the creation of "family homesteads". The movement, which originally came from Russia, is based on a series of novels by the Russian author Vladimir Megre. Matthias Quent, an expert on right-wing extremism, classifies the movement as racist and anti-Semitic because it exhibits comparable

4 A beech lattice wall created by Konstantin Kirsch in 1997 (photo: 2008).

ideological patterns to those of National Socialism.[9] While Kirsch distances himself from right-wing extremist ideas, he effectively contributes to their dissemination by distributing Anastasia literature.[10] Like Wiechula before him, Kirsch also has a certain tendency to wilfully ignore scientific facts. Thus, he is unwaveringly convinced that sooner or later he will move into one of his living structures, even though simple calculations of the biomass production of trees and, in principle also his own experience, tell a quite different story. Herrmann Fritz Block is a little more cautious and speaks of his structures as arbours to be used especially in the warmer seasons. Nevertheless, there is no denying that Kirsch has created an impressive body of Baubotanik work that goes far beyond Wiechula's "paper visions" of growing architecture.

5 a Ash lattice wall created by Konstantin Kirsch in 1993, condition in 2008.
b Detail showing a completely inosculated section of the lattice mesh.

6 Outer wall of the ash tree house in 2018 by Konstantin Kirsch, after about 25 years of growth.

The Tree Circus by Axel Erlandson in California

The farmer Axel Erlandson, born in 1884, can be described as a kind of antithesis to the figure of Wiechula's failed visionary. The son of Swedish immigrants, he set himself the goal of creating something new, unprecedented and above all bizarre with trees. This he undoubtedly achieved with his "Tree Circus", a mixture of amusement park and cabinet of curiosities (→ Fig. 9) comprising bizarrely shaped trees, which opened in 1947 in Scotts Valley (California). In addition to a grown entrance portal (→ Fig. 7) and the tower-like "Basket Tree" (→ Fig. 17), his show garden was filled with trees whose trunks were shaped into rings, knots, hearts and even more complex geometries. As historical photographs and the remaining living specimens prove, he succeeded in shaping trees to his will with impressive precision, letting them grow together at defined points, while keeping them largely vital. To achieve this he drew on his practical knowledge of fruit growing, but also on decades of experimentation. The tree sculptures exhibited at the Tree Circus, for example, were not planted there but were grown at Erlandson's place of residence at the time (Hilmar, California) as early as the 1920s (→ Fig. 8). His skills and knowledge earned Erlandson much attention and admiration, but he kept his techniques and experience in shaping the plants to himself, explaining it away simply as "talking to the trees" whenever he was asked.[11] Despite (or perhaps because of) the secrecy surrounding Erlandson's art, a small fan community arose intent on emulating the work of their idol. One of the protagonists of this enthusiastic movement, Richard Reames, coined the term "Arborsculpture" for it.[12] It is therefore all the more remarkable that Erlandson himself saw little future potential in his own work. In one of his last surviving letters, he wrote: "So in a way it would appear that I have learned a kind of profession so late in life that I cannot carry it to near its ultimate possible attainment. But there may not be much lost if such is the case: because the principle things we need in this world are surely food, clothing and shelter, and growing these kind of trees can hardly help to satisfy any of those needs. Perhaps it could be said about the growing of these trees like they called some activities during the First World War; activities which did not contribute in any way to winning of the war were called 'Non-essential industry'."[13]

To a certain extent he was not wrong: from a functional and architectural viewpoint, Erlandson's tree sculptures offer us little, and even as sculptures they are not of particular artistic value. Economically, too, the Tree Circus was not a resounding success, as the hoped-for stream of visitors never materialised.[14] Nevertheless,

7 Grown entrance gate to the Tree Circus by Axel Erlandson in Scotts Valley, California (photo: 1977).

one should not underestimate its influence on today's — and perhaps future — living architecture. Rather, with reference to Rem Koolhaas,[15] one could call his theme park the "Coney Island of Baubotanik". In his book *Delirious New York*, Koolhaas describes how the amusement parks on Coney Island outside New York became a testbed for new technology and urban systems such as electric lighting or the elevator, which went on to play a fundamental role in the emergence of the high-rise metropolis. So, in a way, it is conceivable that Erlandson's playful and whimsical experiments for his Tree Circus have paved the way for later explorations into how future (i.e. green) metropolises could come about. For the field of Baubotanik, the fact that a large number of the complex shaped trees still exist today, continuing to grow after decades, is a stroke of luck, making it possible to conduct wide-ranging investigations to trace and reconstruct their development with a view to validating growth simulations (→ Chapter 8, pp. 196–197).

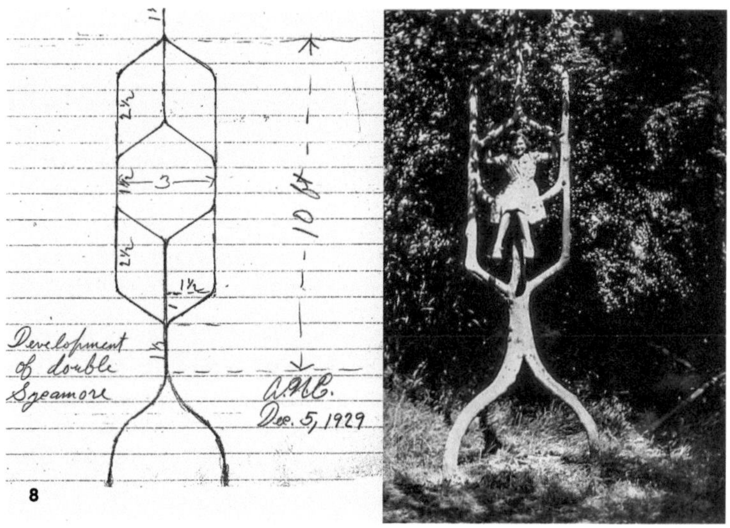

8

8 Axel Erlandson, Sketch for the development of a tree sculpture from American sycamore or Occidental plane tree (*Platanus occidentalis*) by shaping and connecting the shoots, 1929. The photo on the right shows the precision with which Erlandson succeeded in realising his plans (1938).

9 Axel Erlandson's Tree Circus at the time of its opening in 1947. The living trees were transplanted to this site, though many suffered in the process. Many of those seen in this photo recovered soon after, and other tree sculptures were also presented as non-living exhibits (photo: 1946).

The Vegetal City by Luc Schuiten

The Belgian architect and draughtsman Luc Schuiten has been working on a vision of a "baubotanical metropolis" for many years. In the coloured pencil drawings and watercolours of his "vegetal city", trees and buildings often merge to form structures in which grown tree forms flow into organically shaped, technical structures.[16] Starting from a fundamental critique of a modern architecture disconnected from the needs of people and nature and sacrificed to the pursuit of profit, Schuiten develops a counter-model in which not only ecology and sustainability, but also the factor of time in particular play an important role. His urban visions are therefore frequently radical transformations of existing cities such as Brussels or Shanghai. The path to the new, much greener and more people-friendly states he imagines is portrayed as a process lasting many years or even centuries. His design for the "Cité des Vagues" is built on a particularly process-based concept (→ Fig. 10 a, b). This fictitious city, situated on a lake, wanders along the shore over time, its progress and development guided by the change in "capacity" of the forest or the trees that form the basic structure of the architecture: an area of young, growing trees tended to by "gardener-architects" is followed by the "adult" part with strong and vital trees that is also the area inhabited by people. Another part is meanwhile in a state of decay and dying, and destined to become fertile ground from which new trees can grow.[17]

On closer examination, these visionary designs are of course just as unrealisable as Wiechula's fantastical drawings. They are classic architectural utopias that offer a glimpse of a better, but not (necessarily) possible future. By highlighting the aspects of time and process, however, they strike a chord with living architecture and can serve as an inspirational conceptual reference for the design of baubotanical architecture and cities. Their applicability to future

10 a

10 Luc Schuiten: **a** bird's eye view and **b** interior of a living space of the Cité des Vagues.

10 b

projects also results from Schuiten's own history as a visionary architect. Born in 1944, he has not only created an impressive oeuvre of drawings over the past decades, but also an extensive body of actual built works. Alongside a series of residential buildings, he was a pioneer of ecological building and realised an energy-autonomous house as far back as 1977. Formal references such as organically shaped windows with subdivisions reminiscent of branches, evoke diverse connections between his actual built works and visionary drawings. As such they oscillate between formal analogies and structural or systemic principles, just like his drawings. Schuiten also tests the practical realisation of his ideas of living architecture through experimental buildings and installations. The first and so far only comprehensive and permanent project of this kind is the Cité végétale d'Arte Sella. While not actually a city, the project featuring four 10 m high "tree tepees" at Arte Sella land art park in northern Italy nevertheless built an entirely viable bridge between Schuiten's large-scale urban visions and a possible, perhaps equally far-reaching future way of realisation (→ Fig. 11). In concrete terms, around 50 birch and rowan trees along with climbing plants form a "living façade" around the rooms constructed from round timbers. In one of these rooms, a centrally arranged spiral staircase leads to a platform on the first floor, from which one can reach the first floor of another dome via a bridge also constructed of round timbers. The fact that the architect regularly returns to the site to maintain and guide the development of the living structures together with the park's gardeners can be seen as a corresponding real-life variant of the processual character of his visions.

Schuiten's drawing style and formal language, as well as his approach in general, align most readily with the genre of solar punk. This optimistic variety of science fiction postulates a future in which humankind has succeeded in renouncing fossil fuels and nuclear power and has found a more harmonious way to coexist with the environment. Electricity is generated by solar, wind and water power and cities have been transformed into green metropolises. The climate crisis and pollution have been overcome, and inclusion and diversity are a self-evident part of human coexistence. Other protagonists working in the genre, or more precisely at the transition between the visions of solar punk and actual planning and related research, include the work of the New York-based group Terreform One headed by Mitchell Joachim, specifically their Fab Tree Hab and "Home Alive" concepts.[18]

11 The "tree tepees" planted by Luc Schuiten in Arte Sella in northern Italy in 2012 form a bridge between his visionary drawings and a possible real-life variant of them.

The Botanic Architecture of Mark Primack

Although the genre of solar punk only emerged some ten years ago, the visions developed by Mark Primack in the 1970s would fit the genre. Primack's fantastical pencil drawings show plants inhabited by humans, in particular vast leaf formations that the inhabitants have caused to swell and grow, much like gall wasps, through targeted biochemical manipulation of their growth (→ Fig. 12).

The series of drawings, that often resembles comics, evolved as part of Primack's thesis on Botanic Architecture (1974) at the Architectural Association (AA) under the then director Peter Cook (archigram). A short time later, the graduate moved to California, where, by chance, he learned of the existence of the Tree Circus (→ pp. 179—180). After some searching, Primack was able to locate the park, which by then was not only completely overgrown but also under threat of destruction: sold as building land, the bulldozers were ready to clear it. At literally the last minute, Primack and a group of friends, calling themselves "Commando Gardeners", managed to have the clearing work temporarily postponed. With the help of grant funding, Primack used his drawing talent to document the remaining pieces of tree sculpture in meticulously accurate pencil drawings, which he later used as a basis for further speculative designs (→ Fig. 13). For these, he used frontal black-and-white photographs over which he drew a grid (→ Fig. 14). The fragments of the wall structure shown on the left, resembling a Gothic arched window, no longer exist today, but the remains of the structure on the right, reminiscent of the posts and headbands of a traditional half-timbered gate, still exist in a

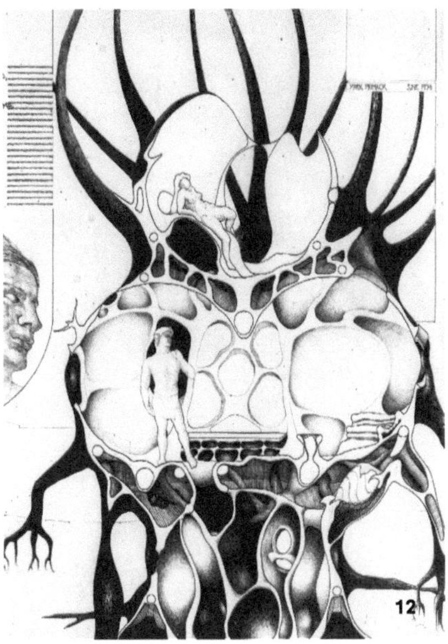

12 According to Mark Primack's vision of Botanic Architecture (1974), humans could in future live in nodule-like plant galls that emerge through biochemical manipulation of plant growth.

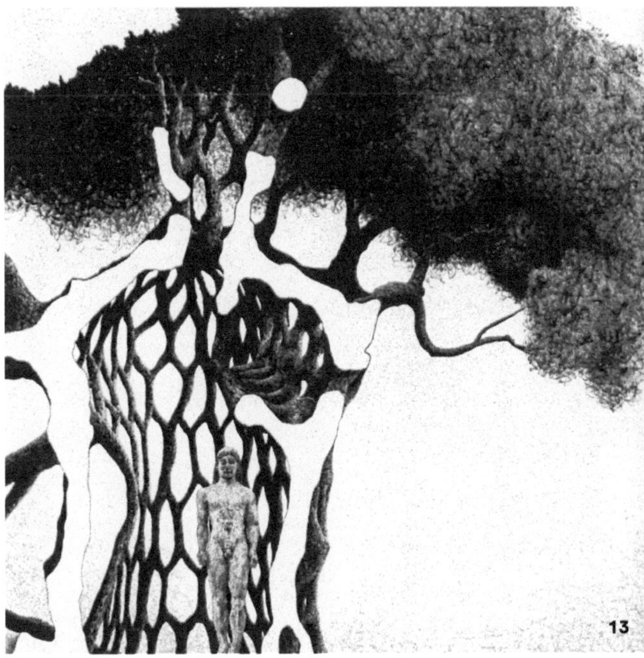

13 Detail from a drawing by Mark Primack (primitive hut — section 2) from 1979, which he developed from a drawing from his documentation of the Tree Circus.

similar form. They are the only trees sculpted by Erlandson to survive on the original Tree Circus site, and stand somewhat forlornly in the corner of a car park in front of a two-storey commercial building: the "Tree Circus Center".

The fact that 25 more of Erlandson's tree sculptures have survived to this day is due to the fact that Primack's activities attracted the attention of the entrepreneur and tree lover Michael Bonfante. Bonfante, sensing a business opportunity in the making, sold the supermarket chain he inherited and invested more than US $ 100 million in his amusement park "Bonfante Gardens". The centrepiece of the park comprises Erlandson's tree sculptures, which Bonfante had excavated from their original location in 1984 and transported in a perilous undertaking with huge heavy goods vehicles to Gilroy, some 100 km away, where they can still be viewed today—partly from a monorail train specially constructed around them (→ Figs. 15—17). However, this amusement park was barely more economically successful than Erlandson's Tree Circus. It was bought by the city of Gilroy in 2007 to avert bankruptcy and has since been known as Gilroy Gardens.[19]

14 Overgrown living architectures of the Tree Circus by Axel Erlandson. Mark Primack drew a grid over the photos to make his scale drawings (1978).

15 Erlandson's tree sculptures in what is now Gilroy Gardens. Here one sees the archway shown in → Fig. 7 with Mark Primack standing beneath it (photo: 2017).

16 The "Four-Legged Giant" in the Gilroy Gardens was planted by Axel Erlandson back in 1929 and is the oldest living tree in the series (photo: 2017).

17 One of Axel Erlandson's most famous sculptures: the Basket Tree (photo: 2017).

Baubotanik — between science and vision

The recent past of living architecture is thus full of dazzling personalities and stories that are as fascinating as they are bizarre. This legacy is something of a double-edged sword for the current practice of Baubotanik: if all that people remember are esoteric world views, economically failed ventures and unrealistic ideas, it risks quickly falling into disrepute. Why should anyone believe in bold new visions of living architecture when the past shows that they are unrealisable? One must take a more differentiated view and distinguish between visionary designs and architectural utopias on the one hand and "promises of salvation" on the other. To the latter one can count Wiechula, who touted his fantastical drawings as actual possible solutions, despite the fact that his own experience and scientific knowledge of the day clearly contradicted them. The former — architectural utopias that deliberately open up spaces of possibility and, as an art form, blur the boundary between the possible and the impossible — can be seen in the work of Schuiten and Primack. Their work reveals potential, broadens horizons and the same time elaborates a notion of the inherent characteristics of living architecture. How one engages with these is a matter of personal perspective — do they merely represent a diversion that clouds a clear view of the facts and what is really possible, or are they a challenge and opportunity with the potential to motivate new initiatives. The following and final chapter attempts to identify a possible pathway by interweaving emerging lines of baubotanical research and engineering with design approaches that draw on visionary precursors without losing touch with well-grounded botanical facts.

18 The Four Legged Giant after transplantation to Bonfante Gardens in Gilroy (photo: 1988).

8 Vers une Arbotecture: Towards a Future Tree Architecture

Between the bold visions of designers like Luc Schuiten and his "Vegetal City" or Mark Primack and his "Botanic Architecture" and the current state of research and practice in Baubotanik lies quite a distance that we have yet to cover. The preceding chapters have discussed manifold potentials of designing and constructing with trees, but also shown the natural limits of growth in Baubotanik. Many of the possibilities at hand are illustrated by the examples presented in → Chapter 6, most of which are historical projects, landscape or artistic installations and experimental structures that explore the constructional, design and ecological possibilities of living structures. However, to make a lasting and more far-reaching contribution to improving our living conditions, Baubotanik must progress beyond the niche of experimental constructions and be applied at a broader scale and in diverse ways in all manner of urban landscapes. To achieve this, two things are needed: first, research and testing of new tools and approaches that enable true co-design between humans and trees, and second, systematic exploration of new hybrid tree architectures in concrete designs.

A new interplay between trees and people

To properly leverage the potential of the interplay between tree growth and design by humans in Baubotanik, it is instructive to take another look at the Khasi people's living bridges. As with all forms of vernacular architecture, their development is characterised first of all by the fact that no construction plan is drawn up at the outset to describe their form and construction. The only goal is the intention to overcome a topographical obstacle such as a gorge or river as safely and comfortably as possible. This then serves as the impetus for initial design decisions, such as where to plant the trees whose aerial roots will later form the bridge. Over time, the respective state of development is compared year for year against the intended objective, and suitable techniques are then chosen to get one step closer to it by influencing the structure's growth. There is still no set construction or design solution, rather the path is constantly sought anew depending on the actual state of development and accompanying boundary conditions influencing it. This complex approach draws on centuries-old knowledge, traditionally passed down orally, as well as on the individual experience of the master bridge builders, who are able not only to assess the current condition, but also to intuitively forecast the tree's growth and development and incorporate these into the design and maintenance decisions they make.[1]

How then can the essence of this approach be made useful for the conception, design and ongoing maintenance of works of modern living architecture? Classical architectural design and planning tools focus primarily on drawing forms or constructions and thus hardly seem suitable for mapping complex and dynamic processes. That is also probably the reason why iterative and ongoing design processes — which take into account plant development as well as suitable guiding measures has rarely been used in Baubotanik, or for that matter in other areas of architecture and landscape architecture. However, new methods of computer-aided design, mechanical modelling, simulation of plant growth and innovative technologies for capturing complex geometries and structures do offer ways of addressing this complexity. At the Baubotanik Research Group at the Technical University of Munich, digital workflows are therefore being investigated that make it possible to design and continuously manage different forms of living architecture.[2]

Digital capture of dynamically changing structures

To understand the growth processes of baubotanical structures, a way of continually recording their changing geometry is indispensable. New optical methods for documenting the three-dimensional form of trees and other geometrically complex constructions have developed in recent years that produce 3D point clouds. These include various laser scanning (LiDAR) approaches or the much more cost-effective method of photogrammetry in which a digital point cloud is constructed from multiple relative camera positions. In 2018/19, the Baubotanik Research Group undertook the first comprehensive photogrammetric 3D documentation of living architecture, including extensive scans of nine aerial root bridges in Meghalaya. Using digital point clouds, one can examine and classify the intergrown (inosculated) nodes in greater detail and record and evaluate significant details such as injuries, callus formations as well as decayed areas. By evaluating certain parts of the point clouds, "sections" can be made of plant shoots, which can be used, for example, to estimate the load-bearing capacity (→ Figs. 1, 2 a—c).[3]

To be able to use these 3D data for physiological and mechanical investigations of the baubotanical structure, structural models need to be generated from the point cloud data that accurately map the connection points and axis lines between them. Geometric features that are important for material transport, growth and biomechanics such as thickness, curvature and length of the elements, must be retained, while at the same time reducing the overall amount of data. In the case of the living bridges, which are highly complex and have very dense inosculated root structures, a special procedure was developed to generate a skeleton model from the point clouds in successive steps (→ Fig. 3 a—d). The procedure can be used both for individual nodal points and for large and complex inosculated structures (→ Fig. 4 a, b).[4] It provides an important basis for undertaking meaningful structural calculations and making reliable development forecasts—which is essential for the broader application of Baubotanik in urban contexts that are more challenging. The structural models, and the calculations and simulations derived from them, similarly serve as an important basis for decisions regarding the maintenance, training and shaping of roots and shoots, as well as for the addition of technical elements. As such, they represent a starting point for the evolution of iterative, development-responsive design approaches, and are, in effect, a digital equivalent of the Khasi's intuitive approach based on their experiential knowledge.

1

1 Point cloud of the bridge in Nongbareh, India, and the riverbed beneath which is exposed during the dry season.

2 a

2 b

2 c

2 a Point cloud of a complex inosculated node. The camera positions are shown in blue. **b** Point cloud of a simple cross-inosculation. **c** Section of a point cloud for assessing the load-bearing bridge cross-section.

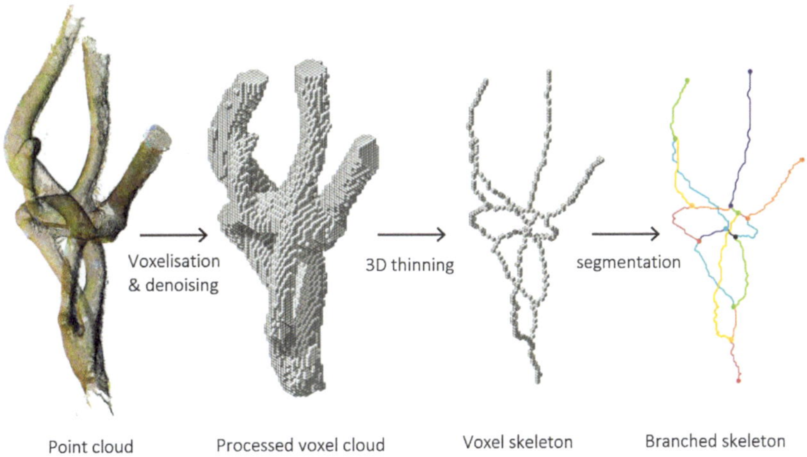

3 a 3 b 3 c 3 d

3 Abstraction steps for generating **d** a structural model from **a** a point cloud via **b, c** voxel models. Complex node created by the knotting of aerial roots.

4 a

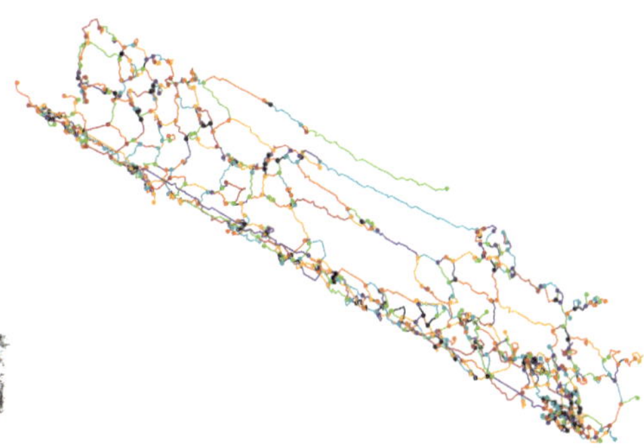

4 b

4 a Point cloud and **b** skeleton model of a section of a bridge.

A continuous computer-aided design process

A pilot project for this approach was Arbor Kitchen, a Baubotanik pavilion for an outdoor kitchen in Wald-Ruhestetten (Germany). The project, which was conducted as part of a design studio,[5] took a group of plane trees (*Platanus × hispanica*) planted on an oval ground plan nine years beforehand as its starting point. Since their planting, the trees had been directed first upwards at an angle and then towards the centre at a height of about 3 m with the intention of one day supporting a roof. Aside from this, however, there were no concrete plans or construction drawings for the actual roof structure. This served as the starting point for a digital workflow comprising the photogrammetric survey and abstraction of the tree structure, the parametric design of a corresponding technical roof construction and the subsequent prefabrication and installation of the resulting components.

After generating photogrammetric point clouds of the tree structures with the help of a drone, skeleton models of the main trunks and the most important branches were made. The basic geometry of the roof structure was then derived from the shape of the upwards-arching branches and translated into a parametric model of the space frame which holds the roof cladding and into which the branches can grow (→ Fig. 5 a—c). The branches can then continue to grow below the roof, meeting at the ridge, where they will be partially connected so that over time they form a tree crown that extends above the roof. In keeping with this design, the space frame was manufactured as a filigree, lightweight structure consisting of steel rebars with a diameter of only 8 mm. This structure was then installed in the tree, which had previously been pruned back to its main branches. A roof cladding of semi-transparent plastic shingles was then applied (→ Figs. 6, 8).

During assembly, no significant modifications were necessary and almost all the prefabricated technical components showed a deviation of less than 1 % from their planned position. This demon-

5 Form-finding process of the roof structure of the Arbor Kitchen, Wald-Ruhestetten, Ferdinand Ludwig, Wilfrid Middelton, Qiguan Shu and project team.
a Photogrammetric point cloud.
b Skeleton model of the main trunks and branches.
c Space frame of the roof structure.

5 a

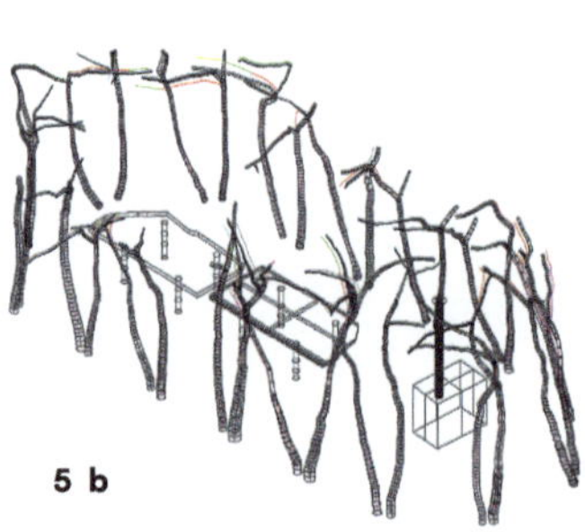

5 b

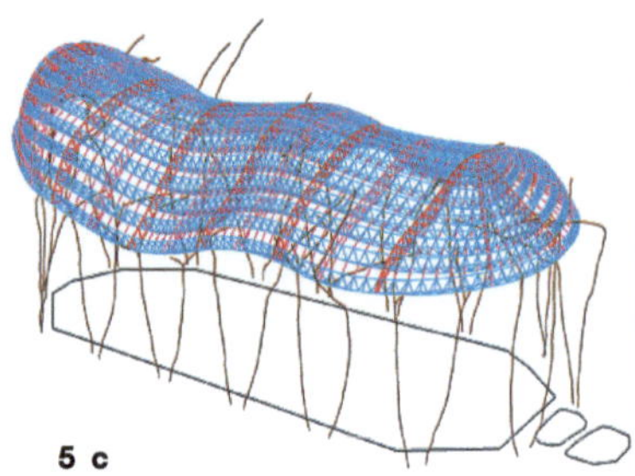

5 c

6 Arbor Kitchen, Wald-Ruhestetten. Installation of the space frame on the pre-formed branches (2021).

strates the potential of digital tools for Baubotanik, as without them such an exact adaptation of the technical parts to the tree geometry and thus a response to tree growth would not be possible (→ Fig. 7). As the trees grow, regular laser scans document shoot development, thickness growth and the overgrowth of technical components by the trees, providing a basis for making decisions on maintenance and design measures to maintain or further improve the load-bearing capacity of the construction and functionality of the roof, depending on the pattern development. To make properly informed decisions, however, one also requires models describing the response of trees to growth conditions and maintenance measures, and thus also how their mechanical performance develops.[6]

7 Arbor Kitchen, Wald-Ruhestetten. Overlay of a laser scan with the digital planning after installation of the roof construction.

8 Arbor Kitchen, Wald-Ruhestetten. In the first summer after the installation of the roof, the trees of the baubotanical structure sprout at the eaves and the ridge (photo: summer 2022).

8

Simulation of thickness growth and load-bearing behaviour

The application of living structures has until now been held back by, among other things, insufficient knowledge of future growth states and their corresponding mechanical properties. The aim of research in this field is therefore to apply already extensive expertise from forestry and horticultural sciences, plant biomechanics, tree statics and structural design to developing growth simulations and mechanical modelling or computational methods for the structural design and assessment of the mechanical performance of living structures.

In tree statics, nowadays standardised experimental procedures and statistical methods for assessing the stability and safety of trees have been established while for naturally grown trees, mechanical models allow for simulating static and dynamic loads.[7] By combining three-dimensional structural models with functional plant models,[8] the physiological processes can be described, making it possible to model growth patterns in response to environmental factors or interventions in the structure (such as pruning).[9] In Baubotanik, however, trunks, branches or roots are joined to form complex structures that through their inosculations acquire new mechanical and physiological properties. Here the existing models are insufficient and need either further development or supplementing with additional models. To this end, a prototypical design tool was developed that makes it possible to predict growth in thickness and with it relevant information on the development of mechanical and physiological parameters.[10] The basis for these calculations is the relationship between water transport (xylem flow) and growth in thickness described in → Chapter 2, pp. 47—49 according to the pipe model theory and the resistance model that describes how the xylem flow in an inosculated structure takes the path of least resistance. Using this model basis, and a skeleton model of a designed or existing growing structure, the tool then simulates the thickness growth of the individual sections. This can be used to estimate the potential development consequences of a design decision or maintenance measure for the structure and its parts so that one can determine where growth will flourish or decline, and which areas are at more risk of dying than others. To demonstrate the applicability of the tool for more complex situations, it was tested on several typical cases, as well as some of the complex inosculated structures (→ Fig. 9 a, b) at the Tree Circus in California described in → Chapter 7, pp. 179—180.[11]

These growth forecasts provide an important basis for predicting a structure's mechanical properties. However, determining or computing the load-bearing capacity proves to be extremely challenging, especially with respect to the complex internal structure of wood at the inosculation points.[12] Anatomical studies have, however, shown that inosculations can be realistically described in mechanical terms as two-sided branch junctions.[13] This means that research findings on the biomechanics of branch junctions can be transferred to inosculated joints. Initial measurements and finite element calculations on approximately ten-year-old inosculations indicate that the joints do not usually constitute weak points in the overall system. Once appropriate measurement methods have been established it will in principle be possible to compute the load-bearing behaviour of a baubotanical structure at any point in its development in the same way as that of trees in tree statics.

9 a "Needle and Thread Tree" at the Tree Circus. **b** The diameter relations of the development prognosis determined by the Baubotanik Research Group correspond almost entirely to the actual development (software: Rhino7/Grasshopper).

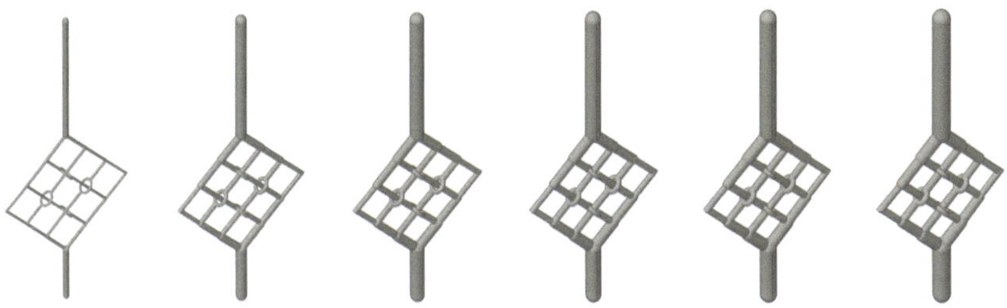

9 b

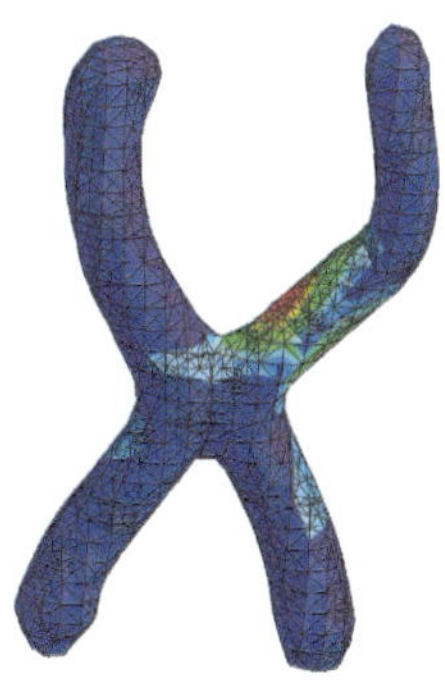

10 b

10 a Preparation of a pulling test on a crosswise inosculation with elastometers to measure the strain in the material and inclinometers to measure the deflection (W. Middleton, Q. Shu et al., Baubotanik Research Group with A. Detter, Tree-Consult, Munich). **b** Modelling the deformation in a finite element model of a comparable inosculation (W. Middleton, H. Erdal).

Designing new tree architecture

The development of future forms of living architecture using trees is about finding a productive synergy between systemic and technical factors and design and atmospheric aspects. For this we must question and rethink some key approaches and established methods of architectural and urban design. The following examples from the work of Office for Living Architecture (OLA)[14] explore a range of possible approaches to tree architecture with a view to providing an outlook on aspects that could become central to a future "Arbotecture".

12

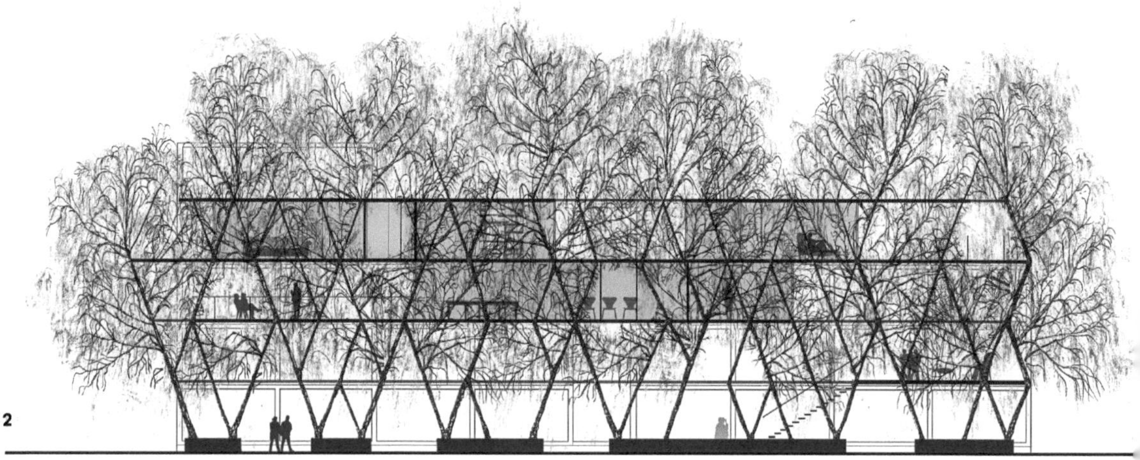

Inhabited trees

While for traditional tree houses, an already-grown tree provides the framework for its technical construction, in baubotanical design it is the growth of a plant and its associated development that are the primary defining aspects. On the one hand, this represents one of the greatest challenges when designing, but on the other it also presents a unique way of conceiving of architectural concepts in the fourth dimension by relating programmatic and structural changes to natural growth. The competition entry Grow! (→ Figs. 11, 12) by Office for Living Architecture (with Isabel Finkenberger) for Hubland, a new urban district in the city of Würzburg (Europan 11, open single-stage urban planning ideas competition, 2011) connects the timeline of the evolution of a new urban district with the growth of baubotanical constructions. The concept acknowledges that a neighbourhood development plan can never cater for or fully anticipate all the needs of its future residents, and that needs and space requirements will change over time. To address these, the project proposed baubotanical structures between the buildings that will "grow" as the needs of the neighbourhood gradually evolve, providing new spaces with distinctive atmospheric qualities. These new spaces are located in the crowns of the baubotanical structures and can be accessed

11 Grow! Visualisation of vertically arranged private outdoor space as an expansion of residential living space into the "baubotanical tree crown".

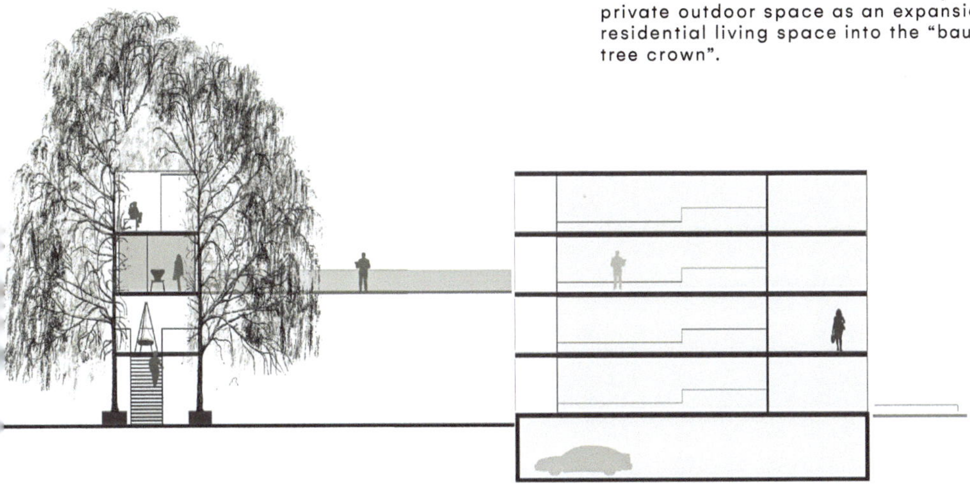

12 Grow! Elevation and section from a competition entry by OLA for the new Hubland district of Würzburg, 2011. Living, growing constructions create new inhabitable spaces in the tree canopy that can be used as an extension of living space after a few years of development.

via walkways from the flats or balconies. Once the living structures have acquired sufficient load-bearing capacity, they will be made available for use and for fitting out with technical components such as façade elements. As green spaces with special spatial and sensory qualities, the living structures contribute to the unique identity of the neighbourhood from the very beginning. At the same time, the future prospect of being able to gain private outdoor space as an expansion of one's living space increases the residents' sense of identification with the tree constructions and creates a strong incentive for them to look after them and ensure their health and growth.

Urban transformations

The distinctive possibilities that Baubotanik offer for accompanying, influencing and enhancing urban transformation can be seen in the competition entry Prato in Caelo by OLA[15] (→ Figs. 13–16, Invited two-phase competition, 2016, 2nd prize) for a new urban park in Prato, Italy. For the conversion of a former hospital site into a public green space, a series of "acts" was proposed much like in a theatre production: the gradual deconstruction of the hospital, the successive opening of the site and the emergence of new public spaces are accompanied by the growth of green structures in the park. The focus here is not on an end result and its finished form but on experiencing the process of change and transformation that is ultimately never entirely finished.

Topographical and architectural elements from various previous phases of use are retained and made legible. To this, a series of iconic baubotanical towers is added as a new layer complementing the skyline of Prato, which already has numerous buildings of varying height from different epochs. Comprising the preserved access towers from the hospital and trees jointed into baubotanical structures, the tree towers symbolically link the past with the future. The project proposed pre-cultivating the trees in a publicly accessible nursery on the site, and then attaching them to the towers at different heights, connecting them to each other using the method of plant addition. After ten to 20 years, the plants will have fused into one organism that can sustain itself independently from the soil (→ Chapter 3, p. 81). In future, the inosculated structures with their concrete cores — the reused stairwells and lift shafts of the hospital — will bear witness to the profound social, cultural, ecological and economic transformation of Prato.

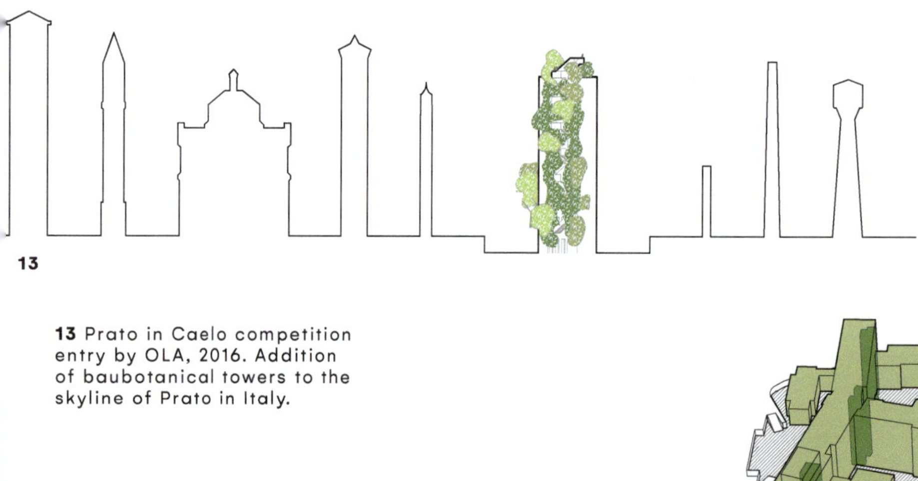

13

13 Prato in Caelo competition entry by OLA, 2016. Addition of baubotanical towers to the skyline of Prato in Italy.

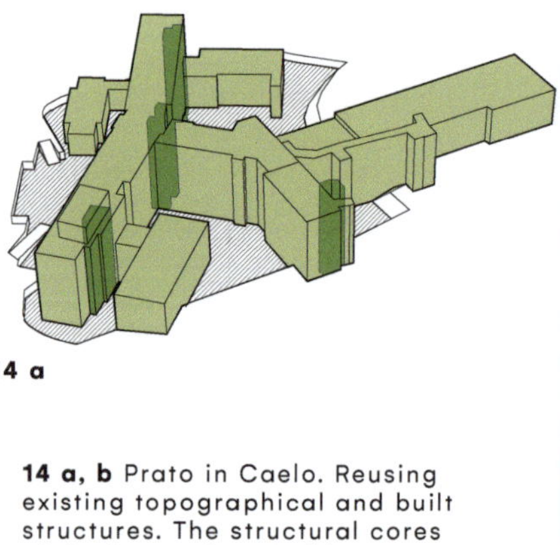

14 a

14 a, b Prato in Caelo. Reusing existing topographical and built structures. The structural cores of the former hospital housing the lift and stair shafts are transformed into the internal support structure of the baubotanical towers.

15

15 Prato in Caelo. Visualisation of how the park with its baubotanical towers and public tree nursery (in the background) could look in 20 to 30 years.

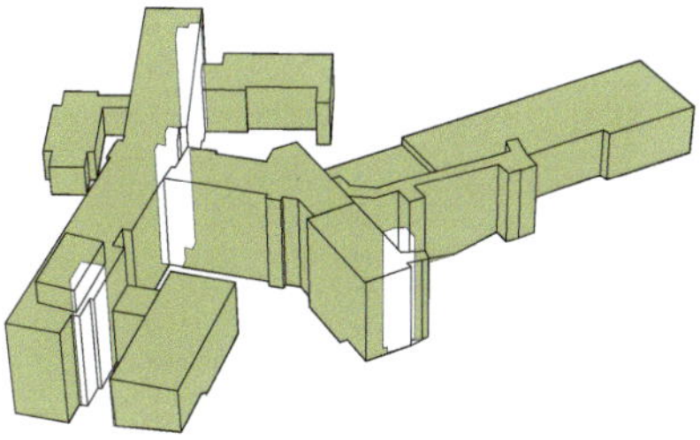

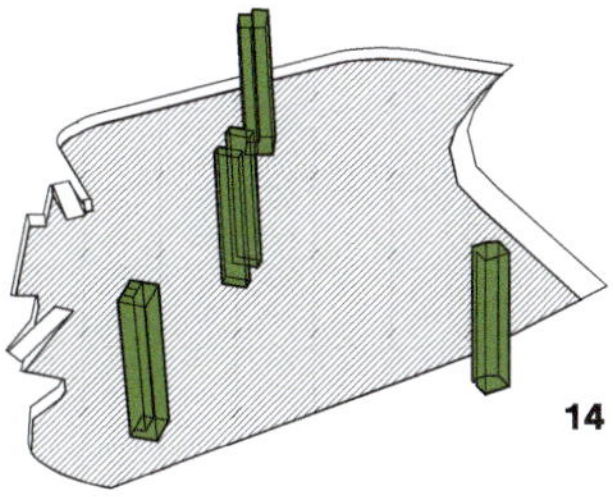

14 b

16 a, b, c Prato in Caelo. Creation of the baubotanical towers through plant addition. The trees would be pre-cultivated in a publicly accessible nursery on the site. Unsuitable plants remain as a "park of invalid trees".

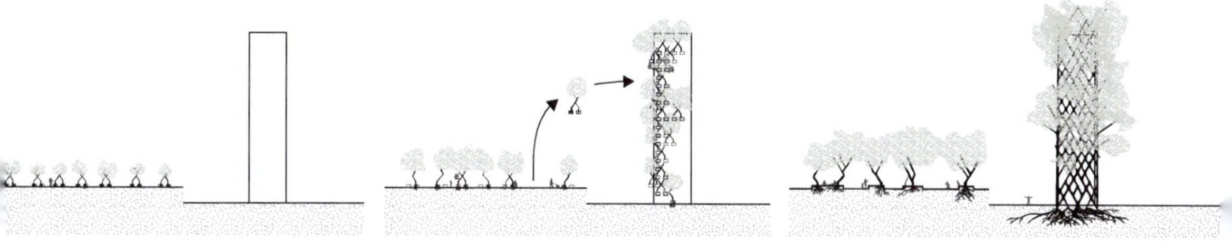

16 a

16 b

16 c

Vertical parks

As cities become increasingly more built-up, the need for high-quality green spaces grows while land resources become ever more scarce. One response to this competition for space is to design vertically usable green outdoor spaces.[16] Baubotanik can play a key role here as trees are essentially self-supporting and can—depending on the tree species—also reach great heights. The Park-Haus Züblin is a model project developed in 2016 as part of the KLIMOPASS[17] research programme (→ Figs. 17—19) and focuses on ways in which neighbourhood parks can be created in inner-city locations that, as part of a city's urban green infrastructure, offer high amenity and recreational value on a small surface area while also playing an active role in urban water management. The objective is to transform urban heat islands into cooling oases with high biodiversity, and in the process to upgrade the surrounding urban districts in their design and what they offer their residents.

The design project proposes converting existing buildings for use as vertical open spaces, thereby retaining the grey energy stored within them rather than investing primary energy in their demolition and a new construction. As a model project, the design proposes the selective deconstruction of parts of a multi-storey car park so that a continuous series of dense green horizontal and vertical spaces results. The remaining, robust parts of the structure can serve as meeting places, public facilities for sports and exercise or for cultural uses. In the initial stages, they can also temporarily house plant support facilities and a rainwater retention cistern for supplying the plants of the baubotanical structure. Once the inosculations are sufficiently advanced and the plants have merged and can feed themselves from the soil at ground level, these can then be successively removed. The resulting vertical park contributes to the urban climate and can be described as a publicly accessible and barrier-free inhabitable tree canopy that can be used for a variety of urban uses.

17 KLIMOPASS model project Park-Haus Züblin, Stuttgart, Ferdinand Ludwig, Daniel Schönle and Moritz Bellers, 2015. Section showing the different uses such as climbing, walking or skateboarding. The space is characterised by an interplay of complex inosculated trunks and the exposed concrete structure.

17

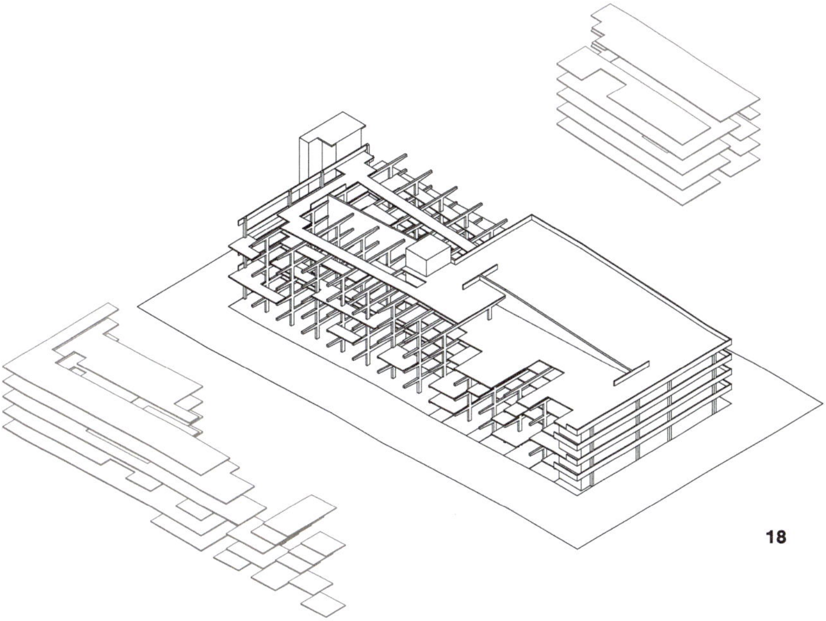

18

18 Park-Haus Züblin. Partial deconstruction and partial reuse of the existing building fabric of the multi-storey car park.

19 Park-Haus Züblin. Visualisation of the interior of the vertical park.

Street tree façades

In discussions on improving the urban climate, a conflicting situation often arises that can't easily be solved using traditional landscape architecture or urban design solutions. While mature street trees provide shade and cool the local microclimate, they can also impair the flow of fresh air that ventilates urban spaces and thus negatively impact the local urban climate (→ Chapter 5, pp. 112–113). The merging of street trees into the building frontage to form "tree façades" could potentially defuse this conflict. The Baubotanical Street Typologies model project (→ Figs. 20–22), which was also developed as part of the KLIMOPASS research programme, uses a district in the development stage as an example to show how new urban building blocks can combine the ecological potential of innovative tree architecture with high quality outdoor experiences and multiple uses. The result is a very large green volume that effectively cools and shades the building façades while at the same time, due to its linear placement in the plane of the building façades, ensures that the street space is well ventilated.

Two building types were developed for different building orientations: where house fronts face east or north, the tree canopy serves as a semi-public access zone. The baubotanical layer can be seen here as a kind of vertical front garden that turns each residential unit into a house in the tree canopy. For apartments facing west or south, the baubotanical layer serves as a filter to the public space and as a visual screen between the separate residential units. Here, the layouts of the flats are extended outwards using projecting oriels and balconies into the baubotanical layer, creating diverse relationships with the tree canopy and street space.

20

20 KLIMOPASS Model Project Baubotanical Street Typologies, Stuttgart, Ferdinand Ludwig, Daniel Schönle and Moritz Bellers, 2015. Axonometry of a south-west facing façade with projecting bay windows and balconies in the tree canopy.

21 Baubotanical Street Typologies. Green access balconies and stairs serve as a semi-public vertical green space providing access to the apartments.

22 Baubotanical Street Typologies. Two facing rows of houses with integral baubotanical façades create a new type of street space that is at once green but also well ventilated.

Houses as trees

As a pioneering form of green architecture and ecological urban landscapes, Baubotanik stands for the closer interweaving of technical building processes and natural growth processes. Inevitably, this leads to greater uncertainty in the way that structures arise and age over time. Because they question classical design, construction and maintenance processes, and at the same time continuously change in their appearance, baubotanical projects are also emblematic of an increasing awareness of processual aspects in architecture and urban planning. They are always changing, their outcome remains uncertain and their condition unfinished.

In the competition entry by OLA[18] for the House of the Future in Berlin (→ Figs. 23—27, open two-phase planning competition, 2012, 3rd prize), the entire building is enveloped in a baubotanical construction so that it presents itself to the city as a large, artificially formed tree. Behind this outer screen, a wide ramp winds upwards directly adjoining the tree-glass façade, so that visitors can experience the tree canopy at different levels. The exhibition spaces, divided into themed galleries, are situated in the solid core of the building, which also houses all the other main functions.

As detailed in the competition brief, the House of the Future sees itself as a window into the world of tomorrow. Its aim is to help people and society understand the opportunities and risks of science-based innovations, and to discuss their sustainability and how to respond to them in an enlightened manner. The proposed design addresses this challenge with the idea of a building whose future is uncertain — a building that is growing and that we cannot predict exactly how it will look. Its uncertain appearance is not, however, a problem; rather, it reflects the programmatic purpose of the building, which is intended to show us things that we do not yet know how they will look.

At the same time, the baubotanical façade is an integral part of the climatic building concept: both the exterior and interior benefit from the cooling effect of the inosculated tree structure. Rainwater and grey water that arise on the site are collected and stored as a resource for supplying the plants with water, and thus indirectly for the building's air conditioning, in turn making a virtue of a disposal problem.[19] The project proposal therefore combines design, ecological and programmatic aspects into a holistic concept and illustrates the diverse potential of Baubotanik in the design of buildings.

23

23 Competition entry for House of the Future, Berlin, OLA, 2012. Situated on the Spreebogen, the building seems at first sight to be a large "tree" in the otherwise hard urban landscape of Berlin. The drawing shows how through Baubotanik, the urban figure ground plan and the green plan coincide.

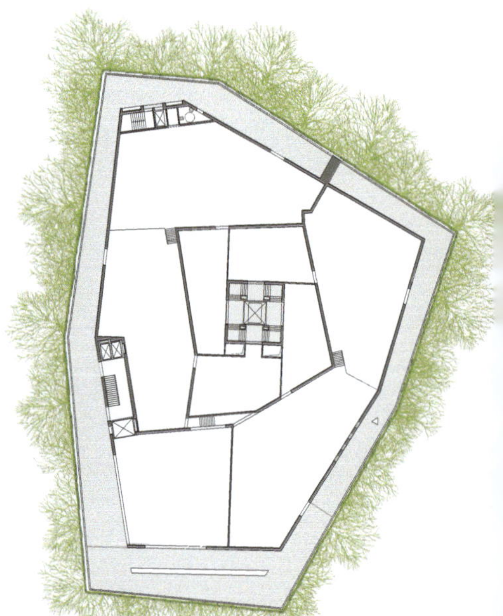

24

25 a

25 b

25 House of the Future. Elevation of the façade development over time.
a After approx. five years (left) and after ten years (right) when the column-like planters can then be gradually removed.
b After approx. 20 years.

26 House of the Future. Energy and water management concept. The building is supplied almost exclusively by locally available resources. The baubotanical façade is an integral part of the climatic concept.

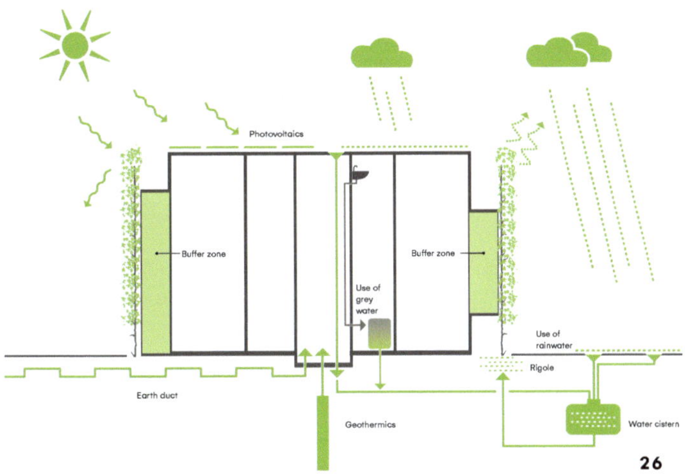

26

24 House of the Future. Floor plan of an exhibition area. The exhibition spaces, which are staggered in height, are accessed via a ramp inside the perimeter of the baubotanical façade.

A paradigm shift

The sharp differentiation between city or house on the one hand and landscape or nature on the other has become increasingly fragile in recent decades and is beginning to erode. The old notions that protecting nature means renouncing building, or that expanding cities means consuming landscape are being increasingly challenged. Architecture, landscape architecture and urban planning are gradually getting the better of a dilemma that has paralysed the disciplines for decades. Thinking only in terms of either-or suggests that any form of building or redesign of the environment entails destroying nature. However much we declare our commitment to sustainability, it does little to appease our sense of guilt and our bad conscience, because ultimately sustainable construction and management only limits the ecological damage we cause; we cause it all the same. The idea that we can improve the natural balance through built interventions is not inherent to this way of thinking. "Regenerative design", by contrast, goes a decisive step further. It begins by undoing a traditional opposition: humans are not a counterpoint to nature, but a co-creating part of nature. In this scenario, the person who designs and builds takes on the role of a gardener, and the environment that of a garden, rather than a placeholder for "pure nature". A gardener does

27 House of the Future. Visualisation of the building from the south. Its appearance changes over the years and with the seasons.

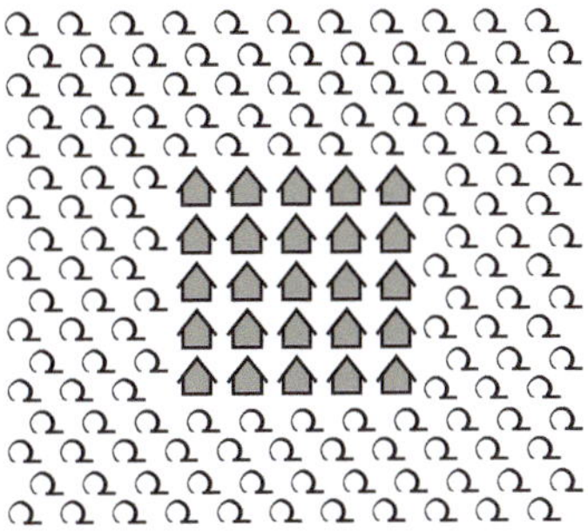

28 a

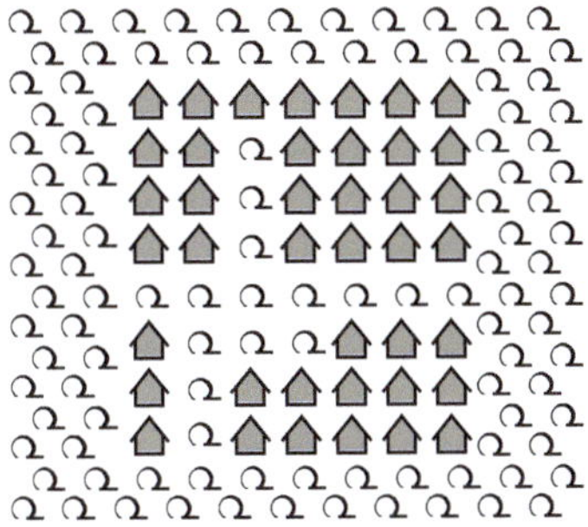

28 b

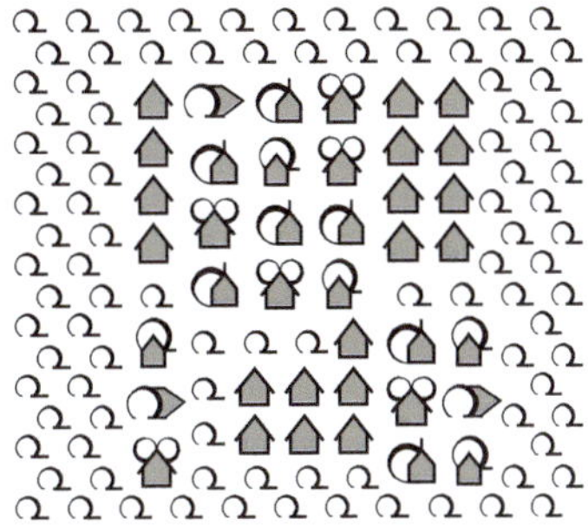

28 c

28 When with Baubotanik trees and buildings merge, the city becomes an inhabited forest.
a Separation — yesterday,
b interpenetration — today,
c fusion — tomorrow.

not "make" a garden but must develop an understanding of the processes at work in the garden in order to make well-considered decisions about how and where to intervene in its development to promote its health and growth.[20] As such, a person who designs and builds cannot themselves create an ecosystem; they can only be entrusted with making wise decisions that influence whether ecosystems and environments improve or deteriorate over time. More than 20 years ago, the landscape architect, trained gardener and horticulturalist Gilles Clément published his ecological manifesto "The Planetary Garden", in which he called for us to treat and care for the planet entrusted to us as carefully as a gardener would cultivate and tend the piece of land entrusted to them. It is, therefore, imperative that we act with and not against the natural ecosystem of the (planetary) garden so that we may maintain and develop its complexity and diversity of life.[21]

The paradigm shift we so urgently need is, therefore, not to treat nature less badly but rather to create a better world than the one we find.[22] The principles of Baubotanik and the approaches to fusing trees and buildings described in this book are intended as building blocks to assist in effecting this paradigm shift so that we may overcome the perceived opposition between nature and architecture (→ Fig. 28 a—c).

References

1 Introduction

[1] Ludwig, F., and W. Middleton (2018). "Growing Bridges", in: Almut Grüntuch-Ernst and IDAS Institute for Design and Architectural Strategies (eds.). *Hortitecture — The Power of Architecture and Plants*, Berlin, Jovis, 177-183; Ludwig, F., W. Middleton, F. Gallenmüller, P. Rogers and T. Speck (2019). "Living Bridges Using Aerial Roots of *Ficus elastica* — An Interdisciplinary Perspective", *Scientific Reports* 9(1), 1-11; Middleton, W., A. Habibi, S. Shankar and F. Ludwig (2020). "Characterizing Regenerative Aspects of Living Root Bridges", *Sustainability* 12(8), 3267.

[2] The origins and development of the Peesten dance linden tree are described in more detail in → Chapter 6, pp. 132—135; See Graefe, R. (2014). *Bauten aus lebenden Bäumen*, Aachen, Berlin, Geymüller Verlag.

[3] Ludwig, F., W. Middleton, F. Gallenmüller, P. Rogers and T. Speck (2019). "Living Bridges Using Aerial Roots of *Ficus elastica* — An Interdisciplinary Perspective", *Scientific Reports* 9(1), 1—11.

[4] Summer lime trees often grow very old even under natural conditions, but the oldest age is usually assumed to be about 1000 years. See https://de.wikipedia.org/wiki/Schenklengsfeld, last accessed 13 January 2022.

[5] Doernach, R., and G. Heid (1982). *Biohaus für Dorf und Stadt. Lebensgemeinschaft von Pflanzen, Tieren und Menschen*, Frankfurt am Main, Fischer Taschenbuchverlag.

[6] Kalberer, M., and M. Remann (1999). *Das Weidenbaubuch: Die Kunst, lebende Bauwerke zu gestalten*, Aarau, AT Verlag.

[7] The history of the dance linden trees discussed above are largely based on research undertaken by Rainer Graefe; see Graefe, R. (2014). *Bauten aus lebenden Bäumen*, Aachen, Berlin, Geymüller Verlag.

8 See Wessolly L., and M. Erb (2014). *Handbuch der Baumstatik und Baumkontrolle*, Berlin, Hannover, Patzer Verlag. Structural analysis is supplemented by other methods such as the "Visual Tree Assessment" (VTA) developed by the physicist Claus Mattheck. See Mattheck C., and H.-J. Hötzel (1997). *Tree Inspections with VTA*, Freiburg, Rombach.

[9] See van Dooren, N., and A. B. Nielsen (2018). "The Representation of Time: Addressing a Theoretical Flaw in Landscape Architecture", *Landscape Research* 44(8), 1—17; Grosse-Bächle, L. (2005). *Eine Pflanze ist kein Stein: Strategien für die Gestaltung der Dynamik von Pflanzen. Untersuchung am Beispiel zeitgenössischer Landschaftsarchitektur*, dissertation, Leibniz Universität Hannover Institute of Landscape Architecture.

[10] Kardan, O., et al. (2015). "Neighborhood Greenspace and Health in a Large Urban Center", *Scientific Reports* 5(11610).

[11] See Waldheim, C. (ed.). (2006). *The Landscape Urbanism Reader*, New York, Princeton Architectural Press; Mostafavi, M., and G. Doherty (eds.). (2010). *Ecological Urbanism*, Zurich, Lars Müller Publishers; Fassbinder, H. (2012). "Stadt als Natur: eine Kehrtwende in Architektur und Stadtplanung", Conference paper for "Livet i staden 2012", Movium, Swedish Landscape University, Alnarp, biotop-city.org.

[12] See Hensel, M. (2013). *Performance-Oriented Architecture: Rethinking Architectural Design and the Built Environment*, New York, Wiley.

2 Botanical Foundations

[1] See, for example, Klug, P. (2016). *Praxis Baumpflege — Kronenschnitt an Bäumen*, Gammelshausen, Arbus; Wessolly, L., and M. Erb (2014). *Handbuch der Baumstatik und Baumkontrolle*, Berlin, Hanover, Patzer Verlag. See also the journals *Urban Forestry & Urban Greening* (Elsevier), *Arboricultural Journal* (Taylor and Francis) and the series of books *Jahrbuch der Baumpflege* (Haymarket Media).

[2] https://en.wikipedia.org/wiki/Hyperion_(tree), last accessed 5 November 2020.

[3] https://en.wikipedia.org/wiki/Methuselah_(tree), last accessed 5 November 2020.

[4] https://en.wikipedia.org/wiki/Pando_(tree), last accessed 5 November 2020.

[5] Mock, K. E., et al. (2008). "Clonal Dynamics in Western North American Aspen (*Populus tremuloides*)", *Molecular Ecology* 17(22), 4827—4844; Rogers, P. C., and J. A. Gale (2017). "Restoration of the Iconic Pando Aspen Clone: Emerging Evidence of Recovery", *Ecosphere* 8(1), e01661.

[6] The wood stock of a forest is the sum of the actually existing above-ground wood mass, i.e. all the wood including all trunks, branches and twigs.

[7] Polley, H., and F. Kroiher (2006). "Struktur und regionale Verteilung des Holzvorrates und des potenziellen Rohholzaufkommens in Deutschland im Rahmen der Clusterstudie Forst- und Holzwirtschaft", *Arbeitsbericht des Instituts fur Waldökologie und Waldinventuren*, 2006/3.2006/3. See also Riedel, T., H. Polley and S. Klatt (2016), "National Forest Inventories Reports: Germany", in: Claude Vidal, Iciar A. Alberdi, Laura Hernández Mateo and John J. Redmond (eds.). *National Forest Inventories: Assessment of Wood Availability and Use*, Heidelberg, Springer, 405—421.

[8] Ludwig, F. (2012). *Botanische Grundlagen der Baubotanik und deren Anwendung im Entwurf*, dissertation, Universität Stuttgart, 56.

[9] https://de.wikipedia.org/wiki/Massivholzbau, last accessed 5 November 2020. See also https://en.wikipedia.org/wiki/Engineered_wood, last accessed 20 September 2022.

[10] See, for example, https://bwi.info, last accessed 5 November 2020.

[11] Rough calculation based on https://www.lwf.bayern.de/mam/cms04/service/dateien/mb-12-energiegehalt-holz.pdf, last accessed 5 November 2020.

[12] http://www.wmsolar.de/index.php?site=wissen, last accessed 5 November 2020.

[13] The bark of the giant sequoia (*Sequoiadendron giganteum*) can grow up to 90 cm thick; see, for example, https://en.wikipedia.org/wiki/Sequoiadendron_giganteum, last accessed 20 September 2022.

[14] Unless otherwise mentioned, all explanations in this chapter refer to tree species in temperate climate zones with pronounced differences between summer and winter. While the focus here is on deciduous trees, the basic principles are very similar for all trees.

[15] The central cylinder is usually much thinner (0.3 to 0.4 mm) than the central pith of the shoot axis.

[16] All bare-seeded plants (i.e. conifers) have no root hairs. Instead, they usually have protective mechanisms to prevent excess water evaporation. The lack of root hairs is partly compensated for by symbiosis with fungi.

[17] Root hairs have a diameter of a few micrometres and are about twice as thick as a human hair.

[18] https://en.wikipedia.org/wiki/Rhizodermis, last accessed 20 September 2022; Bresinsky, A., C. Körner, J. W. Kadereit, G. Neuhaus and U. Sonnewald (2008). *Strasburger — Lehrbuch der Botanik*, Heidelberg, Springer Spektrum, 210.

[19] See, for example, Hallé, F., R. A. Oldeman and P. B. Tomlinson (2012). *Tropical Trees and Forests: An Architectural Analysis*, Heidelberg, Springer Science & Business Media.

[20] See Wilson, F. B. (1984). *The Growing Tree*, Amherst, University of Massachusetts Press.

[21] Kostler, J. N., E. Brückner and H. Bibelriether (1968). *Die Wurzeln der Waldbäume: Untersuchungen zur Morphologie der Waldbäume in Mitteleuropa*, Berlin, P. Parey.

[22] Kutschera, L., and E. Lichtenegger (2002). *Wurzelatlas mitteleuropäischer Waldbäume und Sträucher*, Graz, Leopold Stocker Verlag.

[23] Wilson, F. B. (1984). *The Growing Tree*, Amherst, University of Massachusetts Press.

[24] Kutschera, L., and E. Lichtenegger (2002). *Wurzelatlas mitteleuropäischer Waldbäume und Sträucher*, Graz, Leopold Stocker Verlag. See also https://en.wikipedia.org/wiki/Quercus_robur, last accessed 20 September 2022.

[25] See Balder, H. (1998). *Die Wurzeln der Stadtbäume: Ein Handbuch zum vorbeugenden und nachsorgenden Wurzelschutz*, Berlin, P. Parey; FLL (2015). *Empfehlungen für Baumpflanzungen — Teil 1: Planung, Pflanzarbeiten, Pflege*, Bonn, Forschungsgesellschaft Landschaftsentwicklung Landschaftsbau e. V. (FLL); FLL (2010). *Empfehlungen für Baumpflanzungen — Teil 2: Standortvorbereitungen für Neupflanzungen; Pflanzgruben und Wurzelraumerweiterung, Bauweisen und Substrate*, Bonn, Forschungsgesellschaft Landschaftsentwicklung Landschaftsbau e. V. (FLL).

[26] Yoda, K., T. Kira, H. Ogawa and K. Hozumi (1963). "Self-thinning in Overcrowded Pure Stands Under Cultivated and Natural Conditions", *Journal of the Institute of Polytechnics*, Series 14, 107—128.

[27] See Pretzsch, H. (2000). "Die Regeln von Reineke, Yoda und das Gesetz der räumlichen Allometrie", *Allgemeine Forst- und Jagdzeitung* 2000(11), 205—210.

[28] Sloboda, B., and D. Gaffrey (1999). *Dynamik der Stammorphologie*. Abschlussbericht zum Forschungsprojekt Az.: SI 11/6-1, Göttingen, Universität Göttingen, Institut für Forstliche Biometrie und Informatik, 6.

[29] Speck, T. (2009). "Baubotanik, Bionik, Biotechnologie", in: G. de Bruyn, F. Ludwig and H. Schwertfeger (eds.). *Lebende Bauten — Trainierbare Tragwerke*, Münster, Lit Verlag (Kultur und Technik. Schriftenreihe des Internationalen Zentrums für Kultur- und Technikforschung der Universität Stuttgart, 16), 63—77, here 68.

[30] The relationship between wind and tree growth is in fact far more complex than the simplified explanation given here. See, among others, Coutts, M., and J. Grace (1995). *Wind and Trees*, Cambridge, Cambridge University Press; Mayer, H. (1987). "Wind-Induced Tree Sways", *Trees* 1(4), 195—206.

[31] Nicoll, B. C., and D. Ray (1996). "Adaptive Growth of Tree Root Systems in Response to Wind Action and Site Conditions", *Tree Physiology* 16, 891—898.

[32] Metzger, K. (1893). "Der Wind als maßgeblicher Faktor für das Wachsthum der Bäume", Mündener forstliche Hefte. Quoted after Büsgen, M., and E. Münch (1927). *Bau und Leben unserer Waldbäume*, Jena, Verlag Gustav Fischer, 164.

[33] See the summary and discussion of relevant research results in Mitchell, C. A., and P. N. Myers (1995). "Mechanical Stress Regulation of Plant Growth and Development", *Horticultural Reviews* 17, 1—42.

[34] Mattheck, C. (1995). "Biomechanical Optimum in Woody Stems", in: B. L. Gartner (ed.). *Plant Stems: Physiology and Functional Morphology*, San Diego, Academic Press, 75—90; Mattheck, C., and H. Kubler (1997). *Wood — The Internal Optimization of Trees* (2nd ed.), Berlin, Springer.

[35] Slater, D. (2016). "An Argument Against the Axiom of Uniform Stress Being Applicable to Trees", *Arboricultural Journal* 38(3), 143—164.

[36] Ludwig, F., W. Middleton, F. Gallenmüller, P. Rogers and T. Speck (2019). "Living Bridges Using Aerial Roots of *Ficus elastica* — An Interdisciplinary Perspective", *Scientific Reports* 9(1), 1—11.

[37] Quirk, J. T., and F. Freese (1976). "Effect of Mechanical Stress on Growth and Anatomical Structure of Red Pine: Compression Stress", *Canadian Journal of Forest Research* (6), 195—202; Marsh, M. (1989). *Biomechanische Modelle zur Quantifizierung der Tragfähigkeit von Einzelbäumen und Beständen gegenüber Schnee- und Windbelastung sowie darauf aufbauende Bestandsbehandlungsmaßnahmen mit Hilfe eines Simulationsmodells, dargestellt am Beispiel der Fichte*, dissertation, Technische Universität Dresden.

[38] Jaccard, P. (1913). "Eine neue Auffassung über die Ursachen des Dickenwachstums", *Naturwissenschaftliche Zeitschrift für Forst- und Landwirtschaft* (11), 241—279.

[39] Shinozaki, K., K. Yoda, K. Hozumi and T. Kira (1964). "A Quantitative Analysis of Plant Form — The Pipe Model Theory: I. Basic Analyses", *Japanese Journal of Ecology* 14(3), 97—105; Shinozaki, K., K. Yoda, K. Hozumi and T. Kira (1964). "A Quantitative Analysis of Plant Form — The Pipe Model Theory: II. Further Evidence of the Theory and its Application in Forest Ecology", *Japanese Journal of Ecology* 14(4), 133—139.

[40] See Zimmermann, M. H. (1978). "Hydraulic Architecture of Some Diffuse-Porous Trees", *Canadian Journal of Botany* 56, 2286—2295.

[41] Leakey, R. R. B., and K. A. Longman (1986). "Physiological, Environmental and Genetic Variation in Apical Dominance as Determined by Decapitation in Triplochiton scleroxylon", *Tree Physiology* (1), 193—207.

[42] Wareing, P. F., and T. A. A. Nasr (1961). "Gravimorphism in Trees: 1. Effects of Gravity on Growth and Apical Dominance in Fruit Trees", *Annals of Botany* 25(99), 321—340.

[43] Ballare, C. L., and A. L. Scopel (1990). "Far-Red Radiation Reflected from Adjacent Leaves: An Early Signal of Competition in Plant Canopies", *Science* 247(4940), 329—332; Casal, J. J., and H. Smith (1989). "The Function, Action and Adaptive Significance of Phytochromes in Light-Grown Plants", *Plant, Cell & Environment* 12(9), 855—862; Gilbert, J. R., G. P. Seavers, P. G. Jarvis and H. Smith (1995). "Photomorphogenesis and Canopy Dynamics: Phytochrome-Mediated Proximity Perception Accounts for the Growth Dynamics of Canopies of *Populus trichocarpa × deltoides 'Beaupré'*", *Plant, Cell & Environment* 18(5), 475—497.

[44] This section is based on the following source: Dujesiefken, D., and W. Liese (2008). *Das CODIT-Prinzip: Von den Bäumen lernen für eine fachgerechte Baumpflege*, Braunschweig, Haymarket Media.

[45] In exceptional cases (e.g. poplars), wound callus can also develop from the bast.

[46] Shigo, A. L. (1994). *Moderne Baumpflege: Grundlagen der Baumbiologie*, Braunschweig, Thalacker.

[47] Measured on poplar roots; data according to: Bruder, G. R. (1998). *Finite-Elemente-Simulation und Festigkeitsanalysen von Wurzelverankerungen*, Karlsruhe, Forschungszentrum Karlsruhe, 100. See also Masselter, T., and T. Speck (2008). "Quantitative and Qualitative Changes in Primary and Secondary Stem Organization of *Aristolochia macrophylla* during Ontogeny: Functional Growth Analysis and Experiments", *Journal of Experimental Botany* 59, 2955—2967.

[48] See Millner, E. M. (1932). "Natural Grafting in *Hedera helix*", *The New Phytologist* 31(1), 2—25.

[49] See Storz, O. (2009). "Wachstum und Tragfähigkeit in der Baubotanik", in: G. de Bruyn, F. Ludwig, H. Schwertfeger et al. (eds.). *Lebende Bauten — Trainierbare Tragwerke*, Münster, Lit Verlag (Culture and Technology. Schriftenreihe des Internationalen Zentrums für Kultur- und Technikforschung der Universität Stuttgart, 16), 45—62; Ludwig, F., et al. (2012). "Living Systems. Designing Growth in Baubotanik", *Architectural Design Journal* 82(2), 82—87.

[50] Ludwig, F. (2012). *Botanische Grundlagen der Baubotanik und deren Anwendung im Entwurf*, dissertation, Universität Stuttgart, 94—95.

[51] See, among others, Basnet, K., F. Scatena, G. E. Likens and A. E. Lugo (1993). "Ecological Consequences of Root Grafting in Tabonuco (*Dacryodes excelsa*) Trees in the Luquillo Experimental Forest, Puerto Rico", *Biotropica*, 28—35.

[52] See, among others, Tarroux, E., and A. Des Rochers (2011). "Effect of Natural Root Grafting on Growth Response of Jack Pine" (*Pinus banksiana*; Pinaceae), *American Journal of Botany* 98(6), 967—974.

[53] The processes that can be observed, and are described here, are based on the work of Millner (1932) who examined and documented different developmental stages in detail using the example of *Hedera helix* (common ivy). In ivy, inosculations are frequently observed, as the climbing shoots often cross one another and are pressed relatively firmly together thanks to their anchoring with the substrate (adhesive roots). See Millner, E. M. (1932). "Natural Grafting in *Hedera helix*", *The New Phytologist* 31(1), 2—25. Further studies and descriptions of grafting can be found, among others, in: Loehle, C., and R. H. Jones (1990). "Adaptive Significance of Root Grafting in Trees", *Functional Ecology* (4); Bormann, F. H. (1962). "Root Grafting and Non-Competitive Relationships Between Trees", in: T. T. Kozlowski (ed.). *Tree Growth*, New York, Ronald Press Company. Anatomical representations of inosculations can also be found in Schweingruber, F. H. (2007). *Wood Structure and Environment*, New York, Springer.

[54] It is not known in detail how these growth processes are controlled. However, phytohormones probably play an essential role.

[55] Garner, R. J. (1988). *The Grafter's Handbook* (5th ed.), London, Cassell.

3 Techniques and Tree Species

[1] A comprehensive overview of the cultural history of hedges and woven fences is provided by: Müller, G. (2013). *Europas Feldeinfriedungen: Wallhecken (Knicks), Hecken, Feldmauern (Steinwälle), Trockenstrauchhecken, Biegehecken, Flechthecken, Flechtzäune und traditionelle Holzzäune*, Stuttgart, Neuer Kunstverlag.

[2] See, for example, the explanations on the pleasure garden in Wimmer, C. A. (1989). *Geschichte der Gartentheorie*, Darmstadt, Wissenschaftliche Buchgesellschaft, 27—28.

[3] In addition to this horticultural application, the shaping of shoots has a long tradition in order to produce trunks of a certain geometry and structure, e.g. for shipbuilding. See Cattle, C. (2010). *Grown Furniture: A Move Towards Design for Sustainability*, dissertation, Brunel University.

[4] See, for example, Lees, S. (1982). "Hedge-Laying: Conserving a Traditional Craft", *Nature in Cambridgeshire*, 25, 32—34; Maclean, M. (2015). *Hedges and Hedgelaying: a Guide to Planting, Management and Conservation*, Ramsbury, Crowood Press.

[5] Becker, H. (1987). "Architektur aus gezogenen Bäumen: Wiechulas 'Lebende Häuser'", *Daidalos. Architektur, Kunst, Kultur* 23 (Baum und Architektur/Tree and Architecture), 70—81; Wiechula, A. (1925). *Wachsende Häuser aus lebenden Bäumen entstehend*, Berlin, Naturbau-Gesellschaft.

[6] See Block, F. H. (2008). *Wir pflanzen eine Laube*, Staufen bei Freiburg, Ökobuch Verlag; Kirsch, K. (1996). *Naturbauten aus lebenden Gehölzen*, Xanten, Organischer Landbau-Verlag Lau.

[7] Kirsch, K. (2009). "Metallfreie Baumverbindung", http://www.konstantin-kirsch.de/2009/10/metallfreie-baumverwachsung.html, last accessed 13 October 2022.

[8] See Stobbe, H., D. Dujesiefken and K. Schroder (2000). "Tree Crown Stabilization with the Double-Belt System Osnabruck", *Journal of Arboriculture* 26(5), 270—274; Detter, A. (2019). "Grundlagen der Kronensicherung und Einsatzmöglichkeiten nach der neuen ZTV-Baumpflege", *Jahrbuch der Baumpflege* 23, 90—108.

[9] See also Official Garnier Limb, https://treehouses.com/garnier-limb/, last accessed 21 September 2022; Zeller, M., and I. Münch (2022). "Befestigung von Bauwerken in Bäumen mit Baumankern und doppelter Umreifung", *Bautechnik* 99, 1—10.

[10] Cattle, C. (2010). *Grown Furniture: A Move Towards Design for Sustainability*, dissertation, Brunel University. See also https://fullgrown.co.uk/.

[11] See Reames, R. (2005). *Arborsculpture: Solutions for a Small Planet*, Williams Oregon, Arborsmith Studios.

[12] For the sake of simplicity, all tree species are listed by their common name, shortened to the superordinate species, i.e. willow, plane, beech, etc. In each case the actual trees are varieties of the respective species.

[13] From 2009 onwards, the black locust trees (*Robinia pseudoacacia*) were not cultivated any further, as all attempts at stimulating intergrowth using the connection techniques investigated were unsuccessful. In 2011, the ash trees were taken out of cultivation due to heavy infestation with ash shoot dieback. In winter 2011/12, significant losses among the beech, hornbeam and oak trees resulted in their removal from the trials. The latter can be attributed to growing in containers and one cannot draw any conclusions from this about the suitability of these species.

[14] Dujesiefken, D., and W. Liese (2008). *Das CODIT-Prinzip: Von den Bäumen lernen für eine fachgerechte Baumpflege*, Braunschweig, Haymarket Media, 89—91.

[15] See, among others, Frei, E. R., K. Streit and P. Brang (2018). "Testpflanzungen zukunftsfähiger Baumarten: auf dem Weg zu einem schweizweiten Netz", *Schweizerische Zeitschrift für Forstwesen* 169, 347—350.

[16] Gloor, S., and M. G. Hofbauer (2018). "Der ökologische Wert von Stadtbäumen bezüglich der Biodiversität", *Jahrbuch der Baumpflege*, 22, 33—48.

[17] See Schönfeld, P. (2019). "Klimabäume — welche Arten können in Zukunft gepflanzt werden?" Bayerische Landesanstalt für Weinbau und Gartenbau; Faní Stratópoulos-

Le Chalony, L. M. (2020). *Klimabäume für die Stadt: Über die Rolle einer angepassten Arten- und Sortenwahl für die Kühlleistung von Straßenbäumen*, dissertation, Technische Universität München.

[18] See GALK (2018). GALK Straßenbaumliste, Deutsche Gartenamtsleiterkonferenz Arbeitskreis Stadtbäume; Röhrig, E., N. Bartsch and B. von Lüpke (2020). *Waldbau auf ökologischer Grundlage*, Stuttgart, UTB GmbH.

[19] See Niklas, K. J., and H.-C. Spatz (2010). "Worldwide Correlations of Mechanical Properties and Green Wood Density", *American Journal of Botany* 97, 1587—1594; Wessolly, L., and M. Erb (1998). *Handbuch der Baumstatik und Baumkontrolle*, Berlin, Patzer Verlag; Ross, R. J. (2010). *Wood Handbook: Wood as an Engineering Material*, USDA Forest Service, Forest Products Laboratory, General Technical Report FPL-GTR-190,

[20] Roloff, A. (2013). *Bäume in der Stadt*, Stuttgart, Ulmer Verlag, 117. See also Arnold, Henry F. (1993), *Trees in Urban Design* (2nd ed.), New York, Van Nostrand Reinhold, 100—103.

[21] Prinz, M., and N. Sauberer (2015). "Die Brutvögel im Schlosspark Tribuswinkel im Jahr 2015 unter spezieller Berücksichtigung der in Baumhöhlen brütenden Arten (Stadtgemeinde Traiskirchen, Niederösterreich)", *Biodiversität und Naturschutz in Ostösterreich*-BCBEA 1(2), 304—317.

[22] Wulf, A. and H. Butin (1987). "Krankheiten und Schädlinge der Platane", *Nachrichtenblatt des Deutschen Pflanzenschutzdienstes* (Braunschweig) 39(10), 145—148.

[23] Börker, T. (2019). *Mykologische und holzanatomische Untersuchungen zur Massaria-Krankheit an Platanen*, dissertation, University of Freiburg.

[24] See, for example, Vrinceanu, D., O. N. Berghi, R. Cergan, M. Dumitru, R. C. Ciuluvica, C. Giurcaneanu and A. Neagos (2021). "Urban Allergy Review: Allergic Rhinitis and Asthma with Plane Tree Sensitization", *Experimental and Therapeutic Medicine* 21(3).

[25] Unless otherwise stated, the comments on *Salix alba* here refer to: Schirmer, R., and B. Stimm (2004). "Salix alba", in: A. Roloff, H. Weisgerber et al. *Enzyklopädie der Holzgewächse: Handbuch und Atlas der Dendrologie*, Weinheim, Wiley, 1—16.

[26] An exception here is the black locust (*Robinia pseudoacacia*), which as a fast-growing pioneer tree species forms a very durable wood.

[27] See, for example, Florineth, F. (2004). *Pflanzen statt Beton. Handbuch zur Ingenieurbiologie und Vegetationstechnik*, Berlin, Patzer Verlag.

[28] See Beat Wermelinger (2013). "Weidenbohrer — Cossus cossus", *WSL — Waldschutz Schweiz*. https://www.wsl.ch/forest/wus/diag/index.php?TEXTID=100&MOD=1, last accessed 16 April 2021.

[29] See Kalberer, M., and M. Remann (1999). *Das Weidenbaubuch: Die Kunst, lebende Bauwerke zu gestalten*, Aarau, AT Verlag.

[30] Roloff, A., and U. Pietzarka (2004). "Acer platanoides", in: A. Roloff, H. Weisgerber et al. *Enzyklopädie der Holzgewächse: Handbuch und Atlas der Dendrologie*, Weinheim, Wiley, 1—16.

[31] Dujesiefken, D., and W. Liese (2008). *Das CODIT-Prinzip: Von den Bäumen lernen für eine fachgerechte Baumpflege*, Braunschweig, Haymarket Media, 89.

[32] Burgdorf, N., and L. Straßer (2020). "Aktuelle pilzliche Erkrankungen bei Ahorn", *LWF aktuell* 124, 46-49.

[33] Götz, B., and C. Wolf (2004). "Tilia cordata", in A. Roloff, H. Weisgerber et al. *Enzyklopädie der Holzgewächse: Handbuch und Atlas der Dendrologie*, Weinheim, Wiley, 1—16.

[34] Gloor, S., and M. G. Hofbauer (2018). "Der ökologische Wert von Stadtbäumen bezüglich der Biodiversität", *Yearbook of Arboriculture* 22, 33—48.

[35] The name "hornbeam" derives from the Old High German "haganbuoche" (*hag* = fence, hedge). See Müller, G. (2013). *Europas Feldeinfriedungen: Wallhecken (Knicks), Hecken, Feldmauern (Steinwälle), Trockenstrauchhecken, Biegehecken, Flechthecken, Flechtzäune und traditionelle Holzzäune*, Stuttgart, Neuer Kunstverlag.

[36] See Kurz, P., and M. Machatscheck (2008). *Alleebäume: Wenn Bäume ins Holz, ins Laub und in die Frucht wachsen sollen*, Vienna, Böhlau Verlag.

[37] Boratynski, A. (2004). "Carpinus betulus", in: A. Roloff, H. Weisgerber et al., *Enzyklopädie der Holzgewäch: Handbuch und Atlas der Dendrologie*, Weinheim, Wiley, 1—12.

[38] Pflanzenhandel Lorenz von Ehren (ed.). (2015). *Stadtbäume fit für die Zukunft*, brochure, Hamburg.

4 Fusion of Trees and Buildings

[1] Boeri, S. (2015). *A Vertical Forest: Instructions Booklet for the Prototype of a Forest City*, Mantova, Corraini edizioni; Giacomello, E., and M. Valagussa (2015). *Vertical Greenery: Evaluating the High-Rise Vegetation of the Bosco Verticale*, Milan, published in conjunction with the Council on Tall Buildings and Urban Habitat (CTBUH), Arup, and Università Iuav di Venezia.

[2] Czaja, W. (2015). "Architekt Stefano Boeri: 'Stundenlang über meine Fehler sprechen'", *Der Standard*, 1 March 2015.

[3] Philipps, T. (2017). "'Forest Cities': The Radical Plan to Save China from Air Pollution", *The Guardian*, 17 February 2017.

[4] Clémençon, P. (2013). "Was der Wind sät: Die verrückten Bauten des Edouard François", *Wohnen* 5/2013, Verband der gemeinnützigen Wohnbauträger.

[5] François, É. (2014). *La hauteur pour tous*, Paris, Éditions l'œil d'or.

[6] See Hoffmann, O. (1987). *Handbuch für begrünte und genutzte Dächer*, Leinfelden-Echterdingen, Verlagsanstalt Alexander Koch.

[7] Hundertwasser, F. (1999). *Hundertwasser Architecture*, Cologne, Taschen, 80—85.

[8] See Well, F., and F. Ludwig (2020). "Blue-Green Architecture: A Case Study Analysis Considering the Synergetic Effects of Water and Vegetation", *Frontiers of Architectural Research* 9(1), 191—202.

[9] See "Paradeiser und Schneebergblick — Wohnpark Alt Erlaa: Dorfleben im Hochhaus" (2014), in: Reinhard Seiß (ed.). *Harry Glück. Wohnbauten*, Salzburg, Müry Salzmann, 65—73; Fischer, Silke (2020). "Alt-Erlaa Residential Park, Vienna: Harry Glück & Partner 1968—85", in: Gerhard

Steixner and Maria Welzig (eds.). *Luxury for All: Milestones in European Stepped Terrace Housing*, Basel, Birkhäuser, 138—170.

[10] Wenning, A. (2022). *Treehouses and Other Modern Hideaways (4th and exp. ed.)*, Berlin, DOM Publishers, 20; Garve, Roland (2019), »Tree Houses of the Korowai«, in: Christian Schittich (ed.). *Vernacular Architecture. Atlas for Living Throughout the World*, Basel, Birkhäuser, 278—285.

[11] See Hallé, F. (2021). *Le Radeau des Cimes: Trente années d'exploration des canopées forestières équatoriales*, Arles, Actes Sud.

[12] The team also included the botanist Patrick Blanc, who was inspired by the epiphytes found in the treetops to create his now world-famous vertical gardens.

[13] Wenning, A. (2022). *Treehouses and Other Modern Hideaways (4th and exp. ed.)*, Berlin, DOM Publishers, 8—9.

[14] Ibid., 36.

[15] http://www.baumraum.de/, last accessed 23 September 2022.

[16] An exception here is Edouard François, who explores the relationship between nature and architecture anew in every project and therefore does not consider his green buildings per se as prototypical solutions for green urban planning.

5 How Living Structures Interact with Their Environment

[1] See Hensel, Michael (2013). *Performance-Oriented Architecture: Rethinking Architectural Design and the Built Environment*, New York, Wiley.

[2] See Grunewald, Karsten, and Olaf Bastian (eds.). (2015). *Ecosystem Services — Concept, Methods and Case Studies*, Heidelberg, Springer Spektrum.

[3] The field of restoration ecology/renaturation ecology examines the question of how suitable starting or boundary conditions can be created so that ecosystems such as forests can emerge and develop anew. See, for example: Kollmann, J., A. Kirmer, S. Tischew, N. Hölzel and K. Kiehl (2019). *Renaturierungsökologie*, Heidelberg, Springer; Zerbe, S. (2022), *Restoration of Multifunctional Cultural Landscapes: Merging Tradition and Innovation for a Sustainable Future*, Heidelberg, Springer.

[4] The field of environmental ethics examines the question of which beings or things in nature can be considered as having an intrinsic value. See, for example, Krebs, A. (1997). *Naturethik: Grundtexte der gegenwärtigen tier- und ökoethischen Diskussion*, Frankfurt, Suhrkamp.

[5] As a result, terms that indicate the system character (such as "urban forest") in this context are often not used. Instead, terms that express the additive or applicative character (such as "building greening") are preferred.

[6] An overview of the benefits of green architecture is provided by Perini, K., M. Ottelé, E. Haas and R. Raiteri (2011). "Greening the Building Envelope, Façade Greening and Living Wall Systems", *Open Journal of Ecology* 1(01), 1. See also Ana-Maria Dabija (2021). *Alternative Envelope Components for Energy-Efficient Buildings* (Green Energy and Technology), Heidelberg, Springer Spektrum.

[7] Kosareo, L., and R. Ries (2006). "Life Cycle Assessment of a Green Roof in Pittsburgh", U.S. Department of Energy, Office of Scientific and Technical Information. https://www.osti.gov/etdeweb/biblio/20861949, last accessed 13 October 2022.

[8] See, for example, Burschel, P., and J. Huss (1997). *Grundriss des Waldbaus*, Berlin, Blackwell-Wissenschaftsverlag.

[9] Kuttler, W. (2004). "Stadtklima, Teil 1: Grundzüge und Ursachen", *Umweltwissenschaften und Schadstoffforschung — Zeitschrift für Umweltchemie und Ökotoxikologie* 16(3), 187—199; Kuttler, W. (2004). "Stadtklima, Teil 2: Phänomene und Wirkungen", *Umweltwissenschaften und Schadstoffforschung — Zeitschrift für Umweltchemie und Ökotoxikologie* 16(4), 263—274. See also Roesler, S., M. Kobi and L. Stieger (eds.). (2022). *Coping with Urban Climates: Comparative Perspectives on Architecture and Thermal Governance* (Klima Polis vol. 2), Basel, Birkhäuser, 28—31.

[10] The thermophysical effects of the environment on humans can be determined in very different ways. The UTCI, Universal Thermal Climate Index, was developed as a globally recognised standard. See: Bröde, P., D. Fiala, K. Błażejczyk, I. Holmér, G. Jendritzky, B. Kampmann, B. Tinz and G. Havenith (2012). "Deriving the Operational Procedure for the Universal Thermal Climate Index (UTCI)", *International Journal of Biometeorology* 56(3), 481—494. See also http://utci.org/, last accessed 24 September 2022.

[11] https://en.wikipedia.org/wiki/2003_European_heat_wave, last accessed 27 June 2021.

[12] Ng, E., L. Chen, Y. Wang and C. Yuan (2012). "A Study on the Cooling Effects of Greening in a High-Density City: An Experience from Hong Kong", *Building and Environment* 47, 256—271.

[13] Pfoser, N., N. Jenner, J. Henrich, J. Heusinger and S. Weber (2013). *Gebäude Begrünung Energie: Potenziale und Wechselwirkungen. Bundesministerium für Verkehr*, Technische Universität Darmstadt, Technische Universität Braunschweig, 177—180. It should be noted, however, that the nature of the ground surfaces is also highly relevant for the cooling performance of trees. See Rahman, M. A., V. Dervishi, A. Moser-Reischl, F. Ludwig, H. Pretzsch, T. Rötzer and S. Pauleit (2021). "Comparative Analysis of Shade and Underlying Surfaces on Cooling Effect", *Urban Forestry & Urban Greening*, 127223.

[14] Hsieh, C.-M., J.-J. Li, L. Zhang and B. Schwegler (2018). "Effects of Tree Shading and Transpiration on Building Cooling Energy Use", *Sustainable Cities and Society* 19, 236249. See also McPherson, E. G., and J. R. Simpson (2003). "Potential Energy Savings in Buildings by an Urban Tree Planting Program in California", *Urban Forestry & Urban Greening* 2, 73—86; Gillner, S., J. Vogt, A. Tharang, S. Dettmann and A. Roloff (2015). "Role of Street Trees in Mitigating Effects of Heat and Drought at Highly Sealed Urban Sites", *Landscape and Urban Planning* 143, 33—42; Pitha, U., B. Scharf, I. Zluwa, C. Pelko, A. Korjenic, T. Salonen and M. Mitterböck (2018). "Vegetationstechnisches und bauphysikalisches Monitoring des 'Vertikalen Gartens' der MA31 in der Grabnergasse 4-6, 1060 Wien", Research Report. TU Vienna and BOKU Vienna.

[15] Berry R., S. J. Livesley and L. Aye (2013). "Tree Canopy Shade Impacts on Solar Irradiance Received by Building Walls and Their Surface Temperature", *Building and Environment* 69, 91—100. See also Ruefenacht, L., and J. A. Acero (2017). "Strategies for Cooling Singapore: A Catalogue of 80+ Measures to Mitigate Urban Heat Island and Improve Outdoor Thermal Comfort", Singapore, *Cooling Singapore*, 2017.

[16] Lang, W., S. Pauleit, J. Brasche, G. Hausladen, J. Maderspacher and R. Schelle (2018). "Leitfaden für klimaorientierte Kommunen in Bayern: Handlungsempfehlungen aus dem Projekt Klimaschutz und grüne Infrastruktur in der Stadt", *Zentrum Stadtnatur und Klimaanpassung*, Munich.

[17] Jacobson, M. Z., and J. E. Hoeve (2012). "Effects of Urban Surfaces and White Roofs on Global and Regional Climate", *Journal of Climate* (25)3, 1028—1044. See also Roesler,

S., M. Kobi and L. Stieger (eds.). (2022). *Coping with Urban Climates: Comparative Perspectives on Architecture and Thermal Governance* (Klima Polis vol. 2), Basel, Birkhäuser.

[18] Lee, D. S., D. Fahey, A. Skowron, M. Allen, U. Burkhardt, Q. Chen, S. Doherty, S. Freeman, P. Forster, and J. Fuglestvedt (2021). "The Contribution of Global Aviation to Anthropogenic Climate Forcing for 2000 to 2018", *Atmospheric Environment* 244, 117834.

[19] See, for example, Baumüller, J., U. Reuter, U. Hoffmann and H. Esswein (2008). *Klimaatlas Region Stuttgart*, Stuttgart, Verband Region Stuttgart.

[20] Beckmann, R. (1982). *Die Hausschutzhecken im Monschauer Land unter besonderer Berücksichtigung ihrer klimatischen Auswirkungen*, Bonn, Dümmler Verlag. See also: Höpfl, L., D. Sunguroğlu Hensel, M. Hensel and F. Ludwig (2021). "Initiating Research into Adapting Rural Hedging Techniques, Hedge Types, and Hedgerow Networks as Novel Urban Green Systems", *Land* 10(5), 529.

[21] Sunguroğlu Hensel, D. (2020). "Ecological Prototypes: Initiating Design Innovation in Green Construction", *Sustainability* 12(14), 5865.

[22] Sunguroğlu Hensel, D. (2021). "Data-Driven Research on Ecological Prototypes for Green Architecture", *Dimensions of Architectural Knowledge*, 1(1) 47—54, here: 51.

[23] Andrade, M. D. F., P. Artaxo, S. G. El Khouri Miraglia, N. Gouveia, A. J. Krupnick, J. Krutmann and I. Scheer (2019). "Air Pollution and Health—A Science-Policy Initiative", *Annals of Global Health* 85(1).

[24] The economic equivalent value of this filtering service is put at around US $ 3.8 billion. See: Nowak, D. J., D. E. Crane and J. C. Stevens (2006). "Air Pollution Removal by Urban Trees and Shrubs in the United States", *Urban Forestry & Urban Greening* 4, 115—123.

[25] Federal Environment Agency (2018). "Nitrogen dioxide has serious impact on health". https://www.umweltbundesamt.de/en/press/pressinformation/nitrogen-dioxide-has-serious-impact-on-health, last accessed 24 September 2022.

[26] Fitzky, A. C., H. Sanden, T. Karl, S. Fares, C. Calfapietra, R. Grote, A. Saunier and B. Rewald (2019). "The Interplay Between Ozone and Urban Vegetation—BVOC Emissions, Ozone Deposition, and Tree Ecophysiology", *Frontiers in Forests and Global Change* 2, 50.

[27] Menke, P., M. Thönnessen, W. Beckröge, J. Bauer, H. Schwarz, W. Gross, J. Hiemstra, E. Schoenmaker-van der Bijl and A. Tonneijk (2008). "Bäume und Pflanzen lassen Städte atmen: Schwerpunkt-Feinstaub", *Forum Die Grüne Stadt.*

[28] See Otto, H. J. (1994). *Waldökologie*, Stuttgart, Ulmer Verlag, 165.

[29] Conversely, large-scale deforestation, often caused by settlement and other land-use changes around the world, can result in up to 30 % less rainfall in a region. See: Teuling, A. J., C. M. Taylor, J. F. Meirink, L. A. Melsen, D. G. Miralles, C. C. van Heerwaarden, R. Vautard, A. I. Stegehuis, G.-J. Nabuurs and J. V.-G. de Arellano (2017). "Observational Evidence for Cloud Cover Enhancement Over Western European Forests," *Nature Communications* 8, 1—7; Spracklen, D. V., S. R. Arnold, and C. Taylor (2012). "Observations of Increased Tropical Rainfall Preceded by Air Passage Over Forests", *Nature* 489, 282—285.

[30] Ellison, D., C. E. Morris, B. Locatelli, D. Sheil, J. Cohen, D. Murdiyarso, V. Gutierrez, M. Van Noordwijk, I. F. Creed and J. Pokorny (2017). "Trees, Forests and Water: Cool Insights for a Hot World", *Global Environmental Change* 43, 51—61.

[31] Forest fires play an important role in many natural forest ecosystems, but in the context of climate change and changes in forest use, there are more and more large-scale forest fires that cause lasting damage to ecosystems and permanent loss of habitats.

[32] See, for example, the comments on the Bosco Verticale in: Well, F., and F. Ludwig (2020). "Blue-Green Architecture: A Case Study Analysis Considering the Synergetic Effects of Water and Vegetation", *Frontiers of Architectural Research* 9, 191—202.

[33] Well, F., C. Morandi and P. Richter (2020). "Regen-und Grauwasser als alternative Wasserquelle für Vertikalbegrünung", *GebäudeGrün*, 20—23; Steger, L., F. Well and F. Ludwig (2020). "Blau-grüne Infrastrukturen: Transformationsstudien urbaner Freiräume am Beispiel Frankfurts", *Transforming Cities* (1), 56—61.

[34] Hoyer, J., W. Dickhaut, L. Kronawitter and B. Weber (2011). *Water Sensitive Urban Design*, Berlin, Jovis.

[35] Well, F., and F. Ludwig (2021). "Development of an Integrated Design Strategy for Blue-Green Architecture", *Sustainability* 13(14), 7944. See also Brears, R. C. (2018). *Blue and Green Cities: The Role of Blue-Green Infrastructure in Managing Urban Water Resources*, Berlin, Springer; Li, H., L. Ding, M. Ren, C. Li and H. Wang (2017). "Sponge City Construction in China: A Survey of the Challenges and Opportunities", *Water* 9(9), 594.

[36] Bayerische Landesanstalt für Weinbau und Gartenbau, Abteilung Landespflege (2013). *Düngung von Straßenbäumen, Substrate, Nährstoffe, Düngung im Projekt "Stadtgrün 2021"*, LWG Veitshöchheim, Abteilung Landespflege.

[37] See, for example, Borgmann, called Brüser, A. (2014). *Möglichkeiten und Grenzen der Revitalisierung von Jungbäumen im urbanen Raum*, master's thesis, Beuth University of Applied Sciences (BHT), Berlin.

[38] However, it must be ensured that adequate dosing of the wastewater does not lead to a leaching of nutrients and thus to overfertilisation or the input of pollutants. See Börjesson, P., and G. Berndes (2006). "The Prospects for Willow Plantations for Wastewater Treatment in Sweden", *Biomass and Bioenergy* 30(5), 428—438. See also Vasudevan, P., A. Thapliyal, R. Srivastava, A. Pandey, M. Dastidar and P. Davies (2010). "Fertigation Potential of Domestic Wastewater for Tree Plantations", *Journal of Scientific & Industrial Research* 69, February 2010, 146—150.

[39] Hundertwasser, F. (1999). *Hundertwasser Architecture*, Cologne, Taschen.

[40] See Balder, H. 1998. *Die Wurzeln der Stadtbäume — ein Handbuch zum vorbeugenden und nachsorgenden Wurzelschutz*, Berlin, Parey Buchverlag.

[41] In Europe, about 17 million m^3 of peat are used in growing substrate every year. For every 10 kg of peat extracted, approx. 18 kg of CO_2 are released. At an average density of 600 kg/m^3, this results in a CO_2 release of approx. 18 million tonnes, which corresponds to approx. 2 % of road traffic emissions. Calculation based on: Altwegg, A. (2011). "Zahlen und Fakten zu Torf", *g-plus—Die Gärtner Fachzeitschrift* 17, 4—6. See also Piedmont Master Gardeners (2022). "A Growing Controversy: Should We Stop Using Peat?", https://piedmontmastergardeners.org/a-growing-controversy-should-we-stop-using-peat/, last accessed 25 September 2022.

[42] Glaser, B., G. Guggenberger and W. Zech (2003). "Organic Chemistry Studies on Amazonian Dark Earths", in: J. Lehmann, D. C. Kern, B. Glaser, W. I. Wodos (eds.), *Amazonian Dark Earths*, Heidelberg, Springer, 227—241.

[43] However, in order to achieve a globally relevant climate effect, large parts of the entire earth's surface in question would have to be managed accordingly—the architectural and urban planning scale of baubotanical projects can only make a small contribution here. See Teichmann, I. (2014). "Klimaschutz durch Biokohle in der deutschen Landwirtschaft: Potentiale und Kosten", *DIW Wochenbericht* 81, 3—13.

6 Designing with Trees and Time

[1] See Graefe, R. (2014). *Bauten aus lebenden Bäumen*, Aachen, Berlin, Geymüller Verlag, 94—100.

[2] Ludwig, F. (2008). "Baubotanik — Möglichkeiten und Grenzen des Konstruierens lebender Tragwerke", in: B. Baier, R. Koenen, J. Müller and S. Scherbach, *Konstruktion und Gestalt — leichte Konstruktionen*, Aachen, Universität Duisburg-Essen, 59—85.

[3] Ludwig, F., W. Middleton, F. Gallenmüller, P. Rogers and T. Speck (2019). "Living Bridges Using Aerial Roots of *Ficus elastica*—An Interdisciplinary Perspective", *Scientific Reports* 9(1), 1—11.

[4] See ibid. and Neelima Vallangi (2015). "India's Amazing Living Root Bridges", http://www.bbc.com/travel/story/20150218-indias-amazing-living-root-bridges, last accessed 25 September 2022.

[5] See Middleton, W., A. Habibi, S. Shankar and F. Ludwig (2020). "Characterizing Regenerative Aspects of Living Root Bridges", *Sustainability* 12(8), 3267; Shankar, S. (2015). "Living Root Bridges: State of Knowledge, Fundamental Research and Future Application", *IABSE Symposium Report: Structural Engineering: Providing Solutions to Global Challenges*.

[6] See Graefe, R. (2014). *Bauten aus lebenden Bäumen*, Aachen, Berlin, Geymüller Verlag, 94—100.

[7] See Andrews, J. (1999). *The Sculpture of David Nash*, Berkeley, Los Angeles, University California Press, 98—113.

[8] Baumann, M. (2002). *Freiraumplanung in den Siedlungen der Zwanziger Jahre am Beispiel der Planungen des Gartenarchitekten Leberecht Migge*: Halle, Trift-Verlag. See also Gadient, H., S. von Schwerin and S. Orga (2019), *Migge. The Original Garden Plans. 1910—1920*, Basel, Birkhäuser.

[9] See Giulio, D., and R. Carugati (2004). *Giuliano Mauri*, Milan, Electa.

[10] This is not an officially approved means of access, just a simple way of reaching the walkway to walk on the experimental structure for testing and demonstration purposes.

[11] See Ludwig, F., and O. Storz (2005). "Baubotanik—Mit lebenden Pflanzen konstruieren", *Baumeister* 11, 72—75.

[12] Ludwig, F., and D. Schönle (2017). "Plane Tree Cube Nagold", in: D. A. Bach, *Architecture Today: Landscape*, Barcelona, Loft Publications, 170—173.

[13] See Connop, S., P. Vandergert, B. Eisenberg, M. J. Collier, C. Nash, J. Clough and D. Newport (2016). "Renaturing Cities Using a Regionally-Focused Biodiversity-Led Multifunctional Benefits Approach to Urban Green Infrastructure", *Environmental Science & Policy* 62, 99—111.

7 Utopias and Visions: Living Architecture between Science and Fiction

[1] Wiechula, A. (1925). *Wachsende Häuser aus lebenden Bäumen entstehend*, Berlin, Naturbau-Gesellschaft, 39.

[2] Ibid., 40.

[3] Ibid., 179.

[4] All that was found was the developmental stage of a weaving hedge. See Kirsch, K. (1996). *Naturbauten aus lebenden Gehölzen*, Xanten, Organischer Landbau-Verlag Lau.

[5] Letter to the editor in the *Schlesisch-ländliche Genossenschaftszeitung* by A. Woll on 19 February 1930, quoted after ibid., 33.

[6] See Ludwig, F. (2012). *Botanische Grundlagen der Baubotanik und deren Anwendung im Entwurf*, dissertation, Universität Stuttgart, 201ff.

[7] See Kirsch, K. (1996). *Naturbauten aus lebenden Gehölzen*, Xanten, Organischer Landbau-Verlag Lau. See also http://www.naturbauten.org/. After many years of good development, the vitality of the trees had declined sharply in recent years, probably due to ash shoot dieback.

[8] See Block, F. H. (2008). *Wir pflanzen eine Laube*, Staufen bei Freiburg, Ökobuch Verlag.

[9] https://www.tagesschau.de/investigativ/kontraste/anastasia-bewegung-101.html, last accessed 24 October 2021.

[10] See also the guest article by Stephan Trüby in the *Frankfurter Rundschau* "Extreme völkische Rechte: 'Ewiger Wald und ewiges Volk'" from 17 March 2022. https://www.fr.de/meinung/gastbeitraege/heimatschutzbewegung-extreme-voelkische-rechte-ewiger-wald-und-ewiges-volk-90243608.html, last accessed 22 October 2022.

[11] See the publication by his daughter Wilma Erlandson: Erlandson, W. (2001). *My Father "Talked to Trees"*.

[12] See Reames, R. (2005). *Arborsculpture: Solutions for a Small Planet*, Williams Oregon, Arborsmith Studios.

[13] Lecture by Mark Primack at the TU Munich, Chair for Green Technologies in Landscape Architecture, 13 November 2017.

[14] See the video documentary "The Man Who Talked to Trees". https://www.youtube.com/watch?v=OWEK1pNgTDA, last accessed 28 September 2022.

[15] See Koolhaas, R. (1978). *Delirious New York: A Retroactive Manifesto for Manhattan*, Oxford, Oxford University Press.

[16] Schuiten, L., and A.-C. Labrique (2009). *Luc Schuiten: Vegetal City*, Brussels, Editions Mardaga.

[17] See in particular the explanatory texts accompanying the exhibition "Exposition sur Grilles": http://www.vegetalcity.net/en/exposition-grilles/, last accessed 28 October 2021.

[18] See Arbona, J., L. Greden and M. Joachim (2003). "Nature's Technology: The Fab Tree Hab House", *Thresholds*, 48—53. See also https://terreform.org/home-alive, last accessed 28 September 2022; Joachim, M., and M. Aiolova, Terreform One (2020). *Design with Life: Biotech Architecture and Resilient Cities*, Barcelona, Actar Publishers.

[19] Wikipedia https://en.wikipedia.org/wiki/Gilroy_Gardens, last accessed 27 October 2021.

8 Vers une Arbotecture: Towards a Future Tree Architecture

[1] See Middleton, W., A. Habibi, S. Shankar and F. Ludwig (2020). "Characterizing Regenerative Aspects of Living Root Bridges", *Sustainability* 12(8), 3267.

[2] These include the project "Urban Green Systems 4.0 — A Computational Framework for Novel Urban Green System Design" from 2022 funded by the German Research Foundation DFG, the sub-project "Designing Urban Green Infrastructures as Dynamic Processes" of the DFG Research Training Group "Training Next Generation Professionals for Integrated Urban Planning Research" from 2022 and the projects "Design and Analysis for Living Architecture — A Twinned Research and Educational Project" and "Next Generation Living Architecture — Digital Design for Urban Settings" from 2021 funded by the Ove Arup Foundation.

[3] Middleton, W., Q. Shu and F. Ludwig (2019). "Photogrammetry as a Tool for Living Architecture", *The International Archives of Photogrammetry, Remote Sensing and Spatial Information Sciences* 42, 195—201.

[4] Middleton, W., Q. Shu and F. Ludwig (2022). "Representing Living Architecture Through Skeleton Reconstruction from Point Clouds", *Scientific Reports* 12(1), 1—13.

[5] Project management and idea: Ferdinand Ludwig, Wilfrid Middelton, Qiguan Shu. Cooperation partners: Cornelius Hackenbracht, Michael Hensel (TU Vienna), Verena Vogler (McNeel). Design team: Alessandra Brembati, Baiyu Chen, Xi Chen, Denise Gordeev, Peter Grasegger, Marlena Hellmann, Stella Kampffmeyer, Tsz Ying Ng, Ke Sun, Tobias Winkler and Zhiqing Zhou.

[6] Shu, Q., W. Middleton and F. Ludwig (2021). "Teaching Computational Approaches in Baubotanik — Developing a Design-and-Build Workflow for a Living Architecture Pavilion", Responsive Cities Symposium, *Design with Nature. Symposium Proceedings*, Barcelona, 212—221.

[7] See, among others, James, K., N. Haritos and P. Ades (2006). "Mechanical Stability of Trees Under Dynamic Loads", *American Journal of Botany* 93(10), 1522—1530; Esche, D., P. Schumacher, A. Detter and S. Rust (2018). "Experimentelle Überprüfung der Windlastanalyse für statische Zugversuche", *Jahrbuch der Baumpflege 2018* (22nd ed.), 229—236; Wessolly, L., and M. Erb (2014). *Handbuch der Baumstatik und Baumkontrolle*, Patzer Verlag, Berlin.

[8] Functional Structural Plant Models (FSPM). See, among others, Godin, C. (2000). "Representing and Encoding Plant Architecture: A Review", *Annals of Forest Science* 57(5) 413—438.

[9] Prusinkiewicz, P., et al. (1994). "Synthetic Topiary", *Proceedings of SIGGRAPH 1994.*

[10] Ludwig, F., B. Mihaylov and T. Schwinn (2013). *Emergent Timber: A Tool for Designing the Growth Process of Baubotanik Structures. Transmaterial Aesthetics: Experiments with Timber in Architecture and Technology.* Berlin. Conference Proceedings Manuscript, https://www.researchgate.net/publication/320058050_Emergent_Timber_A_tool_for_designing_the_growth_process_of_Baubotanik_structures.

[11] Shu, Q., T. Roetzer, M. Hensel and F. Ludwig (in preparation). "Tree Information Modeling: Bring Living Trees into Building Systems".

[12] Studies on the anatomy of intergrowths (in early stages of development) are also being carried out at TU Delft. Wang, X., W. Gard, N. de Vries and J.-W. van de Kuilen (in preparation). "Anatomical and Mechanical Features of Self-Growing Connections in Plants", https://papers.ssrn.com/sol3/papers.cfm?abstract_id=3970513.

[13] Ludwig, F., M. A. Rahman, M. D. Mylo, O. Speck, C. Fleckenstein, Q. Shu and T. Speck (in preparation). "Joining Trees for Future Cities: A Long-Term Inosculation Study for Living Architecture".

[14] The Office for Living Architecture was founded in 2022 by the authors together with Jakob Rauscher and emerged from the preceding office ludwig.schönle Baubotaniker Architekten Stadtplaner founded in 2010.

[15] Office for Living Architecture together with umschichten, allmannsattlerwappner, Sergio Sanna, Carlo Scoccianti, green4cities.

[16] See Ludwig, F., and I. Zintl (2018). "Vertikale Freiräume — Chancen für die dritte Dimension in der Landschaftsarchitektur", *Stadt + Grün* 67, 44—49.

[17] Klimawandel und modellhafte Anpassung in Baden-Württemberg, Teil 2 Angewandte Forschung und Modellprojekte. Final report of the research project: Ludwig, F., D. Schönle and M. Bellers (2015). Klimaaktive baubotanische Stadtquartiere, Bautypologien und Infrastrukturen: Modellprojekte und Planungswerkzeuge. Klimopass. Landesanstalt für Umwelt Baden Württemberg LUBW. Institut Grundlagen Moderner Architektur und Entwerfen (IGMA), Universität Stuttgart Institut für Landschaftsplanung und Ökologie (ILPÖ), Universität Stuttgart.

[18] Office for Living Architecture with Stark Ingenieure (structural design), Transsolar Stuttgart (energy consulting), TOP Stuttgart (fire protection consulting), Prof. Dr. Christian Stoy, and Christopher Hagmann (cost estimate), Dr. Ulrich Pantle and Alexander Wäsch (concept consulting).

[19] See Eisenberg, B., F. Well and F. Ludwig (2019). "Integrierte Strategien zur Stärkung blau-grüner Infrastrukturen: Verbesserung des Stadtklimas und der Aufenthaltsqualität als Maßgabe zukunftsfähiger Stadtentwicklung", *Transforming Cities* (3), 56—59; Well, F., and F. Ludwig (2020). "Blue-Green Architecture: A Case Study Analysis Considering the Synergetic Effects of Water and Vegetation", *Frontiers of Architectural Research* 9(1), 191—202.

[20] Benne, B., and P. Mang (2015). "Working Regeneratively Across Scales — Insights from Nature Applied to the Built Environment", *Journal of Cleaner Production* 109 42—52. See also de Bruyn, G. (2009). "Der Dornröscheneffekt: Architekturtheoretische Überlegungen zur Baubotanik", in: G. de Bruyn, F. Ludwig, H. Schwertfeger et al. (eds.). *Lebende Bauten — Trainierbare Tragwerke*, Münster, Lit Verlag (Kultur und Technik. Schriftenreihe des Internationalen Zentrums für Kultur- und Technikforschung der Universität Stuttgart, 16) 127—133.

[21] Clément, G. (2015). *The Planetary Garden and Other Writings*. Philadelphia, University of Pennsylvania Press.

[22] See, for example, Lyle, J. T. (1996). *Regenerative design for sustainable development.* John Wiley & Sons; Mang, P., and B. Reed (2012). "Regenerative Development and Design". *Encyclopedia of Sustainability Science and Technology*, Heidelberg, Springer, 8855—8879.

About the Authors

Ferdinand Ludwig is Professor of Green Technologies in Landscape Architecture at the Technical University of Munich. He studied architecture at the University of Stuttgart, completing his doctorate on Botanical Foundations of Baubotanik and their Application in Design under Prof Dr Gerd de Bruyn and Prof Dr Thomas Speck (Plant Biomechanics Group, University of Freiburg). In 2007, he founded the research group Baubotanik at the Institute for Architectural Theory and Design (IGMA) at the University of Stuttgart, which is now based at the TU Munich.

His research and teaching focus on architectural concepts in which plants play a central role. Their functional and conceptual integration into architecture and design not only provides answers to the pressing ecological questions of our time, such as adaptation to climate change, but also poses a methodological challenge as to how to approach aspects of growth and decay, chance and probability in the design of our environment.

Daniel Schönle runs his own architecture and urban design office in Stuttgart, addressing projects at all scales and with a particular passion for conceptual issues. He studied architecture and urban planning at the University of Stuttgart, graduating in 2002 under Prof Wolfgang Schwinge at the Institute for Architectural Theory and Design (IGMA). In the following years, he worked at bueroschneidermeyer in Stuttgart and in private practice; varying interdisciplinary collaborations often led him abroad.

Parallel to his design work, Daniel Schönle also teaches and researches at various universities. In 2010 and 2011, he was a research assistant under Prof Dr Johann Jessen at the Department of Fundamentals of Local and Regional Planning at the Institute of Urban Planning and Design of the University of Stuttgart, and from April 2016 to September 2019, he was acting head of this department as interim professor.

As partners of OLA — Office for Living Architecture Ferdinand Ludwig and Daniel Schönle, together with Jakob Rauscher, develop baubotanical projects at a variety of scales. Their work seeks to find new ways of exploiting the spatial, aesthetic, ecological, constructional and processual potential of plants in architecture, with a view to developing sustainable approaches and solutions for a range of applications.

Sonja Dümpelmann is a landscape historian and professor at the University of Pennsylvania Weitzman School of Design. She is the author of several books, including the award-winning *Seeing Trees: A History of Street Trees in New York City and Berlin* (Yale University Press, 2019), and the editor of *Landscapes for Sport: Histories of Physical Exercise, Sport, and Health* (Dumbarton Oaks, 2022). She lectures internationally and was a senior fellow in Garden and Landscape Studies at the Dumbarton Oaks Research Library and Collection in Washington. In 2020—2021, she was a fellow at the Berlin Institute for Advanced Study (Wissenschaftskolleg zu Berlin).

Acknowledgements

This book is the result of many years of baubotanical research and practice, which started at the Institut für Grundlagen Moderner Architektur IGMA at the University of Stuttgart. This work was made possible to a large extent by Professor Dr Gerd de Bruyn, who supported our endeavours from the very beginning, not least by creating an open environment at IGMA in which Baubotanik could develop. The authors are immensely thankful to him for his support. We would also like to thank the University of Stuttgart and the Deutsche Bundesstiftung Umwelt for funding and supporting our work on Baubotanik.

We thank the Werner Konrad Marschall and Dr-Ing Horst Karl Marschall Foundation for their financial support of this publication and Ria Stein for her editing and for her extraordinary commitment to the conception and realisation of the book. Likewise, we would like to thank Markus Nießner for his excellent work and cooperation in its layout, cover design and typesetting.

Without the extensive and wide-ranging expertise of the team of the Chair of Green Technologies in Landscape Architecture at the Technical University of Munich and the office of Daniel Schönle, this book would not have been possible. In particular, the authors would like to thank Ute Vees for her vital contributions to Baubotanik and her extensive research and assistance in the writing of the manuscript. Thanks are also due to Barbara Hefner, Johannes Schmidt, Kristina Pujkilovic, Lorenz Boigner, Christoph Fleckenstein, Qiguan Shu, Wilfrid Middleton, Aly Elsayed, Jan-Timo Ort, Sarah Ann Sutter, Andreas Desuki and Oliver Teiml for their help in preparing the drawings and in undertaking the research and projects presented here. In addition, the authors would like to thank all those who provided photos and drawings, especially Ragani Haas for her drawings and her input on the conception, graphics and layout, and also Siegfried Ludwig for his proofreading and feedback on the manuscript.

The experimental buildings, studies and research work shown in this book are the product of a network of contributors. We would like to thank all those involved in the various projects, from clients and sponsors to design partners and contractors. The Plant Biomechanics Group in Freiburg, in particular Professor Dr Thomas Speck, are to thank for their assistance in the scientific evaluation of the tests. The long-term experiments were made possible by the support of the Gewächshauslaborzentrum Dürnast, the Baumschule Bruns, the Versuchsstation für Gartenbau Hohenheim and the Kunstverein Wagenhalle e.V. And finally, we would like to thank our various collaborators for their contributions over the years in which we have worked together, most notably Hannes Schwertfeger and Oliver Storz, Cornelius Hackenbracht, Christoph Roesler and Susanne Hackenbracht, and especially Jakob Rauscher—who, together with the authors, is a founding partner of the Office for Living Architecture OLA.

Illustration Credits

Cover: Markus Niessner with Ferdinand Ludwig, Daniel Schönle and Melly Müller with material by Skalgubbar

p. 2 Photo: Ferdinand Ludwig

1 Introduction
pp. 8—25

1, 3, 4 Photo: Amos Chapple
2, 6 Photo: Wilfrid Middleton
5 Photo: Anselmrogers/WikiCommons
7, 10 Photo: Ferdinand Ludwig
8 Photo: Reiner Lippert/WikiCommons
9 Photo: Reinhold Möller/WikiCommons
11 Photo: Cira Moro
12 Drawing: Ferdinand Ludwig and Daniel Schönle, with material by Ragani Haas
13 Photo: Ferdinand Ludwig/OLA

2 Botanical Foundations
pp. 26—61

2 after: Lüttge, U., and M. Kluge (2012). *Botanik — Die einführende Biologie der Pflanzen* (6th ed.), Weinheim, Wiley-Blackwell, 392.
4 after: https://eschooltoday.com/learn/leaf-structure/.
5 after: Raven, P., et al. (1985). *Biologie der Pflanzen*, Berlin, De Gruyter, 467.
7 after: Pretzsch, H. (2000). "Die Regeln von Reineke, Yoda und das Gesetz der räumlichen Allometrie", *Allgemeine Forst- und Jagdzeitung* 11, 205—210, Fig. 7.
11 after: Shinozaki, K., K. Yoda, K. Hozumi and T. Kira (1964). "A Quantitative Analysis of Plant Form — The Pipe Model Theory: I. Basic Analyses", *Japanese Journal of Ecology* 14(3), 97—105.
12 after: Mohr, H., and P. Schopfer (1992). *Pflanzenphysiologie* (4th ed.), Berlin, Springer, 500.
13 after: Mattheck, C., and H. Kubler (1997). *The Internal Optimization of Trees* (2nd ed.), Berlin, Springer.
18 partially after: Millner, E. M. (1932). "Natural Grafting in *Hedera helix*", *The New Phytologist* 31(1), 2—25.

3 Techniques and Tree Species
pp. 62—97

1—5, 7—22 Photo: Ferdinand Ludwig
6 Photo: Christoph Fleckenstein
24—30 Photo: Ferdinand Ludwig
31 Photo: Cira Moro
32, 34, 41, 42 Photo: Hans Braxmeier/Pixabay
33 Photo: Erich Westendarp/Pixabay
35 Photo: Sabine Fassbender/Pixabay
36 Photo: Eero Kolehmainen/Pixabay
37, 40 Photo: Pixabay
38 Photo: Susanne Jutzeler, suju-Photo/Pixabay
39 Photo: Włodzimierz Wysocki/WikiCommons
43 Photo: My2100/WikiCommons
44 Photo: Jeff Buck
45 Photo: Rosenzweig/WikiCommons
46 Photo: wertyfy2/Pixabay
47 Photo: Jean-Pol Grandmont/WikiCommons
48 Photo: Daderot/WikiCommons
49 Photo: Dietmar Rabich/WikiCommons
50 Photo: Couleur/Pixabay

4 Fusion of Trees and Buildings
pp. 98—109

1 Photo: Mauro Gambini/Flickr
2 Photo: Laura Gatti
3 Courtesy of Maison Edouard François/Photo: Nicolas Borel
4 Courtesy of Maison Edouard François
5, 6 Photo: Dirk Junklewitz
7 Photo: Frank Geissler/Pixabay
8 Photo: Thomas Ledl/WikiCommons
9 Photo: Carsten ten Brink/Flickr
10 Courtesy of Francis Hallé
11 Courtesy of Tom Chudleigh
12 Courtesy of Schneider + Schuhmacher Architekten/Photo: Helene Schiffer
13 Courtesy of Andreas Wenning
14 Photo: Kristina Pujkilovic

6 Designing with Trees and Time

Living root bridge, Wah Thyllong, pp. 128—131
5 Photo: Sameer Gurung
6, 8, 9 Photo: Ferdinand Ludwig

Dance linden tree, Peesten, pp. 132—135
11 Photo: Benreis/WikiCommons
12, 14, 15 Photo: Ferdinand Ludwig
16 Lithography: Carl August Lebschée

Ash Dome, pp. 136—137
17, 18 Courtesy of David Nash
19 Photo: Colin McPherson

Wacholderpark Pergolas, pp. 138—139
21, 22 Photo: Dirtsc/WikiCommons

Cattedrale Vegetale, pp. 140—141
24, 25 Courtesy of Arte Sella/Photo: Giacomo Bianchi

Torre Verde, pp. 142—143
27 Photo: Thilo Folkerts
28 Photo: Ferdinand Ludwig

Baubotanik Footbridge, pp. 144—149
30—34, 36, 37 Photo: Ferdinand Ludwig

Bird Watching Station, Waldkirchen, pp. 150—151
39 Photo: Oliver Storz

Steveraue Platform, pp. 152—153
41 Courtesy of Bureau Baubotanik/Photo: Heine&Becker

Village de Gîtes les Tropes, pp. 154—157
43, 47, 48 Courtesy of Gîtes les Tropes/Photo: Céline Guillaume
45 Courtesy of Maison Edouard François
46 Courtesy of Maison Edouard François/Photo: Nicolas Borel

Baubotanik Tower, pp. 158—161
49, 51 a, b Photo: Ferdinand Ludwig
51 c Model view: Boris Miklautsch
53 Photo: Cira Moro

Plane Tree Cube, Nagold, pp. 162—169
54 Photo: Ferdinand Ludwig
56, 57 Drawing: OLA
58 Courtesy of BIOCOM AG
59, 62, 63 Photo: OLA
60 Visualisation: OLA
61, 64 Photo: Ferdinando Iannone

Green Living Room, Ludwigsburg, pp. 170—173
65 Courtesy of Helix Pflanzen
67, 68 Photo: OLA

7 Utopias and Visions: Living Architecture between Science and Fiction
pp. 174—187

1—3 Drawing after: Arthur Wiechula (1925). *Wachsende Häuser aus lebenden Bäumen entstehend*, Berlin, Naturbau-Gesellschaft.
4, 5 Photo: Ferdinand Ludwig
6 Photo: Lena Bonengel
7—9, 14, 18 Courtesy of Archive Mark Primack
10 Courtesy of Luc Schuiten
11 Courtesy of Arte Sella/Photo: Giacomo Bianchi
12, 13 Courtesy of Archive Mark Primack/ Drawing: Mark Primack
15—17 Photo: Ferdinand Ludwig

8 Vers une Arbotecture: Towards a Future Tree Architecture
pp. 188—209

1, 2 Photogrammetric drawings: Wilfrid Middleton
3, 4 Photogrammetric drawings: Wilfrid Middleton and Qiguan Shu
5 Photogrammetric drawings: Design studio Prof Ludwig (TU Munich)
6 Photo: Qiguan Shu
7 Drawing: Wilfrid Middleton and Qiguan Shu
8 Photo: Kristina Pujkilovic
9 a Courtesy of Archive Mark Primack
9 b Simulation: Qiguan Shu
10 a Photo: Wilfrid Middleton
10 b Simulation: Wilfrid Middleton, Halil Ibrahim Erdal
11, 12, 23—27 Drawing: OLA
13—16 Drawing: OLA/competition team
17—22 Drawing: OLA/project team KLIMOPASS, courtesy of LUBW

All illustrations, unless otherwise stated, are by the authors or the project teams named in the chapter texts and acknowledgements, produced under the direction of the authors.

Index